ABSOLUTE TRUTH

THE CATHOLIC CHURCH IN
THE WORLD TODAY

Edward Stourton

VIKING

VIKING

Published by the Penguin Group
Penguin Books Ltd, 27 Wrights Lane, London W8 5TZ, England
Penguin Putnam Inc., 375 Hudson Street, New York, New York 10014, USA
Penguin Books Australia Ltd, Ringwood, Victoria, Australia
Penguin Books Canada Ltd, 10 Alcorn Avenue, Toronto, Ontario, Canada M4V 3B2
Penguin Books (NZ) Ltd, Private Bag 102902, NSMC, Auckland, New Zealand

Penguin Books Ltd, Registered Offices: Harmondsworth, Middlesex, England

First published 1998
1 3 5 7 9 10 8 6 4 2

Set in 11.5/14pt Monotype Bembo
Typeset by Rowland Phototypesetting Ltd,
Bury St Edmunds, Suffolk
Printed in England by Clays Ltd, St Ives plc

A CIP catalogue record for this book is available from the British Library

ISBN 0-670-87967-3

Contents

Acknowledgements

This book began life in the fertile mind of Mark Damazer, head of Weekly Programmes at BBC News and Current Affairs. An agnostic with a passion for ideas, he asked me to present a series of programmes on the modern Church.

The BBC team who produced the series were so generous in their help with the book that their names should by rights be alongside mine on the cover. Farah Durrani is a Muslim; the determination with which she mastered Catholic theology and Church politics was awesome, and she has a flair for bringing ideas to life through human stories. Ewa Ewart has unrivalled contacts in Poland, Moscow and the Vatican, and came to the project with the enthusiasm of one who lived through events in Poland in the late 1970s and early 1980s. John Thynne's research was tireless and always enlightening, and Fiona Murch, the executive producer, guided us all with an instinctive sense for the right balance between encouragement and discipline. She was mercifully tolerant when scripts appeared late for the programmes because I was lost somewhere in the book.

Others at the BBC I would like to thank include Irene Ozga, David Lines, Ian Lavelle, Sarah Hann, and my colleagues on the *One o'Clock News*, who were as tactful as they could have been about dragging my mind back to the daily news agenda. Our camera crews – Matt Gray, Keith Conlon, Wolf Truchsess, Peter Reuter, Alan Duxbury, Andrew Morton, Jacek Czerwinski and Tomasz Ksiazak – were engaging travelling companions and the sounds and pictures they recorded have been an inspiration. Several of the images reproduced in this book were taken from video shot by Matt Gray, Alan Duxbury and Jacek Czerwinski.

Just before I began writing a friend who is an experienced author told me and my wife that he was hesitating about a new book because he feared it would lead to a divorce. At the time we thought he was joking. This book has been written at breakneck speed and I am deeply grateful to my wife and our children for putting up with me while I was doing it.

Juliet Annan courageously backed a novice. If she had moments of doubt she was kind enough not to let it show. She and her team at Viking, Hannah Robson and Antonia Till, guided me through the last-minute remedial surgery needed to put the material in respectable shape, and the end result was immeasurably improved by the attention they gave it. Hazel Orme's copy-editing was meticulous and sympathetic.

I am especially indebted to my agent, Vivienne Schuster: her loyal support sustained me through the inevitable moments of crisis.

Finally I am grateful to the dozens of people all over the world who gave up their time to talk to me.

Picture Credits

All pictures are from the BBC TV series *Absolute Truth* (© BBC News), except for: Pope John XXIII (© Loomis Dean/Camera Press London); Pope Paul VI (©Patrick Morin/Camera Press London); Second Vatican Council, 1962 (© Camera Press London); Confirmation in Zambia (© author).

Chronology

1958 October   Cardinal Angelo Roncalli, Patriarch of Venice, is elected pope and takes the name John XXIII.

       December   Franz König, Archbishop of Vienna, is created cardinal.

1959 January   Fidel Castro ousts the Batista regime in Cuba, and installs a Communist government.
                     John announces his decision to call an Ecumenical Council of the Church.

1962 October   The Second Vatican Council opens.
                     The Cuban missile crisis brings the United States and the Soviet Union to the brink of nuclear war.

       December   The first of the four sessions of the Vatican Council closes.

1963 March   The Pontifical Commission for the Study of Population, Family and Births is created to consider the Church's position on artificial contraception.

       April   John publishes his encyclical *Pacem in Terris* – Peace on Earth – which revolutionizes the Church's relationship with Communism.

       June   John XXIII dies of cancer.
                     Cardinal Giovanni Battista Montini is elected pope and takes the name Paul VI.

       October   The Pope's birth-control commission meets for the first time.

       December   Karol Wojtyła becomes Archbishop of Kraków.

1964	October	At the third session of the Second Vatican Council the conservatives try to bury the Declaration on Religious Liberty.
		Nikita Khrushchev is deposed as Soviet leader, and Leonid Brezhnev takes his place as head of the Communist Party of the Soviet Union.
		Cardinal Suenens delivers his 'Galileo' speech to the Vatican Council, begging the bishops to consider changing the Church's teaching on contraception.
	November	The Crowleys are invited to join the Pope's birth-control commission.
1965	October	Paul VI becomes the first pope to address the United Nations in New York.
	December	The fourth and final session of the Second Vatican Council ends.
1966	February	Camilo Torres, a priest who had joined the guerrilla movement in Colombia, is killed by the Army, and becomes a symbol of the new Church in Latin America.
	June	The birth-control commission concludes its work and delivers its report to Paul, recommending a change in Church teaching.
1967	April	Paul publishes *Populorum Progressio*, his only social encyclical, giving the Church's blessing to radical ideas emerging from the developing world.
1968	July	Paul publishes the encyclical *Humanae Vitae* – On Human Life – which reasserts the Church's traditional ban on artificial means of birth control.
	August	Paul travels to Colombia to open the conference of Latin-American bishops at Medellín, which commits the Church to the option for the poor.
	October	Fifty-five British priests write a letter of protest against *Humanae Vitae* to *The Times*.
1969	May	The leaders of the Indian Church meet for the Bangalore Seminar, which lays the foundations for a distinctively Asian Catholicism.

	July	Paul becomes the first pope to visit Africa. While there, he consecrates Emmanuel Milingo as Archbishop of Lusaka.
1970	December	An increase in the price of food provokes riots in Poland, and Polish troops fire on Polish demonstrators. Hans Küng publishes *Infallible? An Inquiry*.
1971	February	Edward Gierek becomes First Secretary of the Polish Communist Party and leader of Poland in the wake of the country's food riots.
1973	March	Dom Paolo Evaristo Arns, Archbishop of São Paulo, is created cardinal.
1975	August	The Final Act is signed in Helsinki. It recognizes Europe's post-war borders and commits the nations of Eastern Europe to work towards respect for human rights.
1976	May	Basil Hume, Archbishop of Westminster, is created cardinal.
1977	February	Oscar Romero becomes Archbishop of San Salvador.
1978	August	Paul VI dies. Cardinal Albino Luciani, Patriarch of Venice, is elected pope and takes the name John Paul I.
	September	John Paul I dies.
	October	Cardinal Karol Wojtyła, Archbishop of Kraków, is elected pope and takes the name John Paul II.
1979	January	John Paul travels to Latin America for the meeting of Latin-American bishops at Puebla.
	March	John Paul publishes his first encyclical, *Redemptor Hominis*, in which he develops his ideas on human dignity and social solidarity.
	June	John Paul II's first visit to Poland.
	December	Hans Kung's right to teach as a Catholic theologian is withdrawn.
1980	March	Oscar Romero is assassinated.

	August	A strike at the Lenin shipyard in Gdańsk leads to the birth of Solidarity.
	September	Edward Gierek is forced out of power in Poland.
	November	Ronald Reagan wins the American presidential election.
1981	May	John Paul II is shot and wounded in St Peter's Square.
	November	Cardinal Joseph Ratzinger becomes Prefect of the Sacred Congregation for the Doctrine of the Faith.
	December	General Wojciech Jaruzelski declares martial law in Poland.
1982	April	Archbishop Milingo is summoned to Rome to face an investigation over his faith healing.
1983	June	John Paul's second visit to Poland. He meets Lech Wałęsa and General Jaruzelski.
	July	Martial law in Poland is lifted.
1984	September	Leonardo Boff is summoned to Rome to justify the ideas in his book *Church, Charism and Power*.
	October	Father Jerzy Popiełuszko is murdered in Poland.
1985	March	Mikhail Gorbachev becomes leader of the Soviet Union.
1989	November	The Berlin Wall comes down. Six Jesuits are murdered at the University of Central America in El Savador.
	December	Mikhail Gorbachev and John Paul meet in the Vatican.
1990	July	Tissa Balasuriya publishes *Mary and Human Liberation*.
1991	August	A coup against Mikhail Gorbachev collapses, and the Communist Party is suspended.
	December	The Soviet Union disintegrates.
1993	August	John Paul publishes his encyclical *Veritatis Splendor*, setting out his ideas on the nature of Truth.
1995	January	John Paul visits Sri Lanka. Buddhist leaders boycott his meeting with members of other faiths.

1997 January Tissa Balasuriya is excommunicated after refusing to retract the challenges to orthodox Catholic teaching in his book.

1998 January Tissa Balasuriya is received back into the Church after an international campaign against his sentence.
   John Paul visits Cuba and attacks the United States' economic embargo.

       May John Paul becomes the longest-serving pope of the twentieth century.

Introduction

At the age of twelve I found a half-eaten sausage in the holy-water stoop of the chapel of my Catholic boarding school in Sussex. The experience defined much of my understanding of what it was to be a Catholic, and even today I often think of it when I cross myself on entering a church.

This was not a harmless piece of schoolboy naughtiness; it was an act of rebellion and of sacrilege. The perpetrator had chosen a symbol of all that was most precious and sacred to deliver a calculated insult, an iconoclastic rejection of the Natural Order as we understood it. My fellow prefects and I went about our search for the culprit with a grim determination. When we found the wretch, it was apparent from his quivering demeanour that he understood the gravity of his offence. We all knew that we were in the presence of Evil.

One of the principal lessons I learned while preparing this book is that time and place can determine the character of Faith. The school where the sausage-bandit and I spent most of our lives between the ages of eight and thirteen was – for a certain type of outgoing, self-confident boy – a Garden of Eden. The park around it had been planted out with magnificent cedars, deodars, beeches and chestnuts in the days when it had been a stately home, and we had free rein to climb any we liked. My chief memories of those years are of hazy summer fields seen from the top of a tree – and of a religion that seemed as unchanging and settled as the English countryside around me.

This was the late 1960s, and the Second Vatican Council had just ended. We were dimly aware that something had been going on in Rome: our parents and some of our teachers would shake their heads and grumble about the loss of a mystical dimension in their worship with the disappearance of the Latin Mass. But since the reforms of the Council took a little time to work through there was still a strong flavour of the old Catholicism in our daily diet of religious teaching and practice, and the occasional intrusion of the modern world rather shocked us. I still remember the scandal caused by a huge American priest who turned up to say Mass one Sunday. The school vestments were too short for him, and clearly revealed that he was wearing open-toed sandals during the service. Since we were required to wear black lace-ups on Sundays instead of our usual weekday sandals, this seemed a terrible mark of disrespect.

It is sometimes said that pre-Conciliar Catholicism was a religion built on fear and not on love. But it was also deeply rooted in our yearning to understand the magical in the world around us – and I use the word magical without any of its pejorative connotations of witchcraft. In a world where God could become Man and Man could rise from the dead, anything was possible. Our regular encounters with a transcendent God in the school chapel and the easy familiarity we acquired with the miracles of the New Testament seemed very much of a piece with the numinous beauty of the world around us. The Faith that has always somehow influenced what I have thought and done – often in ways I have not understood – will for ever be rooted in the image of chestnut trees in bloom in the Sussex sun.

We were taught that we were part of a 'universal' Church, but we cannot possibly have been expected to understand what that meant. Those of us – the majority – who went on to Catholic public schools began to get a sense of it as we came to realize that our Catholicism set us apart from most of our contemporaries; to compensate for our feeling of alienation in our home country, we were taught that we belonged to the 'best and biggest club in the world'. But it was not until the journeys I made for this book that I came close to appreciating the breathtaking scale of the Church's ambition in its claim to univer- sality.

I have spent time describing the sights, sounds, colours, buildings, and politics of the places I have visited because they have been just as powerful an influence on the faith of others as my chestnut trees were on mine. As I encountered the diversity among my fellow members of the worldwide Catholic club – a diversity that has been allowed to flourish by Vatican II, that earthquake in Rome, which seemed such a distant rumble in the Sussex countryside — I was forced to recognize the limitations that time and place had put on my own faith.

'My object in writing,' says Hilaire Belloc, in *Europe and the Faith*, 'is to show that the Roman Empire never perished but was only transformed; that the Catholic Church which it accepted in its maturity caused it to survive, and was, in that origin of Europe, and has since remained, the soul of our Western civilization.' In India in 1997 I heard a venerable archbishop denounce Belloc as the worst kind of Eurocentric Catholic triumphalist; at Ampleforth — the Benedictine monastery where my education continued from the age of thirteen — in the 1970s everything about the way we were taught and the way we lived was designed to weave together the ideas of Europe and Catholic faith in our minds.

During an argument over the Maastricht treaty a prominent Eurosceptic once accused me of being a Europhile because of my religion; a Catholic education, he said, had made me suspicious of British institutions. At the time I was incensed that someone I thought of as a friend could use religion as a weapon in a political argument, but there was a kind of warped justice to the gibe. Benedictinism is a far older institution than the nation state: when the order was founded more than fifteen hundred years ago, the idea of England had no meaning, and that of Great Britain was many centuries in the future. During the Dark Ages, the monks more or less kept Western civilization alive; their librarians and their scholars preserved classical culture, husbanding the seeds of the Renaissance during Europe's long winter. And because of tradition's place at the heart of the Benedictine life, that heritage still imbued the community in the North Yorkshire valley where Basil Hume presided as abbot over more than a hundred monks, some seven hundred boys and a wonderfully eccentric and gifted collection of lay teachers.

It meant that the Benedictines were uniquely well qualified to offer our young minds a coherent world-view — a point of reference to which everything we studied could be made to relate. Latin was alive to us because we prayed in it on Sundays. History meant more because we were taught by men whose whole lives were devoted to ideals that had been developed many centuries ago, and at almost every turn of the textbook page in the story of Europe you will find others like them. Almost all the literature we read – English, European, and American – was easier for us because its Christian roots were part of our everyday intellectual furniture. When we studied the great Renaissance painters the subject matter was instantly familiar. An appreciation of classical music seeped into even the most tone-deaf of us – myself included – with every motet the choir sang at Mass in the abbey church on Sundays. Benedictines love knowledge, so science was encouraged as much as the arts; the Prior taught biology, and talked quite freely about its challenges to the Church's teaching on sexual morality.

Far from being something apart from the world, Catholicism, for us, was at its heart. Even those who declared themselves atheists – and it was one of the glories of my Benedictine education that the monks accepted the value of intellectual inquiry even when it led their pupils away from faith – did so in the context of a civilization they understood to have been formed by Christianity. We felt plugged into centuries of knowledge and feeling and thought and inspiration; the concept of Christendom was lodged deep within us. The wire that linked us with Newman and St Thomas More and Michelangelo and Chaucer and Dante and St Benedict and St Augustine of Hippo and Charlemagne and Constantine and St Peter and Virgil and Plato was live – and Christ made it pulse.

Two facts hit us in the outside world when we left the monastic community's embrace at the age of eighteen. The first was that in our own society the Faith we had come to accept as naturally as breathing was regarded as a freakish oddity, the second that it was shared by more human beings than any other creed.

The first of those facts encouraged the tribalism that is an undeniable part of English Catholicism. Huddled together during centuries of persecution, English Catholics developed a strong sense of their own identity, and the shadow of the priest-hole lay across the otherwise sunny landscape of my Catholic education. Persecution bred tenacity: the proportion of Mass-goers among Catholics is significantly higher in England than it is in France or Italy where Catholicism is the majority religion. But it also fostered a sense of separateness, which can be unhealthy. The survival of the Faith in England was closely tied up with the history of a few aristocratic and squirearchical families – and we became ever more closely intertwined because the codes of both religion and class compelled us to intermarry as the centuries went by. The priests who were trained at the English College in Rome and then smuggled back across the Channel, the country-house owners in Yorkshire, Lancashire, Worcestershire and Wiltshire who gave them refuge, the grandees who steadfastly paid their fines for recusancy even when it brought them to the point of bankruptcy, all belonged to the same tiny caste.

It means that in English Catholicism snobbery is blessed by sanctity. Martyrdom is an extraordinarily powerful phenomenon. All over the world the influence of men and women who died for their faith echoes down the years. In England many of those executed during the sixteenth and seventeenth centuries were noble – in the social as well as the moral sense. So the English vice of fawning to grand ancestry and the Catholic veneration for sacrifice in the cause of the Faith are mixed in a lethally self-indulgent cultural cocktail.

When I was a teenager my family lived in West Africa, and Sunday services in the cathedral of Accra, the Ghanaian capital, gave me the first real sense of what the idea of the Church in the World really meant. The opportunity to encounter a Church outside Europe provided an empirical experience of the catholicity of Catholicism and gave me an advantage over most English Catholics. Even so, most of those nine hundred million souls who share my faith remained an abstraction. For a concrete sense of the way in which they related to my own religion I had to wait until a visit to an ashram in the Hindu holy city of Benares – or Varanasi, as it is now known.

The very idea of a Catholic ashram requires some extraordinary cultural somersaults, and I shall return to it in Chapter 13. The foreignness of the concept was reinforced by the visual impact of the place. In a makeshift, open-sided building I saw row upon row of dark faces above brightly coloured clothes, and ahead of them, the focus of their attention, stood a tall figure, one arm upraised in the exhortation to prayer. White-robed and bearded, he looked the very image of a guru, but he was a Catholic priest. Sister Lioba, who showed us round, explained that those he was addressing were low-caste Hindus, who felt betrayed by their religion and had come to hear a different message.

One or two of the nuns helping out wore the familiar white and blue of Mother Teresa's Missionaries of Charity, but Sister Lioba was dressed in a saffron sari, not a habit I recognized, and I assumed she belonged to a home-grown Indian order. She told me she was a member of the Institute of the Blessed Virgin Mary.

The IBVM is best known in Britain for running smart Catholic girls' boarding schools. They are extremely good – I can write that with some authority, since they educated both my wife and my daughter. But there was a time when they took the idea of 'reconverting England from the top down' perhaps a little too seriously; one, in particular, had such a grand reputation that it attracted ancient and aspiring Catholic families from all over the world, and at one stage counted a Grimaldi and a Marcos among its pupils. The Institute was founded in York in the early seventeenth century by Mary Ward, an English gentlewoman with ideas about women's potential far in advance of the Stuart era in which she lived – she believed that 'in time women will do much' in the Church.

Mary Ward – with her white ruff and stern-looking black dress – looks down on my daughter and her schoolfriends in the handsome chapel of St Mary's School in Dorset. One of the purposes of my book is to tease out the threads that link her and them to the saffron-robed sister and her Hindu pilgrims by the Ganges. The historical links are easily explained by colonialism and the missionary work that accompanied it; but what do those links mean today? Are they strong enough to constitute a family tie? Or are these exotic Catholic cousins so different that we are part of the same family in name only? Those questions are central to the battles currently being fought over the Church's future; there can be no limit to the size of the club, because that would make nonsense of its catholicity and its claim to offer a universal message, but thrashing out the essential rules of membership is a tough business when the club grounds spread over so many acres.

I have taken the Second Vatican Council as a starting point because it began a revolution in the world's oldest institution. The man who called it, Pope John XXIII, said it would 'shake the heavens and the earth', and everything that has happened in the Church since and is happening in it today is a result of the Council's decisions. It was a hugely ambitious enterprise: to reverse in little more than three years the course of the Church over centuries, so that it looked forward instead of backwards. Then, there were many who judged it a reckless gamble – and today there are those who argue that the events of the past three decades have proved them right: that John squandered the Church's inheritance.

It unleashed a period of great turmoil. But it has also been, and continues to be, a period of great vigour, as Catholics all over the world respond to the challenge the Council posed: does our faith have the answers that mankind needs as the third millennium of the Christian era begins?

This book is an attempt to assess whether the Second Vatican Council's ambition to engage with the world has borne fruit in the way the world is ordered; whether Catholicism can still influence politics and society. The unprecedented reach of the papacy of John Paul II makes that question not just legitimate but pressing. How significant was his part in the collapse of Communism? And what does his achievement in Poland mean for the Church's role in society?

If you stepped back in time to survey the intellectual landscape of a century ago, you might be forgiven for concluding that Christianity was destined to become an irrelevant curiosity. The future seemed to belong to ideas that apparently struck at the very heart of religion; Darwin, Marx and Freud were the prophets with history on their side, and Nietzsche had confidently pronounced that God was dead. Yet in the 1990s Catholicism is almost the only 'ism' left on the intellectual field of battle: most other ideologies have been sent scurrying for cover by the forces of free markets, liberal democracy and globalization. Does the Church have real answers to social problems, and how far can or should it seek to impose its ideas on society at large? In Latin America its engagement with the challenges of poverty and oppression led to a deep split within the Church, open conflict between Church and state and martyrs on a scale almost unprecedented in the long history of Catholicism.

Trying to establish the secular influence of a religious institution presents a real conundrum: which set of intellectual tools is appropriate to the job; those of the Church, or those of the world? The problem reflects a dilemma I have long felt in my own life between being a journalist and being a Catholic.

I tried to sum it up in the *Catholic Herald* when I began work on this book and the accompanying BBC TV series: 'The journalistic habit of mind is to treat everything with scepticism and to test every claim against evidence and counter-argument. Faith requires the acceptance of facts even when they fly in the face of reason, and Christ gave a special place to those who "have not seen and still believe".' Or as the Benedictine-educated columnist Hugo Young put it in one of the centenary lectures at Westminster Cathedral: 'There is a sense in which religious truth is for ever alien to the deconstructive procedures of journalism. Religious truth is about otherness, about mystery, about the impalpable . . . God and his interpreters are not properly susceptible to the reductivist simplicities of the *Daily Mail*.'

The easy way out of the dilemma that that tension poses for someone who is both a Catholic and a journalist is to ignore it. In the early eighties, when I was beginning my career in journalism, religion became big news for a while. Pope John Paul's pilgrimages to Poland, his unprecedented visit to Britain in the midst of the Falklands crisis, and the furious debate about Marxism, priests and politics stirred up by events in Latin America created an appetite for religious stories in mainstream news programmes and newspapers, and specialist knowledge was at a premium. Since, by accident of education, I had a good mental road map to work with, I exploited my advantage quite shamelessly. I ought to feel grateful to John Paul for giving me such a helpful leg up in my career.

But once I had established myself, I steered clear of religious journalism. That was partly because I wanted to avoid being typecast: while I have always been happy to be described as a Catholic and a journalist, I most definitely do not regard myself as a Catholic journalist. But it also reflected a certain squeamishness in the face of the tension between the journalistic and the religious approaches to the search for truth. It is frankly awkward to find a contradiction between two such central factors in one's life, and I found I would rather not dwell on it.

Picking apart the Church's impact on the world for this book has brought that contradiction even more sharply into focus. The Church has – in the spin-doctor's phrase – a 'good story to tell' about its role in Poland and Eastern Europe during the 1980s. But as I tried to make sense of the events of the period I realized there are two parallel interpretations of what happened, and they never quite meet. In one, which belongs to the arena of journalistic truth, the Pope features as one factor among many in the collapse of Communism, and his role is analysed as a historical, not a spiritual, phenomenon. In the other he is the Instrument of Divine Providence, by which Catholicism has vanquished Communism. So even when two witnesses to that era come close to agreement, they may not really be talking about the same thing. Mikhail Gorbachev was full of praise for John Paul. But he described him as a 'humanist', and gently but firmly reminded me that there were other forces at work in the Soviet Empire in the 1980s – not least his own reforms.

Lech Wałęsa was equally generous in his praise of John Paul, but his understanding of the events in which they both played such a critical role is rooted in the religious, not the secular, approach to truth. When I asked him what made him a Catholic, he told me that the fear of hell was a powerful factor: 'I might meet Stalin or Lenin down there,' he said, 'and I am terrified about what they would do to me.' It was said with a laugh, but it was not a joke. To a traditional Catholic, hell – like heaven – is an objective reality; both places are filled not with abstract spiritual essences but with individuals – people you know, whether they be your neighbour, your boss or one of your children.

The journalist in me understood what Mikhail Gorbachev was talking about, the Catholic in me understood Lech Wałęsa. Trying to put them together, so that what they said made sense in the same context, has been a slippery business.

So this, for me, is a book about the nature of Truth.

The simple logic of the idea of Truth at the heart of Catholicism has always held an irresistible appeal for me, and even at times when I have doubted the existence of God, I have never doubted that He is a Catholic God if He is there. That sounds arrogant and triumphalist, but for me it is only logical. One God implies One Truth, and the Catholic Church claims to be the One True Interpreter of that Truth. The Oneness of Truth and its absolute quality have always seemed to me to be self-evidently implied in the idea of Godhead. For me the word God has no meaning unless the Truth is singular. That, of course, does not mean that the Church cannot make mistakes; even this most self-confident of popes has apologized for its past crimes. But it does mean that the Church's aspiration to provide a single, coherent set of teachings is justified. I thought all Catholics agreed on that.

Not so: when I finally came to confront the worldwide reality of my Faith, I met people who called themselves Catholics and believed in many truths. Some even dismissed the very basis of my idea of

Truth, condemning linear logic as a European invention with no claim to universality.

And, like the devil, the pluralists have all the best tunes. On most of the concrete issues that confront the Church today, I found their arguments compelling – even as I shuddered at the careless rips they made in the integrity of the Church's Truth. It is a tension that goes to the heart of being a Catholic in the late twentieth century, an experience that is so shot through with contradictions that many people have concluded it is an impossible piece of intellectual contortionism.

It was a great privilege to see the Church at work on four continents: I encountered some pockets of distrust for the media, but by and large was impressed with the willingness of high Church officials to confront difficult questions. By the end I was becoming positively blasé about hobnobbing with cardinals. Of course, there are one or two wooden-headed old bigots around, but you do not rise to the top of an institution as sophisticated and complex as the Church without being bright. I talked to plenty of rebels too, and was struck by the way that even those who had quarrelled most bitterly with the Church retained a deep affection for it.

More by luck than by good judgement, this project has turned out to be extraordinarily well timed. Many of the great figures at the Second Vatican Council are now dead, but I was able to talk to some of those who played a central part in what was one of the great revolutions of the twentieth century, and their memories were still vivid. And far from slipping over the edge of contemporary experience into the world of history, the debate over the Council is, if anything, more alive now than it has ever been – for a Church that has existed for two thousand years, three decades is a mere blink of the eye.

An anniversary of the second great upheaval in the life of the Church in the 1960s has stirred other, more painful memories: 29 July 1998 was the thirtieth anniversary of the encyclical *Humanae Vitae*, the Church's condemnation of birth control. Even by many priests and bishops *Humanae Vitae* is regarded as the Church's dirty secret, two Latin words to be whispered if they are spoken at all. But it was a watershed with implications that went well beyond biology, and the encyclical's thirtieth birthday has served as a reminder of its impact.

And the millennium will be one of those great punctuation marks in the Church's history. In his 1994 letter, *Tertio Millennio Adveniente*,

Introduction

Pope John Paul laid out hugely ambitious plans for this landmark in the life of the world's oldest institution. He has said he wants to lead the Church into the next millennium, and when I saw his frail figure at an audience in St Peter's Square, I could not help thinking that the determination to fulfil that ambition is what keeps him going. The final years of his papacy have been marked by a sense of frantic last-minute housekeeping, as if, like an anxious host, he is rushing to prepare the Church for the arrival of the year 2000. As his papacy and the millennium draw to a close together, the Church is poised midway through a revolution that began when John XXIII called the Council Fathers together in Rome.

Of course, I have not achieved all the ambitions I set myself when I began this book; part of the fun of faith is that it is ultimately beyond 'irritable reaching after fact and reason'. But the journey has been inspirational. Some Catholics regard it as rather disloyal for a Catholic journalist to investigate the Church, but I have always thought that a Church which was not strong enough to face hard questions was not worth belonging to. Nevertheless, I set out with some trepidation – expecting that my faith would be stirred, but fearing too that it might be shaken.

Sometimes I have allowed myself to be led down obscure theological paths, but I have tried to make this book as 'un-churchy' as I can. The Roman Catholic Church is the largest institution in the world. It is the only truly 'supra-national' institution because, unlike the United Nations or the European Union, which seek to unite peoples through their governments, the Church claims to be a family that transcends race, colour and nation, and speaks to individuals without the mediation of their secular rulers. It is eternally enigmatic because it is at once so close to us and so distant; with a political system inherited from a Renaissance court it makes decisions that touch the most intimate areas of our lives.

You may love the Church or hate it, but it is too big to ignore, and almost anyone who has been touched by Western civilization has also been touched by the influence of the Church. Catholicism is about Sex, Power and the Meaning of Life.

Unlocking the Treasury

Walk through the courtyards and corridors of the Swiss Guards' quarters before dawn and you step straight back into Renaissance Italy; a knife between the shoulder-blades would come as no surprise.

The drill yard is a narrow rectangle between high walls just off the Via Santa Anna at the back of St Peter's Square; it is hung with the flags of the Swiss cantons and at one end there is a monument to those who died on 7 May 1527, when a heroic defence of Clement VII by Swiss troops earned the Guards their special place in the papal household. It is here that one of the Catholic Church's regular setpiece dramas begins. At seven a.m. a contingent of Guards forms up; despite the striped doublets and chic sixteenth-century plus-fours, the drill is uncompromisingly soldierly. A brisk march takes them into the long corridor that leads down from the Vatican apartments and out through the vast bronze doors into St Peter's Square. Beneath a sky washed like a watercolour, the world's greatest stage set is being prepared for a papal audience. Both the set and the performance that is about to begin have been designed to encapsulate the essential qualities of the Roman Catholic Church.

The first and overwhelming impression is of grandeur. The chairs and barricades, which have been laid out the previous evening, break down the vast space of St Peter's Square into a geometric pattern, which seems to make it vaster still. The pilgrims flow between them like tributaries of a great river as they look for their allotted seats, and by half past eight the streams are as fast and strong as floodwaters. The central steps cascade down from the canopy under which the Pope will sit, drawing all eyes to the focus of the drama and source of all authority. Yet the way in which the colonnades around the Square encircle the pilgrims is like an embrace, and within the grandeur there is a sense of intimacy. Look closely at the crowds, and you see a mosaic of individual dramas being played out.

A papal usher – echo of a time when this was a royal court – prinks his way towards the dais, feet like a duck and back like a rod, his purple tailcoat faded and the keys of St Peter displayed proudly on his fob. There are several groups of pilgrims from Poland – teenagers in white smocks and sailor-suit collars, women with turquoise scarves like some kind of Scout uniform – each absorbed in its songs, prayers and ostentatiously lively gossip. Just ahead of me a Lithuanian male voice choir arrives, dressed in scruffy military regalia with Ruritanian pretensions; a microphone is placed in front of them and they begin to sing harmonies, not caring much if anyone listens but proud to perform in St Peter's Square. A group of disabled pilgrims are bumped uncomfortably up the steps, their wheelchairs manoeuvred in among the black and purple of the bishops; the Church accords special respect to 'our lords the sick', and they take their place in the area reserved for privileged guests around the papal throne. Everywhere are clusters of nuns, in black, grey, brown, blue and beige.

On the right as you face St Peter's, close to the statue of St Paul, a space is reserved for newly-weds. They come in their wedding clothes, and as the popemobile turns into the central aisle formed by the barricades several of the brides climb on their chairs for a better look. One adjusts her tiara out of the way of her camera as she takes a picture. Another draws her shawl around her shoulders for modesty's sake; she is wearing a long sheath of ivory silk, a hat with a huge bow, and her fine features stand out against the honey-coloured stone behind her. As the Pope passes, in a gesture that perfectly expresses the intimacy of her new estate, she puts a hand on her husband's shoulder to steady herself.

The Catholic Church has a genius for the *mise en scène*, and its special skill is to inspire awe at the same time as convincing every soul it encounters that each has a special place in its affections. Nothing much really happens at a papal audience – there is no beginning, middle or end – but the mix of the grand and the personal is nicely judged. At the one I attended, the gospel was read in Italian, German, French, English and Spanish. The Pope's address – on the Virgin Mary – was repeated in each of those languages, and at the end of each language section there was a pause so that he could give an individual greeting to groups of pilgrims; the English section included some ecumenical-minded Methodists, and we were asked to pray for their leader's wife, who had recently been seriously injured in a car-crash. Everyone among the thousands in the square – scruffy Lithuanian chorister, ivory-clad beauty or habited nun – was made to feel that his or her life story was inextricably bound up with the Church, and that the Church was ineffably grand.

Because the message of Christianity is ultimately beyond the reach of words, the Church has spent centuries developing the means to express it through theatre. For all his saintly simplicity Pope John XXIII understood the power of spectacle – he had after all been patriarch of Venice, the world's most theatrical city – and the opening ceremony of the Second Vatican Council, on 11 October 1962, is burned into the memory of everyone who was there: it was a stunning, peacock display of papal power harnessed in the cause of revolution. Two thousand three hundred and eighty-one bishops processed through St Peter's Square and into the basilica that day. I saw a similar but much smaller ceremony when reporting on the special Synod of Bishops in 1985, and it was unforgettable, a simultaneous affirmation both of the Church's diversity and its unity; every face framed by the uniform of the mitre, but the faces themselves infinitely various, reflecting the character of every race on the planet. In 1962 the Orthodox and Eastern Rite bishops, whose presence had been secured only through hard diplomatic bargaining, added to the cosmopolitan glamour of the scene with their jewelled crowns and flowing beards, and in the old film clips of the day there is something endearingly and unconsciously camp about the way patriarchs and archbishops can be seen adjusting one another's robes and headgear.

There were one or two hitches. The Council Fathers – as the bishops who attended the Council were known – had been divided into groups and spread around the Vatican so that they could be brought into the procession according to a carefully plotted schedule, but one group of archbishops was simply forgotten by its master of ceremonies. 'We were left behind in one of the rooms of the Vatican museum,' remembers the South African Archbishop Denis Hurley of Durban, 'we were suddenly called on to get down quickly and since we couldn't join the procession going into the piazza we had to be ushered along the portico in front of St Peter's.'

Pope John himself brought up the rear of the procession. Though he was launching a Council that would cut the Church adrift from much of its history, he processed with the full panoply of that history, carried on his portable throne, the *sedes gestatoria*, and surrounded by the ostrich plumes due to his office. Father Francis Murphy, who was to gain fame with his leaks from the Council under the pseudonym Xavier Rynne, remembers the Pope weeping under the emotion of the occasion: 'John XXIII looked very small and scared until the crowds shouted, "*Viva il Papa*". Then I saw the tears coming down. At long last his Council had started.'

The Church's timescale extends to eternity, and it sometimes seems to plan its rituals without realizing that others do not see things *sub specie aeternitatis*. The Pontifical Mass with which the Council opened lasted four hours. Even some archbishops found that a challenge. Archbishop Hurley was worried from the moment he found his seat: 'It was very impressive, but being acquainted with Roman liturgical celebrations I knew it would last for hours, and I found myself quite near the front. I was very nervous lest I fall asleep and the TV cameraman take advantage of my sleeping eyes.'

But he, and everyone else, was woken up by the Pope's address. It is difficult to imagine a speech in Latin causing a stir in the late twentieth century, but most of John's immediate audience would have had at least some understanding of the language, and what he said came as a thunderbolt: a clear and unequivocal rebuke to the conservatives – or, to put it in Church code, the pessimists – who had been plotting to undermine the reforming spirit behind the Council since the moment it had been announced.

'It often happens that, in the daily exercise of Our apostolic ministry, We are shocked to discover what is being said by some people who, though they may be fired by religious zeal, are without justice, or good judgement, or consideration in their way of looking at matters. In the existing state of society they see nothing but ruin and calamity; they are in the habit of saying that our age is much worse than past centuries; they behave as though history, which teaches us about life, had nothing to teach them, and as though, at the times of past Councils, everything was perfect in the matter of Christian doctrine, public behaviour, and the proper freedom of the Church.

'It seems to Us necessary to express Our complete disagreement

4

with these prophets of doom, who give news only of catastrophes, as though the world were nearing its end.

'In the present state of affairs, now that human society seems to have reached a turning-point, it is better to recognize the mysterious designs of divine Providence which, passing through the different ages of man, and his works, generally against all expectation, achieve their purpose and guide events wisely for the good of the Church – even those events which seem to conflict with her purposes.'

It may not sound very revolutionary to the modern ear – with all those royal wes and the orotund periods of Ciceronian dimensions which, with their apparently endless sub-clauses building slowly to a climax as they do, would probably read and sound better in Latin. But to the bishops of the Roman Catholic Church in 1962 this was radical stuff. They had been brought up to believe that the Church had long since worked out all the answers; here was St Peter's successor, a man they believed to be infallible, telling them they had to think of new answers in the light of what was happening in the world around them. Cardinal König, who was to become one of the leading lights of the radicals in the Council's debates, told me that until that moment none of them really knew what to expect, because none had experienced a council of the Church or anything like it. Suddenly, he said, 'This old man brought hope into the assembly and gave us the courage to look ahead, [told us] the past is not important, it is the future that is important.'

It would be intriguing to know the thoughts of Cardinal Ottaviani at this point. His senior rank gave him a place just to the right of the Pope at the front of St Peter's. As head of the Holy Office, the guardian of orthodoxy, he had already shown his colours as one of the leaders of the 'prophets of doom', and was to become the chief opponent of König and his ilk in the Council debates. The motto on the Cardinal's coat-of-arms was *Semper idem* – always the same. But when John XXIII said, 'The deposit of faith itself, that is to say the truths contained in our ancient doctrine, is one thing, but the form in which those truths are announced is another,' it was an invitation to change. To Cardinal Ottaviani and his superiors, it must have seemed a direct challenge.

And he must have had the first real inkling of the power of the tide against which he was swimming. Almost all those I spoke to who were there that day shared Cardinal König's memory that it was the moment they came to realize the Council's potential. The Pope had instructed them to experiment with new ideas, and the simple act of processing into St Peter's with the worldwide fellowship of bishops gave them a new understanding of what the Catholic Church meant. Robert Kaiser, who covered the Council for *Time* magazine, gave me this vivid description of the end of the ceremony: 'I saw black faces and brown faces and yellow faces, and ruddy red faces from Ireland and Scotland. I saw all kind of faces. I saw an immense panoply of colour. These bishops and patriarchs were from all over the universe and when they came out they tumbled down the front steps of St Peter's so that from a distance it looked like a waterfall, a waterfall of red and purple and black and every colour of the rainbow. These were the representatives of the Church from around the world. This was the first ecumenical council where we really saw the universality of the Church.'

It is difficult now to re-create the lost world of faith, which was soon to be swept away by that waterfall – despite the best efforts of Cardinal Ottaviani and his allies. To get back into the mind of the pre-Conciliar Catholic requires an imaginative leap that is almost impossible to make. The old cliché 'once a Catholic always a Catholic' does not really do justice to the way in which the Faith was enmeshed in every fibre of the Catholic being, so that even those who tried to escape it defined their rebellion in Catholic terms.

If you looked at the surface of the Church at that period, there seemed no reason for change. In most parts of the world the churches were full, and recruits were pouring into seminaries, convents and monasteries. A younger generation of theologians had begun to create undercurrents of new thought, but they did not really touch the daily life of the Church, and its rituals and sacraments – the baptisms and confirmations, the confessions, marriages, benedictions, stations of the cross, rosaries, novenas, ordinations and extreme unctions – continued as they had done for centuries. Indeed, far from being enfeebled by the atheist ideologies that developed in the late nineteenth century, the Church in the 1950s seemed in some places to be more self-confident than ever before.

The Church in Britain was a good example. Catholics were beginning to spread their wings as the end of legal discrimination worked through into social attitudes. For centuries their hands had been kept from the levers of power in British society, and the top end of society was considered a critical target in the campaign to reconvert the England that was still thought of as 'Mary's dowry'. The big religious schools – such as Ampleforth, Downside and Stonyhurst – set about recruiting and educating as many future politicians, bankers, judges, doctors and opinion-formers as they could lay their hands on. They had expanded energetically in the 1930s, and by the 1950s Catholics could be found at the top of every profession that made up what was about to earn the title 'the Establishment'.

There were clever converts to show off like Evelyn Waugh and Graham Greene, and the writings of Hilaire Belloc and G. K. Chesterton provided powerful ammunition in debate at High Table. At Cambridge the Catholic chaplain, Monsignor Gilbey, was converting the best and the brightest by the pew-load.

Of course, the attitude to authority in society at large was more conducive in the 1950s to the Catholic tradition. Cardinal Hume remembers the joys of exercising authority in those days. He was a housemaster at Ampleforth when he heard word that one of his boys was preaching seditious atheism around the dormitories. He called in the offender and reminded him that the entire monastic community and its school were founded on the conviction that Jesus Christ was the Son of God. The future Cardinal said that if *he* ever stopped believing in that Fact he would leave and get married, and he demanded the same consistency from the offending boy, who was offered a timetable of the buses to York and a choice: believe or leave. 'His crisis of faith was cured overnight,' says Hume, 'but you could only do that in the nineteen fifties.'

The centrality of the Fact of Christ's divinity was what really distinguished the Catholicism of those days and gave it the appeal that held so many – from the Irish labourer in Liverpool to aristocrats and intellectuals at the Jesuit church in Mayfair – in thrall to its spell. The article of faith on which Catholicism rests is at once preposterous and marvellous – indeed, it is marvellous in part because it is so preposterous. If God really did become Man in the person of Jesus Christ, it is a truth so awe-inspiring that it can only dominate every moment of our lives. It means that at a moment in human history, a moment as real as the battle of Hastings or the election of the Attlee government in 1945, there was an intersection between our finite world and the infinite realm of the divine. It makes the existence of that parallel, divine world an ever-present reality at every moment of every day.

Once you had accepted the Fact, everything else made perfect sense. The idea of transubstantiation – the belief that bread and wine are transformed into the body and blood of Christ at Mass – has been much ridiculed as a piece of medieval superstition, but for Catholics it is perfectly logical: if God could become Man in Palestine two thousand years ago, why shouldn't He turn a piece of bread into his Divine Body in our parish church on Sunday morning? Miracles, the Immaculate Conception and the Virgin Birth, the Apparitions of Mary, the Liquefaction of St Gennaro, the preservation of grisly bits of martyred saints, indeed the full panoply of Catholic mysticism – which can be so revolting to some Protestants and so incomprehensible to the scientifically minded – all seem natural and uncontroversial once you have accepted the Divinity of Christ.

Everything about the way the pre-Conciliar Church worshipped revolved around the idea that the intersection between the human and the divine, which took place when Christ was born and was repeated each Sunday, demanded to be celebrated. Great music expressed the enormity of the event that occurred at every Mass. Incense and Latin heightened the sense of mystery surrounding what was being done on the altar. At benediction the consecrated Host was placed in an ornate monstrance and displayed on the altar to be venerated. All sorts of complicated rules were developed to manage the meeting of the physical and spiritual worlds that took place at the consecration: fasting before communion was compulsory, as the idea of God's Body becoming mixed up in that morning's bacon and eggs presented all sorts of theological difficulties. Once consecrated it was too holy to be touched, so it had to be placed directly on the tongue. I remember stories of pious nuns who would cut out and burn bits of the carpet along the altar rail because they had been touched by the divine when a Host fell from a communicant's lips.

The act of consecration itself was considered so sacred that it could only be performed away from the prying eyes of the faithful, so the priest kept his back to the congregation. I remember overhearing one elderly priest, indignant about the changes introduced by Vatican II, saying that asking him to consecrate the Host facing the people was like asking a couple to make love in public.

And, of course, there was the deep satisfaction of certainty – an attraction felt especially strongly by Catholics in this country. There has long been a suspicion of 'enthusiasm' in the English approach to religion, and it has always seemed to me that there is a certain sense of embarrassment at the heart of Anglicanism. The empirical English mind has never really been comfortable with the preposterous aspect of the Christian Fact, and all that talk of bodies and blood and miracles is, after all, in rather poor taste. Anglicans are slightly shamefaced about it all. Not so the Catholic Church – and certainly not the Catholic Church of the 1950s. It was supremely confident about trumpeting the Truth it held. It was comforting to believe that your Church had an answer to absolutely everything. There was no part of human life, no moment of human history and no avenue of philosophical inquiry on which the Catholic Church of those days did not have a view. When I was confirmed at the age of twelve my aunt gave me a prayer-book called simply *Lord God*. First published in the 1930s, it offered me a prayer appropriate for every eventuality a schoolboy might meet: Before an Examination and After an Examination ('Coming, Lord God, straight from the test of my human knowledge I want to offer to thee the success or failure that results . . .'); Before Being Punished ('Lord, I am about to be beaten . . .') and After Being Punished (a joke here: 'There is no set form of words for this occasion. Mental rather than vocal prayer is usually found to meet the case more adequately'). A footnote to the Prayer Before a Match revealed that: 'It is the custom of Ladycross School for the team to pay a visit – *en costume* – to the Blessed Sacrament before playing a match. Practices of this sort might well be extended to other activities of school life . . .' I dimly remember that Ladycross were always rather useful on the rugby field.

We all had a general issue *Simple Prayer Book*, which included special prayers for reducing our sentence in purgatory. The number of days that could be knocked off was precisely stated beneath each prayer – so many days' remission for a Glory Be, so many days for a Hail Holy Queen and so on. Some prayers were more powerful than others: we quickly worked out that you could speed your passage through the purging of the soul by months just by cracking through a few Hail

Marys, while some of the longer prayers like the Creed were only worth a week or two.

If we had followed through the literalism of this approach, we might have detected an inconsistency: if our days in purgatory could be so easily reduced by precise numbers, should we not also have had a table to indicate how many days of punishment were required to expiate each sin – a sentence of X for lying, Y for allowing our attention to wander during Mass? Had it been possible to reach such an equation, I suspect most of us would have found ourselves in credit in the celestial bank. We used to compete to see who could knock off the most years of purgatory with the same fervour we brought to the battle for the champion conker, but none of us was old enough to have done anything very serious; sausages in the holy-water stoop was about as bad as it got. I can still remember racking my brains for a sin to produce at my first confession; it was terribly disappointing to hear that 'not shutting my eyes while praying' was not good enough and, caught in that tortured loop that only a Catholic upbringing can give you, I can remember feeling guilty that I had nothing to feel guilty about.

The impact of all this was to invest every choice we made with immense moral significance. No decision, not the smallest, was neutral. It became second nature to think first about what the Church taught was right and wrong, and only afterwards about what we did or did not want to do. For us, like Lech Wałęsa with his terror of being tormented by Stalin and Lenin in hell, fear of damnation was an ever-present reality.

The itch to offer a prescription for everything extended to the adult world too. It was not just that the Church never admitted to being wrong on any point; the way it understood its claim to be the possessor of Revealed Truth meant it could never admit to having been wrong in its history. In Church fêtes and Catholic attics you can still find dusty books that bear testament to the vast reservoirs of intellectual energy and ingenuity that were poured into the effort to square reality with the Church's understanding of itself as a perfect society which could do no wrong. Here are some of the issues addressed in a book designed to help converts, *Questions and Answers on the Catholic Church*, published by the Catholic Missionary Society in Edinburgh in 1913.

Question:
A fails to keep Friday as a day of abstinence and is according to the teaching of the Catholic Church in mortal sin and deserving of hell. B is an habitual criminal, living in mortal sin, and therefore also deserving of hell. Are both A and B equally guilty?

The answer, intriguingly, reveals that A could, in fact, be more guilty than B if he understands that what he is doing is wrong and B does not, because 'the degree of guilt depends directly on the degree of voluntariness involved in the sin'.

Question:
Is it possible for Protestants to be saved? If so, what is the meaning of the saying, 'No salvation outside the Church'?

Protestants will be delighted to hear that they can be saved, and that this is granted to the best of them because they are really aspirant Catholics:

Protestants in good faith intend to belong to the true Church, and believe they do belong to it, only they are mistaken as to the body which they identify with the Church.

Question:
Does the Roman Catholic Church designate as heretics all Christians who do not hold the doctrines of that Church? Does the Roman Catholic Church consider any or all of the following as heretics: Knox, Whitefield, Wesley, Livingstone, Milton, Bunyan, Penn, Fox, Chalmers, Moody, Dr Horton? Are the whole of the clergy and members of the Anglican Church – or any other Church, e.g. the Wesleyan – considered heretics by the Roman Catholic Church?

Answer:
Yes, every one of them. [It goes on to distinguish between 'formal' and 'material' heretics, who are not in quite so much trouble.]

Question:
Were not the following tortures sanctioned by the Church of Rome, and made use of by the Inquisition – burning to the death, the strappado or pulley, by which the victim's arms were dislocated, the application of live coals to the soles of the feet, the rack, the pouring of huge quantities of water into a linen bag thrust down the throat, iron dice forced into the feet by screws, the application of red-hot irons to the breast and sides, with many others?

The answer is quite brilliant:

The assertion that these practices were 'sanctioned by the Church of Rome', though not untrue in words, gives an impression which is absolutely false . . .

Sadly, this was not all good clean fun. In both my schoolboy prayer-book and the Missionary Society's *Questions and Answers on the Catholic Church* there are a couple of Latin phrases that give a hint of the darker side of the Church's self-confident belief in its monopoly of the truth: *Nihil Obstat* and *Imprimatur*. The *Nihil Obstat* is followed by the name of a censor, and indicates that he has found nothing contrary to Catholic teaching to 'stand in the way' of its publication, and the *Imprimatur*, or 'let it be printed', is endorsed by a senior cleric. Censorship was an automatic Church reflex – indeed, Rome has never really shaken off the habit, as I found when I met some of the rebel theologians and priests I interviewed for this book. Because it believed it spoke Absolute Truth it believed it owned the truth. The other side of the pre-Conciliar Church's emphasis on the mystical and the divine was a ready willingness to condemn scientific conclusions that did not square with the Church's understanding, and to stick by that condemnation long after it had become ludicrous to do so. The other side of its pursuit of beauty in its worship was an excessive addiction to ritualism, and its obsession with prescription was matched by a ferocious intolerance of dissent.

John XXIII's original reasons for calling the Second Vatican Council have never been fully explained. It is said that the idea first came to him during a briefing from his Secretary of State: as Cardinal Tardini went through the day's reports from the Vatican diplomatic service, painting a grim picture of a world in turmoil, the Pope was inspired by the notion that a full Council of the Church – something that had taken place only twice in the previous five hundred years – would enable it to engage with the problems of the twentieth century. But the vague and lukewarm way in which his cardinals and the Curia, the Vatican bureaucracy, initially responded to it suggests that many of them saw it as the dream of a slightly dotty old man. John had been chosen, after all, to serve as a 'transitional pope' – the *papa di passaggio*. When he told eighteen of his curial cardinals of his plans on 25 January at the church of St Paul's Without the Walls, they were so astonished that they were reduced to silence – 'Too moved and too happy to utter a word,' one of them explained later, rather unconvincingly – and the official organ of the Vatican, *Osservatore Romano*, broke the news to the world in a statement so terse that it was almost lost between the announcement of a diocesan synod for the clergy of Rome and plans to update canon law. But the calling of the Council was a recognition of a fact that now, with the hindsight of three decades, seems blindingly obvious: the Church and the world around it were moving in steadily different directions, and however healthy the Church may have appeared on the surface, its intellectual mindset was simply not sustainable in the long-term.

For nearly a century the Catholic Church had lived on its inherited intellectual capital. It was a magnificent inheritance – the intellectual equivalent of the Getty, Astor and Grosvenor millions all rolled into one – and the Church could afford to live handsomely for a while. But by the time Pope John XXIII became its guardian, the coffers were almost empty. The profligate heir who had set the Church on this ruinous course was Pius IX – Pio Nono. By one of those twists that pepper the history of the papacy he had been elected in 1846 as a liberal who could meet the demand for reform in the Papal States, and for a while his openness to change made him the darling of the Roman crowds. But that did not save him when Europe erupted in 1848, the Year of Revolutions, which saw the established order challenged all over the continent. Pio Nono escaped disguised as a servant from the mob besieging his palace, and fled to exile in Naples. The experience turned him into a reactionary of the most entrenched kind, and for the next thirty years of his long rule he went energetically about the task of building a wall around the Church.

Of course, the Church had found itself on the losing side of the intellectual argument for centuries: the Reformation and the Renaissance, the Enlightenment, the development of the natural sciences, the ideas that animated the American Declaration of Independence and the French Revolution all represented a steady march away from the medieval thinking to which the Church had become so firmly wedded. But it was not until Pius IX's papacy that the Church's rejection of the world around it was formalized and codified. In 1854 Pius defied rationalism with the doctrine of the Immaculate Conception of the Virgin Mary. Ten years later the Syllabus of Errors was published, which listed and condemned the heresies of the modern world. And in 1869 he called the First Vatican Council, at which the dogma of Papal Infallibility was declared. The Council set the tone for a period of intolerance and triumphalism, which froze the Church in the Middle Ages.

In 1896 Leo XIII issued a papal bull that condemned Anglican orders as 'absolutely null and utterly void'. It was based on what is now judged to be dubious theology: the bull argues that English reforms undertaken in the sixteenth century undermined the true nature of the priesthood. It was inspired by political opportunism: Cardinal Vaughan, Archbishop of Westminster, was a convert from Anglicanism, and believed that a flood of Anglican ministers would follow him on the road to Rome if the Pope ruled that they were not really priests. It looked like an act of spiteful and belated revenge for the Reformation. A hundred years later Cardinal Hume was conducting the delicate negotiations necessary to convert Anglican priests disenchanted over the ordination of women, and he had to go to Rome to work out a way round the fact that the Church still technically regarded the Anglican priesthood as a fraud.

In 1907 the Church formally condemned 'Modernism' and began hunting energetically for heresy among its own members. Pius X is said to have run a 'secret espionage association', which spied 'even on Their Eminences, the Cardinals'. When Benedict XV became Pope in 1914 he found his own name on the list of suspected Modernists.

The effect was to stop the Church thinking. The intellectual energies that should have been engaged in meeting the challenges of the twentieth century were spent on producing tendentious justifications for the Catholic Missionary Society and prayer-books to tighten the Church's grip on the souls of small boys. Because the intellectual resources at the Church's disposal were considerable, it was done well. But, for all their intelligence and creativity, men like Waugh and Chesterton were simply polishing the family silver to reflect the Catholic view of the modern world more brightly; they did little to reinvest for its future. One of the final documents agreed at Vatican II spoke of 'the treasury out of which the Church continually brings forth new things that are in harmony with the things that are old'. When John XXIII took the throne of St Peter he found that many of the rooms in the treasury had been locked for centuries, and much of the reluctance he encountered to open them up sprang from the embarrassing fact that the keys had long since been lost.

There was also a deep fear of what might be revealed if the doors were opened. Cardinal Hume's explanation of the appeal of pre-Conciliar Catholicism was simple: 'It was safe,' he said. The Catholic Church had had a radical youth and a vigorous, innovative early adulthood, but as middle age approached she became increasingly ossified and set in her ways. On the threshold of her two-thousandth birthday she tried to come out from behind her fortress walls and rediscover her ideals.

For many Catholics the change that began with John XXIII's broadside against the prophets of doom has been every bit as traumatic as a bereavement or a divorce; the story of the Church over the past four decades is the drama of an institution undergoing a mid-life crisis.

2

A Slight Conspiracy

The Second Vatican Council was one of those rare moments when the Church was moving in step with the times. The revolutionary spirit that was to bring free love to Carnaby Street and violence to the campuses of America was just beginning to spread its wings, and all over the world the old order was changing. In the week the Council opened Britain declared independence for Uganda and acquired its first female high court judge. France had just retreated from colonial rule in Algeria, and Martin Luther King's civil-rights campaign was at its height in the states of the American South. When the Council Fathers met they were on the crest of a wave of change.

At the first substantive Council session the Church began an experiment with an idea that most of the Western world had long accepted: democracy. It was a dramatic day and, like many pivotal political moments, it had its roots in an obscure argument about procedure. Its genesis underlined just how far the Church had to go to catch up with the modern world.

The exercise of power in the Roman Catholic Church is a mysterious business, and that suits the body with its hands on most of the levers of power: the Roman Curia. To civil servants from Whitehall to Foggy Bottom in Washington the privileged position enjoyed by a Vatican bureaucrat must seem an impossible dream: imagine being able to appear before a committee of the House of Commons or the American Congress and claim the Holy Spirit as the authority for your actions. The way the Church is governed reflects both its history as a temporal power and its claim to divine inspiration. The Papal States – some sixteen thousand square miles of central Italy – were lost to the Church in the Italian unification of 1870, but the Pope still has a unique place among the world's political leaders: he is head both of the world's smallest sovereign state – the Vatican has some five hundred citizens – and the world's largest institution, with close to a billion members. In addition to the powers he enjoys in this world, he is believed to have special access to the lines of communication with the next: he is the 'pontifex', the bridge-builder between the human sphere and the divine. Both roles encourage the centralization of authority in the papal person. The temporal power the Pope enjoys has its roots in the Middle Ages, and as head of the Vatican state he is Europe's last absolute monarch. His position as the successor to St Peter gives him a special claim to power over the world's Catholics in matters of faith and morals. But the way in which he exercises his authority in both fields is tempered by theology and by the practical difficulties involved in fulfilling such a peculiar mixture of functions.

A modern pope need not be much troubled by the affairs of his city state. The Vatican consists of little more than a post office – much patronized by tourists in search of an unusual postmark – the Swiss Guard and the Vatican museums, which make a healthy profit. There is a small police force and a fire department, but no one pays tax, and the whole enterprise is run with reasonable efficiency by a committee of five cardinals, known as the Pontifical Commission for the Vatican City State, and their staff.

The governance of the Universal Church should, in theory, be shared between the Pope and his bishops. Though he may be St Peter's successor, they are the successors to the other apostles. The way the shared inheritance of the Pope and his bishops – there are now some four thousand worldwide – should be reflected in the running of the Church is one of the most contentious issues in contemporary Catholicism. At the time of the calling of the Council, the College of Bishops had, in practice, very little say in determining the direction of the Church.

The office of cardinal has no biblical foundation, and has arisen from the way in which the Church developed as an institution. Cardinals are princes of the Church, and at one time it was possible to be created one without having been ordained. The cardinals' most important formal function is, of course, to elect a pope, and to run the Church in the interregnum between popes. But they have also become established as the Pope's special advisers, rather like a medieval monarch's favourites at court.

The balance of power between popes, cardinals and bishops has shifted back and forth over the centuries, but whatever happens the Roman Curia seems to endure as a force to be reckoned with. It is the imperial civil service by which the Roman Catholic Church is held together. Because it is permanently based in the Vatican, it is natural for a pope to turn to it for advice much more readily than he does to bishops in their sometimes far-flung dioceses. Even his cardinals must be specially called together for what is known as a 'consistory', if he wants to consult them formally, but the Curia is always there. It is similar to a secular civil service in the sense that it is organized by departments, but its religious dimension gives it a distinctive character. The Curia consists principally of the Secretariat of State and the Pontifical Councils and Sacred Congregations.

The Secretariat of State might be compared in British terms to the Cabinet Office, in American terms to the White House Staff. Based in the Apostolic Palace, it is the body a pope can use most directly to run the Church as an institution and to direct its relations with the rest of the world. Its head, the secretary of state, is sometimes referred to as the Church's prime minister. Through him and his two deputies, the Pope has access to the resources of the Vatican's diplomatic service.

The Congregations and Councils are like civil-service departments, each assigned an area of responsibility, such as the family, the clergy, or Catholic education. Congregations are headed by a prefect, Councils by a president. Most are cardinals, and they run their departments with the assistance of an often surprisingly small staff of officials. Every Congregation and Council is presided over by a kind of board of management, a group in some cases more than fifty strong that meets periodically. Although such groups include outsiders, including lay people, the key players are the curial insiders. Curial cardinals all sit on one another's Congregations and Councils, strengthening the web of contacts that binds the Curia together and makes it an object of such suspicion to outsiders.

Unlike most of the world's civil-service bureaucracies, the Curia is able to go about its business without the tiresome necessity to answer to a democratically elected assembly or an executive arm of govern-ment. The Church claims to be the interpreter of God's will on earth; the Curia sees itself as the instrument by which the process of interpretation is achieved. And just as civil servants in London or Washington may sometimes try to frustrate the will of their elected leaders in what they sincerely believe to be the national interest, so curial officials sometimes seek to obstruct a pope's designs, believing with equal sincerity that they are acting with the best interests of the Church at heart. John XXIII's vision of his Council most definitely did not square with the ideas of the civil servants he needed to realize his ambitions.

At the heart of the curial system of John's day was the Holy Office – or, to give it the title that was once a byword for religious intolerance, the Inquisition. Today it is called the Sacred Congregation for the Doctrine of the Faith, but in all its incarnations its function has been the same: to protect the sacred 'deposit' of the faith bequeathed to the Church by Jesus Christ, and to guard against heresies that might threaten it. At the heart of the Holy Office in 1962 sat Cardinal Alfredo Ottaviani.

He is remembered with great personal affection even by his opponents, but his long and stubborn fight against change earned him the status of an icon who stood for everything backward-looking in the Church. By a grimly symbolic quirk of fate his eyesight grew steadily dimmer as the Council progressed. He fought an energetic bureaucratic rearguard action in the three years of preparation for the meeting of the world's bishops in Rome.

Archbishop Denis Hurley of Durban – one of the youngest archbishops in the Church in the 1960s – was chosen to sit on the Central Preparatory Commission. Individual commissions had been set up to consider different areas of the Church's life and produce reports – or *schemata* – for the Council to debate. The Central Preparatory Commission saw and approved them all before they went forward, so a seat on the Commission should have provided a real opportunity to influence the course the Council took. Archbishop Hurley came gradually to realize that it was not going to work like that. Presented with one conservative draft after another – almost all heavily influenced by the Curia – he and the other Commission members from outside the Roman circle tried to put their own stamp on the texts, painstakingly amending them section by section. But when the documents came back to them in their final form they found that the curial drafters had taken out almost everything they had tried to put in: 'They stayed in Rome and edited the material after we had gone home,' he explained to me. 'We had no say in the final editing . . . By May 1962 I was almost in despair that this Council would be in any way refreshing or innovating . . . It seemed that the system had taken over.'

It looked like a brilliant and highly effective coup by Ottaviani and his allies. But the politics of the Church were changing in a way that neither the Roman faction nor, indeed, the world at large had appreciated. Archbishop Hurley took his frustration to a group of powerful reforming cardinals who became known as the Trans-Alpini – those from 'across the Alps' – who were to challenge Roman hegemony. They included the German-speaking bloc made up of König of Vienna, Döpfner of Munich and Frings of Cologne, plus the French led by Lienart of France, with Suenens of Belgium and Alfrings of Utrecht. And they had a critical ally inside the Curia in the German Jesuit Cardinal Augustin Bea. Their memory still inspires awe among those who saw them perform at the Council, and my meeting with Cardinal König gave me a flavour of what a formidable force these 'giants of the Church' must have been when they worked together in their prime.

Franz König was ordained in 1933, actively opposed the Nazis during the Second World War, and at its end became a professor of theology. In the 1940s he wrote a series of what are now standard reference works on Christianity and world religions, rising to become a bishop in his mid-forties and Archbishop of Vienna in 1956, a post he held for thirty years. He was created cardinal in 1958. By the time I met him, nearly forty years later, he was one of just four of Pope John's cardinals still living. At ninety-two he was still full of intellectual curiosity. His mind, legendary for its brilliance, was focused, and even after two and a half hours of an intensive interview – covering complex ideas and events that happened decades ago – he showed few signs of fatigue. His English remained fluent throughout (he acquired almost complete mastery of ten languages).

Mention of his name provoked fond reminiscences in all sorts of unexpected corners of the globe, many relating to his passion for physical fitness: visiting Chicago in his sixties he astonished his hosts by insisting on water-skiing on Lake Michigan, and Cardinal Hume remembers him jogging round one of the inner courtyards of the Vatican during the two conclaves held to elect popes in 1978, when he was already over seventy. Judging by the number of cardinals I met who maintained their full vigour well into old age – the veteran diplomat Agostino Casaroli, the great champion of human rights Paolo Arns of Brazil, and, indeed, Hume himself – the combination of freedom from anxiety about earthly things and a passion for the heavenly must offer a healthy lifestyle. Having a couple of adoring nuns to do all the washing and cooking probably helps.

The Trans-Alpini group was formed by leaders of the Church in Catholicism's historic European heartland, and that gave them authority and standing among the world's bishops. They also had a reach beyond their home constituencies that few appreciated. The Churches of Africa, Asia and even Latin America lacked the confidence to take the initiative at the Council, but France, Germany and Holland had sent missionaries all over the developing world, and the missionary bishops who arrived in Rome after years of relative isolation in remote dioceses naturally looked to their national leaders for guidance. Finally the progressive Europeans found allies among the North Americans. The Church in the United States had grown steadily in strength but had never really flexed its muscles before. At Vatican II it emerged as a force to be reckoned with.

The last stage of the Roman coup planned by Cardinal Ottaviani and the Curia was to have been completed with the election of a new set of commissions at the opening of the Council, to take over the work of the preparatory bodies, and while the Council sat they were to have the job of turning its debates and decisions into documents that could be endorsed with the full authority of the Church. To ensure their control over the Council, the curialists needed their own men on the commissions, and they prepared a list of approved candidates to be presented for a vote on the morning of the opening Council session.

The progressives had seen it coming. There was, Archbishop Hurley confessed to me, with the charming understatement of an earlier age, 'a slight conspiracy'. The night before the opening session, the Trans-Alpini conferred on the telephone and decided to push for a recess while the Council Fathers formed their own views about candidates for the commissions.

If the Europeans were the ideas men, the Americans knew how to make things happen. Archbishop Hannan arrived at the Council as an assistant bishop for Washington DC. He had studied theology at the Gregorian University in Rome in the 1930s, had served as chaplain to the Second Airborne Division during the war, and returned to Rome full of anti-Communist fervour: 'We felt that the future of the world depended upon our maintaining a great deal of discipline and order because we had freed Europe of one tyranny,' he told me sternly, 'but the world was still faced with the tyranny of Communism.' But he was also a good American democrat, the heir to the traditions of Jefferson and Washington.

Hannan had seen the preparatory drafts that had so dismayed his South African colleague Hurley, and his reaction had been the same: 'Some of them were done by men who had taught me at the Gregorian University. They were done in a rather academic fashion and we didn't see anything new in them . . . we thought there should be a new spirit and that's the reason why we were hesitant about accepting everything that was being produced by the committee in charge of the Council.' He did what good American activists always do: 'organize'.

The night before the opening session he and a group of fellow bishops – he called them 'us young guys' – went round canvassing support for a revolt against the Curia's electoral lists: 'I remember pounding on the door of a nice old archbishop from Kansas City at eleven o'clock at night. Of course he was startled but when I told him what my mission was he agreed with it . . . We American bishops voted largely as a block.'

In fact, a formal vote proved unnecessary.

The agenda on the Council's first morning was the nomination of the 160 members who would sit on the ten commissions. But the moment business began Cardinal Lienart demanded the floor and called for a break in proceedings so that the bishops would have time to make up their minds about the candidates. He was seconded by Cardinal Frings, who said that he had the support of Döpfner and König. Even today the sound of clapping in a church falls oddly on the ear: sacred buildings are designed for more stylized expressions of emotion. In 1962 the applause that echoed round St Peter's from two and a half thousand middle-aged and elderly men in mitres marked a watershed. 'The Council took over its own future from that moment,' says Hurley. Cardinal König told me that the message they were trying to deliver was simple: 'We are the Council, not the Vatican.' To the great confusion of the outside world, the Council was suspended within half an hour of beginning.

It gave the Council Fathers a breathing space to make their own judgements about whom they wanted to see on the commissions, and in informal meetings during the ensuing days lists of candidates were hammered out. The bishops were enjoying the novel experience of seeing their own opinions carry weight in the way the Church conceived of itself and its mission. As an institution it had long acted as a mechanism for transmitting authority downwards; the Council provided the first institutional forum that allowed decisions to flow in the other direction.

It was a pretty odd form of Parliament. Banks of seats were constructed along each side of the nave of St Peter's, like the stands at a football ground or the bleachers in a baseball park. The main sessions began with Mass at nine in the morning, and continued for three hours of full debate until lunch, with each speaker allowed ten minutes to make his point. 'Bishop after bishop, cardinal after cardinal,' Hurley remembers. 'I found the procedures heavy and boring.'

The debates were, of course, conducted in Latin. That presented no difficulties for men like Hurley and Hannan, who as young priests had been students in Rome. They had been immersed in the language: all lectures and classes at the Gregorian University were conducted in it, so the idea of Latin as a spoken language was second nature to them. But bishops from some of the far-flung provinces of the Catholic empire had to sit there for hour after hour with little idea of what was going on. And even the most skilled Latinists sometimes had trouble with the variety of accents – the French and Spanish were often stumped by the pronunciation from the English-speaking world, especially when some of the American bishops were in full flow.

The voting slips were in Latin too: the bishops would tick the box marked *placet* – it pleases me – for yes, *non placet* for no, and *placet iuxta modum* to agree to an amendment. Archbishop Felici, the Council's secretary-general and a Roman curialist through and through, liked to show off his linguistic skills by making Latin jokes and issuing practical bulletins in Latin on matters like car-parking arrangements, which must have amused some and made others feel very small.

But by the standards of most international deliberative bodies – the UN General Assembly, say, or the European Parliament – the Council was effective, and the volume of business it got through was awe-inspiring. Critically, it changed the bishops' thinking about how the Church should take decisions; they caught the democratic bug. All the symptoms of a vigorous adversarial political system began to appear. They began caucusing. The afternoons were devoted to committee work, and while the committees were meeting, groups of bishops from different parts of the world began to form blocs: those from Africa, for example, coalesced around language, so that there were Anglophone and Francophone alliances, and another from the Portuguese-speaking countries. They held discussions among themselves, away from St Peter's and in a language they could all understand. The theologians who were driving the Council debate behind the scenes – men like Hans Küng and Karl Rahner – were invited to address small groups where real debate was possible. The regional blocs forged common positions of their own.

The guerrilla warfare to which skilled politicians everywhere resort in order to speed up the decision-making process and circumvent cumbersome procedure began to surface in St Peter's. Just as the House of Commons has its tea-room, the basilica acquired its version of a Roman street bar. With scholarly facetiousness, it was dubbed the Bar Jonah – which means Son of John in Hebrew, and is a scriptural reference to St Peter. Legend has it that Pope John himself insisted that the bar be installed so that the bishops could smoke, fearing that otherwise they would be 'puffing under their mitres'. It inevitably became the focus for plots, gossip and horse-trading, and – like the House of Commons tea-room during a dull debate – filled up quickly when a poor speaker took the floor.

With the arrival of democratic politics came the Church's first real encounter with the press. It was a painful process, and even today the Church is not really comfortable with the fourth estate. 'Covering Vatican Hill was much like covering Capitol Hill in Washington DC,' Robert Kaiser of *Time* remembers. 'It was a political event. It was a parliament of the world's bishops and therefore it was a very human event. The Holy Spirit may have been there, but the Holy Spirit normally works through human beings. And I could see the human beings busily at work, and there was a huge argument going on. That was what was fun about it.'

Nothing gets the journalistic juices going like secrecy, and the early sessions of the Council were as secret as the Church could make such an enormous gathering. I first encountered the technique known as the 'news blackout' during the 1980s when I was covering superpower summit meetings. There was logic behind the argument that Ronald Reagan and Mikhail Gorbachev could talk more freely without the political pressures that would inevitably have been generated had the substance of their deliberations been made public. It was equally undeniable that in those Cold War days a summit was big news, and the thousands of journalists who attended expected something to report. The American solution was for the presidential spokesman to relay in great detail everything that was not news: what the President and First Lady had for breakfast, what time their alarm had gone off, what kind of car brought the President to his meeting and so on, in tedious detail almost down to the time and quality of the presidential bowel movements. It led to the following memorable exchange on the first day of the Reykjavik summit in 1986.

Larry Speakes, spokesman for the President: '. . . the President then looked at the local papers . . .'

First reporter, shouting from the back: 'But the local papers are in Icelandic.'

Second reporter: 'The man said he looked at the local papers, not that he read them!'

The Vatican had been perfecting the technique of the news blackout at the Council long before the Americans latched on to it. The justification was the same: that real debate was easier without the pressure of public opinion. And the results were sometimes equally ludicrous. Each evening the official Vatican bulletin recorded who had opened the session by enthroning the gospels on the altar that morning, and gave extensive accounts of incidental detail. Robert Kaiser preserved some of the more collectable news items, this from 30 October 1962:

Before the commencement of the discussion, His Excellency Monsignor Felici, Secretary General, announced that the Pontifical Commission for the Vatican City would distribute to each Father an envelope containing a card indicating postal and telegraph rates to all the nations of the world and also two series of stamps issued on the occasion of the Council's inauguration, one cancelled, the other new.

'We began to get official bulletins that said absolutely nothing, so reporters had to fan out around the city and cultivate sources who were inside – the bishops and theologians – and debrief them to find out what was happening,' says Kaiser.

Applications for press accreditation to the Council were accompanied with the instructions that every journalist should have 'an entirely correct attitude to the Holy See', and be endorsed by a clergyman. But the Vatican hopes of controlling the press proved vain: in the end those who try to control the flow of information in democracies almost always lose – and, as we know, the Church was becoming a democracy.

Nine hundred journalists turned up to cover the opening of the Council, and television was there too – the first time its impact had been felt at a critical moment in the Church's history. For the opening ceremony the Vatican's workmen had installed 'fifty kilometres of telephone lines, four and a half kilometres of television cable, three and a half kilometres of microphone cable and eleven kilometres of coaxial cable'. Put all that technology and all those journalists together with nearly three thousand bishops turned politicians, and the result is inevitable: information begins to seep out all over the place, and the official bulletins seem irrelevant.

The Americans as a group – bishops and theologians as well as reporters – can claim much of the credit for pushing the Vatican to become more media-friendly. Archbishop Hannan was responsible for liaison with the English-speaking press. 'The first year,' he says, 'was a rough year.' He came under pressure from major American newspapers and magazines and the broadcast networks who had sent teams to Rome only to find they had nothing to do: 'We got all kind of complaints: "We spent a lot of money sending these people over, we thought there was going to be a story each day and there are no stories . . . we're disgusted. And we are not going to send them back until something is done."' 'Good riddance,' might have been the response of the Roman Curia; the man in charge of the press operation, Monsignor Vallainc, had at one point written to tell a French journalist bluntly, 'We do not need the press.' But Hannan came from a country where the rights of the press were as deeply ingrained as the rights of the Church in Rome: he pressed hard for greater media access, and gradually it worked.

A fellow American was fighting his own more subversive campaign for press freedom. In the Council's second week the *New Yorker* published a startlingly detailed account of the struggles between pro-gressives and conservatives during the preparation for the Council. 'Replete with facts, rumours, gossip and educated guesses', in the words of its author many years later, 'Letter from Vatican City' was printed under the byline Xavier Rynne, and appeared in the magazine for the duration of the Council. There were sixteen letters in all, and they were considered such a reliable source of information that the bishops themselves would sometimes turn to the *New Yorker* to find out what was going on. Even today Xavier Rynne's four-volumes provide one of the most accurate and detailed accounts of the Council that exists.

In consultation with the editor of the *New Yorker* the author, who had a teaching job in Rome, decided to keep his identity secret. 'If we had used my own name I might have been persecuted in Rome,' he told me, from comfortable retirement in Maryland. 'I might have lost my professorship.' In the foreword to the first volume of his account, which came out in 1963, Rynne lists with some glee the identities he has been assigned by Council gossip: 'a disgruntled Catholic clergyman', 'a Roman student who after failing his final exams criticized the Roman educational system', 'a writer inspired by the Vatican Secretariat of State', and 'finally, believe it or not, Jack Kerouac'. The mystery was pursued with the same enthusiasm that later marked the chase for Deep Throat, Woodward and Bernstein's notorious source in the Watergate scandal, and the search for the author of *Primary Colors*, the satirical account of Bill Clinton's election campaign. One or two people noticed that the middle name of a Redemptorist priest, Father Francis Murphy, was Xavier and that his mother's maiden name had been Rynne, but it was not until the twenty-fifth anniversary of the Council in 1985 that he finally made a public confession.

Father Francis was what was known as a *peritus*, or theological adviser at the Council. Many bishops had brought their own advisers to guide them through the debates, and the *periti* might easily find themselves playing the role of what in contemporary politics is called a spin-doctor. Archbishop Hannan – on the conservative wing of the Church on most issues despite his belief in the free press – regarded Rynne as another symptom of the Church's experiment with democracy: the arrival of the politically motivated leak. 'Everything he leaked and the way he leaked it of course focused attention on what he hoped would come out of the Second Vatican Council,' he told me, 'we had so many *periti* over there giving talks to groups . . . and even when the Council did not decide as they had hoped they would put their own spin on it.'

The Council debated the mass media during its first session, and Xavier Rynne provided – as so often – the best account of what was said. The Council document that emerged was neither interesting nor original, but a couple of speeches provided an insight into Church thinking on the press at that time. A Canadian cardinal made a bold statement, which the Church has still not fully understood: 'The power of modern means of communication is so great,' said Cardinal Léger of Montreal, 'that it is ridiculous to try to insulate people against it; rather we must try to adopt it fearlessly, putting an end to the negative type of criticism characteristic of so many churchmen in the past.' The second noteworthy observation was made by the Archbishop of Siena, who 'brought up the subject of the Index of Forbidden Books, and suggested it be abolished'. 'This was,' writes Xavier Rynne, 'something of a surprise coming from an Italian prelate.' It is even more surprising to reflect that in the 1960s there was still a list of books that Catholics were forbidden to read.

A favourite Council anecdote has it that when John XXIII was asked what he meant it to achieve he walked over to his window and opened it as if to let in the fresh air of modernity. The aspiration to escape from the fortress walls behind which the Church had hidden for centuries was at the heart of the project, and was achieved as much by the way the Council reached its decisions as by the decisions themselves. The media played a critical role in the transformation. Robert Kaiser uses the analogy of watching a play then seeing the same play from backstage: 'You see all the wires and the pulleys and you get another view; that's what the mass media were giving. The world was getting a backstage view of the Council and the argumentation was very important.' The hundreds of millions of souls who made up the Church in the world watched their leaders disagreeing. It has taken more than thirty years for the full impact of that to sink in, and the old instincts are not quite dead. But the vast majority of Catholics today claim the same right to argue over ideas and challenge established teaching as the bishops did in the 1960s.

'The twentieth century is about the passing of power from the élite to the people,' says Robert Kaiser, 'and through the media the people were very much present at Vatican II.' The first great Council debate was about taking the worship of God away from the élite and giving it back to the people.

3

Quietly and With Power

A Marxist analysis of the Second Vatican Council would assign to Cardinal Ottaviani the role of class traitor.

The panoply of titles that adorn the Church hierarchy – all the glitter of eminences, my lords, excellencies and monsignors – belied the fact that by 1962 the bishops of the Church came from every walk of life – 'the sons of peasants and princes, of bankers and labourers, of tribal chiefs and trolley conductors', as Xavier Rynne put it in the first of his account of the Council:

Emanuel Mabathoana, Bishop of Maseru, is the grandson of the Lion of the Mountain, Chief of the Basutos in South Africa; Bishop Dlamini of Umzinmkulu is a member of the royal family of Natal. Cardinal Gracias saw the light of day in the slums of Karachi, Cardinal Siri's father was a Genoese longshoreman, and Archbishop Kominek of Vaga was the son of a Silesian miner. The youthful-looking Philippe Nguyen Kim Dien worked as a street-cleaner and rag-picker before entering the seminary . . .

Alfredo Ottaviani, prince of the Church though he was, began life as the son of a baker 'with the black dirt of Trastevere beneath his feet' – and those who knew him speak with affection of the way he maintained the earthy good humour characteristic of the area where he had grown up. Yet his most dramatic intervention in the first session of the Council was a defence of the privileges of the élite. On 30 October 1962 he delivered a passionate attack against plans to change the liturgy of the Mass. How dare the Fathers of the Council contemplate tampering with something that had not changed since the seventh century? 'Are these Fathers planning a revolution?' he demanded. His particular contempt was reserved for the proposal to abandon the use of Latin in favour of vernacular languages. As if to underline its special place in Catholic life, a torrent of Latin poured from his lips for a quarter of an hour, until the president of the day reminded him politely that he had gone well beyond his allotted time. After a further two minutes, as the Cardinal's voice rose to a falsetto of denunciation, his microphone was cut off and, as if to rub salt into the wound, many of the Council Fathers applauded the presiding bishop's decision. For two weeks thereafter the Cardinal boycotted the Council, sulking in his tent as he pondered the unpalatable thought that the answer to his question about a revolution might be yes.

For centuries Latin had been the language of the élite. In the medieval world it had been an instrument of power. Those who knew it were the computer nerds of their age, possessors of a knowledge that set them apart and made them a commodity in high demand; they could interpret the law, say Mass, read the poets and philosophers of an earlier age. And even in the modern Church it defined a kind of spiritual class system, marked a divide between those who understood what they were doing and saying and those who did not. Beautiful, soporific, addictive and uplifting, the Latin Mass provided a justification for Karl Marx's much-quoted observation that religion is the opium of the people. In denouncing the shift from Latin to the vernacular, Cardinal Ottaviani was speaking against the interests of the class from which he had risen.

Generalizations, such as Marx's epigram, fail to explain everything that gave the old liturgy such a powerful hold over so many people. But even in the most sincere expressions of nostalgia it inspires there is an element of the feudal idea of power that went with the old Church. One English priest who was ordained before the Council described the old Mass to me as 'a quiet centre in a noisy world', which gave people a 'space . . . for saying their prayers'. His parish included a large area of working-class homes in the 1960s, and he suggested that the 'quiet space' was especially important to poor families: 'I go down the street,' he remembers, 'every house is full of an Irish family with ten or twelve children . . . back-to-back houses . . . there's not much peace. So often church was a place you could get spiritual refreshment.' That analysis may well be accurate, but it is not difficult to detect the echoes of paternalism it carries with it.

Today it seems self-evident that the congregation should understand what happens on the altar. In 1962 it was a highly controversial notion. All sorts of arguments were advanced against change – that it destroyed the mystique of the Mass, that the use of Latin, a *lingua franca*, united the Church, even that the introduction of communion in both kinds presented a threat to public hygiene. Traditionally, lay Catholics had only received the communion wafer, while the wine that became Christ's blood was reserved for the priest. When it was suggested that this might change, the thorny issue of women's lipstick smearing the communion cup was raised on the floor of St Peter's. But looking back on the debate with the perspective of the intervening decades, it is apparent that it was an argument about the distribution of power in the Church.

The champions of liturgical reform saw it as a way of bringing worship closer to the people: it was not just a question of replacing the language of the élite – Latin – with the language of the people, they also wanted to reform the Tridentine rite – so called because it had existed since the Council of Trent. That Council, which ended in 1563 after meeting sporadically over a period of eighteen years, was the Roman Catholic Church's answer to the Reformation, a defiant rejection of everything the new Protestant churches stood for. It set the course of Roman Catholicism for the next few centuries. The Tridentine rite made the Mass a sacrament performed by a priest with the people as spectators, which encouraged the idea of the Church as an institution run by a priestly caste to whom the laity owed complete obedience. The reformers wanted a liturgy that allowed the people to participate fully in the Mass – and, by implication, in the way the Church was run.

Cardinal König believes that that first furious tussle over the liturgy was the defining moment of the Council. It marked out the differences between those like him who shared Pope John's vision of a modern Church and the 'pessimists' who 'felt the Church has eternal ideas, the message of Christ, so we can't touch it or change it', who did not 'distinguish between what is essential and what depends on the changing times'. The task in hand, König told me, was to adapt the liturgy and, indeed, the Church as a whole, so that it would 'bring people back to understand and to live with the Church'.

The battle over the liturgy also began a process of historical reassessment, which is still going on in the Church today. The scholars who had been given the task of creating a new form of worship argued that much of their work consisted in stripping away the unnecessary ornamentation that had grown up around the Mass over the centuries, and returning it to something closer to the sacrament Jesus had left the early Church. The shorthand of political debate – progressives, liberals, conservatives and so on – is notoriously inadequate for an account of the debate within the Church, and one of the reasons is that in some senses the progressives were more conservative than the conservatives: they looked back to the very early, pre-medieval Church for inspiration. And the more closely they looked there, the more support they found for causes dear to progressive hearts: married priests and elected bishops, for example, were both once the norm.

In the European heartland of Catholicism there was a significant democratic resistance – from many lay people and their parish priests – to the introduction of a democratic Church. For most believers the liturgy defines the Church: Mass on Sundays represents their principal point of contact with their religion – '*lex credendi, lex orandi*' as the old Catholic saying has it, 'the way you pray is the way you believe'. So the shake-up in the liturgy touched their Faith where they felt it most keenly. In France the pain of the transformation led eventually to the emergence of the traditionalist movement under Archbishop Marcel Lefebvre, which culminated in the creation of a schismatic traditionalist sect. In England, Cardinal Hume freely admits today, the Church leadership had done little to prepare their flock for what was coming. The English bishops, he said, were 'very loyal people, very obedient people', and were determined to bring in the changes required of them, but they did a feeble job of selling the revolution to the men and women in the pew. Change came as a shock. 'We did Mass in the old rite up to a certain Saturday,' the Cardinal says, 'and then on the first Sunday of Advent we all changed to English . . . For some people it was just too much.'

The battles between conservatives and progressives on the floor of St Peter's were fought out all over again at the grass-roots. In some parishes the bitterness engendered during that period has not been forgotten. Father John Challenor, who today runs a pressure group called Catholics for a Changing Church, was a priest at the Birmingham Oratory during the years of the Council, and was caught up in one of the most notorious disputes.

The Oratorians in England have a reputation for fogeydom, which is odd when you consider their heritage. Cardinal Newman, who founded the Birmingham Oratory and revitalized the Oratorians, was a revolutionary. His conversion to Catholicism in 1845 scandalized the Anglican world, and he soon found himself in trouble with the authorities in his new spiritual home: he was denounced to Rome for his writings on the laity. His thinking had such a profound effect on the Second Vatican Council that it is sometimes referred to as 'Newman's Council', for he believed that 'to live is to change' – a progressive philosophy if ever there was one.

Unlike most of the community at the Birmingham Oratory, Father Challenor was enthused by the Council. He said, 'It almost had the effect on me the burning bush had on Moses.' He taught in the Oratory School, and began to pass on some of the Council's conclusions to the boys. Their reaction made him realize the depth of conservative sentiment around him: 'I got used to some very surprising feedback. The boys would go home and tell their parish priest that this or that has been decided in Rome, and the parish priest would blow up and say, "You go and tell Father John he's got it wrong."' Parish priests all over England responded to the changes with similar reluctance: 'Conservatism,' says John Challenor, 'had been very effectively sold . . . For the hundred years before Vatican II, the general message of the Catholic Church had been to stick to tradition, distrust innovation and be very suspicious of novelty. Modernism was, after all, a dirty word for Catholics.'

The issue that brought John Challenor's dispute with his fellow Oratorians to a head seems ludicrously trivial with the hindsight of three decades: it was a row over where to put the altar in the Oratory church. But in those turbulent days many Catholics felt that their most fundamental ideas about God and their relationship with Him were being challenged, and such arguments were often fought with all the passion of a debate about the nature of human destiny. The Second Vatican Council had decreed that a priest should say Mass facing the congregation so that they could see what he was doing and be made to feel part of the service. The main church at the Oratory was designed for a priest to say Mass in the traditional way, with his back to the people. Modern churches are built to reflect the Council's concept of worship, and many older buildings proved easy to adapt. But the

Oratory's architecture is stubbornly Tridentine. Twelve massive marble columns – quarried in the Ligurian mountains, shipped in pairs to England by steamer and brought to Birmingham by canal barge – flank the nave beneath a painted tunnel-vaulted ceiling. Stand at the back and your eye is led irresistibly to the distant altar against the far wall. A communion rail separates the sanctuary – a realm set apart for the priest and his acolytes – from the congregation.

John Challenor and a small group of like-minded lay people pushed for the Church to be modernized to reflect the new liturgy endorsed by the Council; the majority of the Oratory fathers were fiercely resistant to such ideas. They feared disturbing what one of them described to me as the 'religious peace' of the lay people. Memoranda were written, bishops were called in to inspect the building, and at one stage a temporary altar was erected on boards under the dome. The old guard regarded John Challenor's group as 'revolutionaries' with 'wild ideas'; the modernizers were so incensed by the resistance to change that one prominent local layman led his family in a walk-out during the offertory. The ill-feeling generated by the episode never really went away, and eventually led to John Challenor leaving both the Birmingham Oratory and the priesthood.

This was not just an argument about furniture: the reform of the liturgy had uncovered a chasm between two different understandings of the meaning of the Mass. 'What the new liturgy gained,' says Cardinal Hume, 'was a sense of a community round an altar. But what it lost was the sense of the numinous, of mystery.' And because the Mass is so central to the life of the Church, a dispute about its meaning becomes a dispute about the nature of the Church. 'You were either a transcendentalist, worshipping a distant deity,' says John Challenor, 'or an immanentist, celebrating the presence of God within the community here and actually doing something about it.'

In Britain and much of Europe the debate over the changes to the liturgy took up so much of the Church's energy that the rest of the Council's work was lost in the fog of war. To many European Catholics Vatican II meant the end of the Latin Mass – for good or ill – and nothing more than that. It was not until the journeys I made for this book that I understood how much more wide-ranging its impact had been in the Church beyond Europe. The debate over the liturgy in the autumn of 1962 was only the starting point for an intellectual revolution that continued on every front right up until the moment the Council closed on the Feast of the Immaculate Conception, 8 December 1965.

Pope John XXIII may have dreamed of that revolution, but he did not live to see it become a reality. He was taken ill during his Council's second month, and although he rallied sufficiently to address the bishops at the end of its first session, cancer did not spare him for long. On 3 June 1963 he died. At the conclave to elect his successor the cardinals chose a man they believed could bring the Council to a successful conclusion. Cardinal Giovanni Battista Montini, Archbishop of Milan, took the name Paul VI.

For the Church in Europe the Council was as much about tidying up the past as preparing for the future. On the day before it closed Pope Paul VI and the Patriarch Athenagoras lifted the 'anathemas' of 1054, by which the Orthodox and Roman Churches condemned each other to damnation. It was not the kind of thing likely to set popular pulses racing in a year when the Beatles got their MBEs, Bertrand Russell tore up his Labour Party membership card over Vietnam, and Jean Shrimpton scandalized polite society by wearing a mini-skirt to the Melbourne races. But the main Council documents looked forward and outward, to the future and the Church in the world. With their glorious Latin titles and self-confident assertion of the power of the Christian message, they are imbued with the spirit of optimism that John evoked in that opening address in St Peter's. *Lumen Gentium*, the Church's new Constitution, begins:

Christ is the Light of nations. Because this is so, this Sacred Synod gathered together in the Holy Spirit eagerly desires, by proclaiming the Gospel to every creature, to bring the light of Christ to all men, a light brightly visible on the countenance of the Church. Since the Church is in Christ like a sacrament or as a sign and instrument both of a very closely knit union with God and of the unity of the human race, it desires now to unfold more fully to the faithful of the Church and to the whole world its own inner nature and universal mission.

And in similar vein its companion document, *Gaudium et Spes*, On the Church in the World, opens:

The joys, the hopes, the griefs and the anxieties of the men of this age, especially those who are poor or in any way afflicted, these are the joys and hopes, the griefs and anxieties of the followers of Christ. Indeed nothing genuinely human fails to raise an echo in their hearts. For theirs is a community composed of men. United in Christ, they are led by the Holy Spirit in their journey to the Kingdom of their Father and they have welcomed the news of salvation, which is meant for every man. That is why this community realizes that it is truly linked with mankind and its history to the deepest bonds.

Those are the words of a Church that has broken down the treasury doors and ransacked the contents to offer them to the world. The pessimism and suspicion that marked the decades between the end of the First Vatican Council in 1870 and the beginning of the Second in 1962 seemed to have been blown away with the cobwebs.

But had they? History is not so easily shaken off, and Cardinal Ottaviani and his allies had not so easily given up. They could not exact their revenge on the liberating influence of the Trans-Alpini bishops until the Council had closed and the Fathers had scattered to the four corners of the globe, but there was a hint of the battle still to come in the debate on one of the Council's most contentious documents: *Dignitatis Humanae*, the Declaration on Religious Liberty.

The Declaration marked the moment when the Church formally embraced the idea of human rights, and its impact has been profound. *Dignitatis Humanae* was inspired by the Americans, specifically the Jesuit and theologian John Courtney Murray, and the very American idea that 'constitutional limits should be set to the powers of government' features prominently in the preamble. It was carried through the Council in part, though, by the enthusiasm of bishops from Eastern Europe. The future Pope John Paul II, Karol Wojtyła, was one of its most energetic champions, and it enjoyed the support of the leaders of the Church in the Soviet empire because it gave them an intellectual framework for their opposition to Communist rule. In the Declaration, the Church recognizes the justice of the demand 'that men should act on their own judgement, enjoying and making use of a responsible freedom, not driven by coercion but by a sense of duty'. It places religious freedom first among all human rights: 'This demand for freedom in human society chiefly regards the quest for the values proper to the human spirit . . . It regards, in the first place, the free exercise of religion in society.'

The Declaration marked a seismic shift in the Church's thinking. Until the Vatican lost the Papal States in the nineteenth century, it had itself been a government, and it had certainly never accepted that there should be any 'constitutional limits' on its power. The idea of a 'theocratic state' – a kind of Catholic equivalent of the mullahs' Iran – was deeply embedded in Catholic thinking, and in most European societies state power and Church power had been interwoven for centuries; the establishment of the Church of England and the presence of its bishops in the House of Lords bear testament to that. Now the Roman Catholic Church was abandoning any claim to assistance from the state in imposing its message.

Moreover, the importance of individual conscience – on which the Declaration's appeal for freedom from government coercion was based – had been at the heart of the Protestant Reformation. The same Church that had brought the world the Crusades and the Inquisition now publicly accepted that 'Man's response to God in faith must be free; no one therefore is to be forced to embrace the Christian faith against his own will' and, in one of the most beautiful sentences to emerge from the entire Council, stated that 'The Truth cannot impose itself except by virtue of its own truth, as it makes its entrance into the mind at once quietly and with power.'

It did not take a theological genius to work out the risks here. The Declaration provided a powerful weapon against governments that abused human rights and sought to stifle dissent. But what about human rights and dissent within the Church? Was the Church giving up its right to discipline its own members in matters of faith and morals? And where did the Declaration leave the old Catholic idea that 'error has no rights'?

Three weeks into the third session of the Council, in early October 1964, the conservative faction planned a coup. By recognizing the value of freedom of thought and by depriving Catholicism of all claims to the protection of the state, *Dignitatis Humanae* hit at the heart of the way they conceived the Church. The Council's secretary-general, Archbishop Felici – one of Cardinal Ottaviani's curial allies – proposed that the text of the Declaration on Religious Liberty should be turned over to a special commission because of a 'desire by the Holy Father that the text be reconsidered and reworked'. He then proceeded to appoint the members of the committee himself, ensuring that it consisted largely of prelates who were known to be opposed to the very idea of religious liberty.

The Archbishop was playing fast and loose with the Council rules but the progressives were to prove themselves equally adept in the black arts of procedural politics: fourteen of them met at the residence of Cardinal Frings to plan a counter-strike. Most of the usual Trans-Alpini suspects were there, Cardinal König among them. He saw the hand of Ottaviani at work: 'The head of the Holy Office,' he said, 'was so afraid of such a document.' The group decided the stakes were so high they had to resort to the nuclear option in Church politics: 'We felt that we were lost, that the Council would give up on changing the fundamental idea of religious liberty,' König told me, 'so we had to ask the Holy Father himself.'

Together they drafted an appeal to Paul. Latin cannot be beaten for endowing a document with a sense of portent: '*Magno cum dolore . . .*' the letter began.

With great sorrow we have learned that the Declaration on Religious Liberty, although in accord with the desire of the great majority of the Fathers, is to be entrusted to a certain mixed committee . . . three of whom appear to be opposed to the orientation of the Council in this matter. This news is for us a source of extreme anxiety and very disquieting.

The cardinals' demand for action is frank to the point of bluntness, phrased in the kind of language a group of cabinet ministers might use if they wanted to force a prime minister's hand in a crisis.

Impelled by this anxiety, we ask Your Holiness with great insistence that the Declaration be returned to the normal procedure of the Council and dealt with according to the existing rules, so that there may not result from it great evils for the whole People of God.

Paul ordered a compromise: there was to be a special commission to study the text of the Declaration on Religious Liberty, but he named the members himself, and ensured that it was balanced between progressives and conservatives. The vote on the Declaration was postponed until the final session of the Council a year later, and in the early months of 1965 Paul wrestled with the dilemma it presented, worrying away at it in characteristic style in conversations with his advisers, and writing himself memos to clear his mind. On 8 May he received a letter from John Courtney Murray, the man who had inspired the Declaration:

Your Holiness,

. . . I think the text has been considerably improved. The doctrinal line is very solid; the human and civil right to religious freedom is based NOT on freedom of conscience (which is dangerous) but on the dignity of the person and on the principles of social order which flow from the dignity of the person. Hence the argument moves entirely in the objective order; the charge of subjectivity cannot legitimately be made.

The method is also sound. The question of religious freedom, as a problem in the civil order, is clearly distinguished from other questions which are of the theological order – in particular freedom and order within the Church.

Fond hope: it is difficult to see the Declaration as anything other than an appeal to the importance of individual conscience, and whatever the detail of the text, the habit of dissent within the Church and the exercise of freedom of conscience have become well established among Catholics everywhere. The Declaration was to prove a powerful weapon in the hands of Karol Wojtyła in Poland – it also began an intellectual trend that was to cause Pope John Paul II all sorts of problems with unruly priests and rebellious lay people.

The Declaration, which was adopted on 21 September 1965 after some of the fiercest debates of the Council, was nothing less than an effort to reconcile the teaching of the Church with the philosophical inheritance of the Enlightenment: they had been moving along lines that diverged ever more widely, and this was an attempt to bring those lines back to an intersection, to find the point at which it is possible to be at once fully modern and fully Catholic.

But there was a chink of light here for the conservatives. Pope Paul, despite his liberal reputation, had shown that he weighed up every question with care and at length, and could be influenced by those around him. He was nicknamed Hamlet, after a man who sometimes thought so long and hard that he found it difficult to come to a conclusion. And throughout the final debates of the Council he seemed acutely conscious of the risk that radical change might split the Church. It was a trait Cardinal Ottaviani was to exploit fully in the second decisive drama of the Church in the 1960s.

4

Intrinsically Evil

I do not think it is a sin, but I am fairly sure it is bad form, to bet on a future beatification. Nevertheless I am tempted to see what odds I can get on an obscure Polish nun I met in Zambia. Unfortunately Sister Leonia is younger than I am, so I will probably not be around to collect my winnings when she becomes a candidate for canonization.

She arrived at the Chilanga community of the Sisters of Mercy of St Charles Borromeo in 1992. A trained nurse, she began working in a shanty-town a mile or so from the convent. The Freedom Compound may have been so named to inspire hope among those who live there, but poverty keeps most enslaved in squalor. Ten is the age at which the girls are considered old enough to offer their services to the community as 'commercial workers' – prostitutes. The official statistics put the number of people infected with the HIV virus in Zambia at 1.4 million – a frightening figure in a country of just nine million inhabitants. But Sister Leonia believed that the government figures did not tell the full story. She conducted a survey of her own in the Freedom Compound, giving HIV tests to all the patients who came to her for more run-of-the-mill complaints like malaria and TB. Of the first 100, 93 were positive.

In the autumn of 1997 Sister Leonia opened the first and only Aids hospice in sub-Saharan Africa. In their homes, she found, Aids victims were often left to die without dignity. Most of the families she works with are very poor and very large – sometimes with ten or twelve children – so 'when someone is very, very sick they are just left in the corner of the house. The priority is given to those who are still alive.' Ignorance about the disease compounds the problem: 'They don't know what to do – they don't know that they can get some help. So they leave the patient in a corner without water, without a mattress and without a blanket.'

The hospice has only fourteen beds. When I visited it, not long after it opened, Sister Leonia had watched twenty-two people die there in the previous six weeks. One had been buried that morning, and she made her way through the Freedom Compound's muddy red laterite roads to see the young man's family. His wife had died of Aids the previous year, and all three of the children they had left behind were HIV positive. It is customary to move the deceased's furniture outside during the period of mourning, and the man's family and friends sat in front of his hut on grubby armchairs and wooden stools, debating the future of his orphans.

Sister Leonia was both cheerful and compassionate in the face of the misery around her, yet unaffected and unfussy in the way she spoke of the religious faith that drove her on. It seemed cruel to put her on the spot, and I desperately wanted *not* to ask her the obvious awkward question: what did she think of the Church's teaching on the use of condoms? Loyal servant of the Church that she is, she took a deep breath before replying.

'We don't promote condoms in the Catholic Church. But only someone who is very far away from this problem could say, "Never, and that's the end of the discussion" . . . If you are in the middle of the problem, you would never say that. I have an example. I am talking to a man, as I am to you now, and he says, "Sister, I know you are a nurse, so you must have condoms, could you give me some? I just came here to work and I shall be working here for a few months." And I see, looking into this man's eyes, that it is useless talking to him about morality. He was so innocent. Of course I can't say, "Get a condom and go ahead," but I do say, "If you can't control yourself it is much better for you, your family and the person you are going to meet to use a condom."'

She said that friends from Poland would tackle her over her departure from the Church's teaching, telling her that she was failing in her duty as a nun; with an expressive lapse in her English she said that she tells them, 'I am also a human being and I am touching the problem. It's my opinion, and I hope God will forgive me for it.'

When the seeds of Sister Leonia's rebellion were sown, Aids was a nightmare in the distant future. The Pontifical Commission for the

Study of Population, Family and Births was created by Pope John XXIII in March 1963. In Europe the debate over artificial contraception has been about self-fulfilment versus obedience. In the developing world it has been and remains an issue of life and death. That dichotomy was reflected in the commission's creation. It was the brainchild of one of the most forceful and prominent of all the progressives, Cardinal Leon Suenens, Archbishop of Malines-Brussels. Informed by the priorities of a sophisticated northern European laity, which was beginning to question the Church's teaching about sex, he suggested the commission to Pope John in the hope that it would lead to 'at least a reform of the old idea, the more children the better'. But part of its appeal to the Pope was the need for an intellectual framework to challenge the growing anxiety over the population explosion in the developing world.

The United Nations' first ever conference on world-population problems was due to be held in 1964. Until then the issue had been kept off the international agenda by what John Marshall, one of the original members of the commission, describes as an 'unholy alliance', which consisted of the Church, Communist governments who believed that a Marxist economy could provide for unlimited population growth, and African nations, which saw population control as a Western plot to keep their numbers down. But once the commission was agreed, the Vatican realized that it needed to sharpen its doctrinal swords.

The way the commission developed provided a new model for theological inquiry, and one that reflected the changes now evident in the working of the Second Vatican Council. While the Council experimented with democracy, the commission took the first steps towards an empirical approach to a theological problem: working through it from the bottom upwards instead of the top down, and giving human experience due weight next to the Church's understanding of revealed Truth. It began in unimpeachably old Roman style: six people, all men, met at a Belgian hotel called the House in the Woods in October 1963. The meeting was a closely guarded secret – indeed, the very existence of the commission had not been officially admitted. 'That's the Vatican way, isn't it?' was the only reason John Marshall could offer me. 'Everything is always a secret. Goodness knows why, but they have always operated on that basis.'

John Marshall was asked to be a member because he had undertaken a study of the reliability of the rhythm method of contraception – 'Vatican roulette', as it had become known. There was one other doctor, an economist, and three priests – a Dominican diplomat and two Jesuits, one a demographer and the other a sociologist. They seem to have had little idea of the explosive and volatile nature of the material they were handling: 'Subsequently it was clear that people's lives had been in turmoil for quite a while, but that had not surfaced then,' says Marshall. There was certainly no sign that they planned to challenge traditional teaching. The Church's view had been laid down by Pius XI in 1930: 'base', 'indecent', 'sin against nature', 'intrinsically vicious' are among the anathemas he hurled at artificial contraception in the encyclical *Casti Connubii*. The six men who met in the country-side near Louvain thirty-three years later described past papal statements on contraception as 'luminous teachings'. Their task was not to challenge those teachings, but to find a palatable and coherent way of presenting them to the world. But they also recognized that the theological basis for the Church's teachings was unclear. Setting a pattern that became a hallmark of the commission's development, they asked for help. Pope Paul – John had died before his commission met – agreed to expand the membership to give the demographers, doctors and economists the theological back-up they needed. The seven new members he named included five theologians, one of whom, Father Bernard Häring, was notoriously liberal. It confirmed John Marshall's conviction that Paul was genuinely open to advice.

From its second session the commission moved to Rome. It was still exclusively male, and its deliberations sometimes had a surreally scholarly quality, which sat uneasily with the intimate issues under debate: 'Occasionally friends of a member who happened to be in Rome would be asked to dinner, and you would see a look of astonishment on their faces as the pros and cons of coitus interruptus were discussed over coffee,' Marshall remembers. But by the summer of 1964 the debate about the Church's position on contraception was being fought out in speeches and articles in the Catholic and secular press all over the world. The commission became a political hot potato. Pope Paul officially confirmed its existence on 23 June, the first anniversary of his papal coronation, and the tone of his announcement seemed to confirm his reputation as a truly modern pope, open to the challenges and opportunities the second half of the twentieth century had to offer: the study of these 'extremely complex and delicate questions' must be undertaken, he said, 'in the light of scientific, social and psychological truths'.

But there was a check in the apparently relentless progress of the progressive agenda – another hint that, with the benefit of hindsight, Paul might not be quite as open to the possibility of change as he appeared. In October the Second Vatican Council was considering the chapter on marriage in what was to become *Gaudium et Spes*, the Pastoral Constitution of the Church in the Modern World. Inevitably, the issue of contraception was raised, even though it was an issue the Pope had reserved for his own judgement and the consideration of his commission. It prompted one of the most famous interventions of Vatican II, a passionate plea for the possibility of change from Cardinal Suenens. In a challenge to the understanding of sex that lay at the heart of the Church's position, he turned to the book of Genesis: 'Hasn't there been too much emphasis,' he asked, 'on the passage "Increase and multiply" and not enough on another phrase, which says, "And they shall be one flesh"?' Before he sat down to prolonged applause, Cardinal Suenens gave special emphasis to this: 'I beg of you, my brother bishops, let us avoid a new "Galileo Affair". One is enough for the Church.'

It was a prophetic warning. It took centuries for the Church to admit it had made a mistake when it condemned Galileo; not until 1992 did the Vatican officially accept that he had been right when he said that the earth revolved around the sun. To many Catholics the Church's continued ban on artificial contraception seems just as absurd as its refusal to accept the truth of Galileo's discovery. But it is caught similarly by the difficulty it has in admitting error.

Several days later, while addressing another topic altogether, Cardinal Suenens made what amounted to an apology for his Galileo speech. It had not been his intention, he said, to call into doubt doctrine 'authentically and definitively proclaimed by the Church's magisterium'. It was generally assumed that the Belgian Cardinal had been rebuked by the Pope for overstepping the mark.

The critical point in the development of the commission, when the possibility of change seemed to become a reality, came with the appointment of lay people to its membership. 'Those of us who were approaching it from a scientific point of view,' John Marshall says, 'realized that the man and woman in the street – or the man and woman in bed – ought also to have a say in the matter. It wasn't just high theology or science, it was human involvement and feelings and experience as well.' It was the first time in the Church's history that non-specialist lay people, women among them, had been asked to help determine the Church's mind on such a momentous question. Patty Crowley still does not know why she and her husband Pat were chosen to be part of it. They were a middle-aged, middle-class Chicago couple. They were grass-roots Catholic activists; they had been deeply involved in the Christian Family Movement, which organized 'cells' to study ways of making the Christian message relevant to modern marriage. But the letter asking them to go to Rome came out of the blue in November 1964.

Years later Patty was convinced that she and the other new lay members of the commission were recruited because they were considered safe. She had been left sterile after the birth of her fourth child in the late 1940s, so the issue did not touch her directly, and she, like all those invited to join, had a record of unswerving loyalty to the Church. She said she had never so much as considered questioning the Church's teaching on birth control: 'We would never have thought to disobey the Church in any way. That's the way we grew up – I think most Catholics who grew up and went to Catholic schools said, "You follow what the Pope says and that's it."'

The commission members who gathered in Rome for its next meeting now numbered fifty-five. The Vatican had not worked out how to handle married couples: when Patty and her husband arrived at the Spanish College, where the commission's later sessions were held, 'Pat had to stay at the monastery while I went down the road a few miles to stay with the nuns. It was quite a shock.' She believes the decisive contribution she and her husband made to the commission's work was put in train almost absent-mindedly: 'We were just an ordinary couple, we weren't doctors, we weren't demographers . . . They didn't know what to do with us. So they asked us to do this survey of couples and what they thought of the rhythm method.'

Using the network they had built up through the Christian Family Movement, the Crowleys quickly produced the widest survey ever made of grass-roots Catholic opinion on such a sensitive issue. They collected responses from some three thousand couples in eighteen countries. The letters and questionnaires are now preserved in the archives of Notre Dame University, and Patty revisited some when she collaborated with the American writer Robert McClory on *Turning Point*, their account of the commission's work. Here is a sample of the catalogue of human pain the Crowleys collected:

I bend over backwards to avoid raising false hopes on my husband's part. This sounds ridiculous, but I stiffen at a kiss on the cheek, instantly reminded that I must be discreet. I withdraw in other ways too, afraid to be an interesting companion, gay or witty or charming, hesitant about being sympathetic . . .

The slightest upset, mental or physical, appears to change the cycle and thereby renders this method of family planning useless . . . My husband has a terrible weakness when it comes to self-control in sex and unless his demands are met in every way when he feels this way, he is a very dangerous man to me and my daughters.

Following my third pregnancy in two years I almost smothered the baby with a pillow because I couldn't stand its crying.

We have three sick kids at home, another kicking in my stomach, and a husband full of booze. I have lived on hope, hope in God, hope in taking a long time for the next pregnancy, hope that someone understands my problem.

'The pain in those letters was heart-rending,' says Patty, 'and we just couldn't imagine that the Church could expect such sacrifice and obedience from couples.'

While the Crowleys were collating the results of their research, Pope Paul was making his unprecedented address to the General Assembly of the United Nations, whose focus was not birth control. He gave a broad overview of what he saw as the challenges facing the modern world, and the speech was famous for a rallying cry that caught the sixties spirit: '*Jamais plus la guerre! Jamais plus la guerre!*' or 'No More War' as the anti-Vietnam war demonstrators would soon be writing on their placards. But he also touched on the population explosion that was causing so much concern to the world's leaders, and there was nothing in what he said to suggest that he was preparing the way for a change in the Church's teaching: 'You deal here with human life, and human life is sacred; no one should dare to assault it. Respect for life, in regard to the great problem of natality, should find here in your assembly its highest affirmation and its most reasoned defence. Your task is so to improve food production so that there will be enough for all the tables of mankind, and not to press for artificial control of births, which would be irrational, so as to cut down the number of guests at the banquet of life.'

When the commission reconvened for its final session in April 1966, the Crowleys took the results of their research with them. In a long and detailed speech, Patty presented the commission with her evidence of what she called 'the anguish experienced by some faithful Catholics', and it was, she believes, 'the letters that convinced the theologians'. She refrained from quoting directly some of the pointed messages for the male celibates around the table – this came from a couple with six children: 'Any priest or bishop who advocates rhythm should take his rectal temperature for a few weeks.'

John Marshall confirms the impact of the Crowleys' letters. It would be wrong to conclude that the commission members who supported the traditional Church line were cruel or had chosen to inflict deliberate pain on the faithful. It was rather that – celibate academics as most of them were – they had no understanding of what ordinary Catholics were suffering. 'Those who had come to it from a purely academic point of view, either in terms of population statistics or theology in the abstract, were increasingly astonished at the openness of these people who were willing to share their experience with the Crowleys,' he says. This powerful empirical evidence of the true state of feeling about birth control in the wider Church came not from dissidents but from loyal Catholics. Their relationship with the Christian Family Movement through which the survey had been conducted proved their commitment, so it was reasonable to assume that their views were, if anything, more loyal than those that prevailed in the Church as a whole.

Beyond the walls of the Spanish College where the commission met, a new way of judging religious truth was evolving in the Church. Cardinal Basil Hume found that his pupils 'didn't want to know what was true when you taught them, they wanted to know what religion meant to you, what you thought about it and whether it had changed your life'. Patty Crowley's letters brought that approach to the heart of the Church as it sought its own mind on an issue that in the past would have been argued through exclusively by theologians. And, like Sister Leonia in Zambia thirty years later, many theologians on the commission changed their minds when they saw the reality of the impact of the Church's laws.

There was a memorable exchange during the subsequent debate. Father Marcelino Zalba, a conservative Jesuit, voiced the perennial Vatican objection to change: that the Church would have to admit that it had got it wrong in the past. 'What then with the millions we have sent to hell, if these norms were not valid?' he demanded.

'Father Zalba,' shot back Patty Crowley, 'do you really believe God has carried out all your orders?'

'Of course I got a kick out of it because everyone started laughing,' she remembers, 'but I didn't think it was funny.'

Those on the other side of the argument did not think it funny either. Fighting alongside Father Zalba was another doughty conservative Jesuit, the American John Ford. A liberal American theologian recalls a late-night debate with Father Ford that ended with this telling insight into the doubts beneath the apparently adamantine certainty of the Jesuit's public position. 'You can give me all the reasons you want,' he said, 'but my problem is much more personal and existential. You might say my whole life has been involved in this. Now, are you telling me, as I'm thinking of retirement, that God allowed me to be wrong all that time, and God allowed the Church to be wrong? Instead of helping people, have we really been hurting them? How could the Holy Spirit allow that to happen?'

Cardinal Ottaviani seems to have spent much of this period snoozing. 'He really just sat there,' says Patty, 'I don't think he participated very much . . . They'd have to end meetings because he was asleep.' John Marshall confirms this: 'Cardinal Ottaviani never gave the impression of really listening to the debates or realizing that a new thinking was afoot.' He believes that the head of the Holy Office disapproved of the commission's very existence. 'He regarded it as a kind of aberration in the life of the Church.'

And there was one intriguing absentee from the commission's final debates: Cardinal Karol Wojtyła had been appointed as an expert in the field. In 1960, as a newly ordained bishop with an academic bent, he had published a philosophy of relationships called *Love and Responsibility*. It was remarkable for combining a modern approach to sex with traditional teaching. It accepted that sex could be for pleasure, not just procreation, but reasserted the Church's stand on birth control.

Would the future pope's view have changed if he had been exposed to Patty Crowley's letters? It is tempting to imagine that her American openness and directness might have made their mark on the Middle European intellectual that he then was; the impact on the future of the Church could have been incalculable. But Karol Wojtyła never took his seat on the Pontifical Commission for the Study of Population, Family and Births. He was too busy with the great mission of his life: the struggle against Communism. The Polish primate, Stefan Wyszyński, had been denied permission to leave Poland by the authorities, and the Archbishop of Kraków stayed at home to demonstrate his solidarity.

Cardinal Ottaviani waited to fight his battle on a field of his own choosing. The commission's final meeting lasted almost three months, from the spring into the early summer of 1966. A steady consensus built for change, and when it fell to the bishops to set the seal on the commission's work, they endorsed the now prevailing view among the theologians, lay people and academic experts. On 24 June, they voted on three questions. Is contraception intrinsically evil? Nine said no, three yes, and three abstained. Could contraception be squared with the Church's teaching and its tradition? Nine in favour, five against and one abstention. Should the Church give a definitive answer on the question as soon as possible? Fourteen said yes, and only one bishop voted against.

Later that day the bishops endorsed *Responsible Parenthood*, the majority report of the commission, which recommended that the Pope should change the Church's teaching, and explained why. Four days later it was presented to Paul VI. In due course the whole world knew what it said: the text was printed in full in the American *National Catholic Reporter* and the British weekly the *Tablet*.

Catholics the world over assumed it was a done deal; they could, at last, enjoy their marriages to the full without having to choose between happiness and obedience to the Church. Back home in Britain, John Marshall talked it over with Cardinal Heenan, then Archbishop of Westminster, who had played a prominent part in the commission's final debates. Heenan was uncertain about the right way forward – he had abstained on the question 'Is contraception intrinsically evil?' – but he was in no doubt about the reality of what was going on in the Church: 'It doesn't matter what the Pope says now,' he told Marshall. 'The people have made up their minds.'

Just over two years later John Marshall was pottering in his garden in Richmond in south-west London when he received a telephone call from the Cardinal: the Pope's long-awaited encyclical was about to be published. The Vatican had been silent since the day the commission ended its work, and Marshall had no more reason than anyone else to doubt that the Pope's conclusions would reflect those of the commission's report: 'The case seemed so convincing that one found it difficult to think that the Vatican would retreat into this bunker mentality,' he says. But Heenan was calling to warn him that that was exactly what was about to happen. They had twenty-four hours to digest the news, and John Marshall drove up to Archbishop's House in Victoria for a conference with the Cardinal.

The Crowleys were asleep when the news came through, and they heard it not from a bishop or a cardinal but from a journalist, who telephoned for a reaction. It was only 2 a.m. Chicago time, but on the morning of 29 July 1968 Europe was buzzing with the news from Rome. 'They told us what the Pope had said,' Patty recalls, 'and we were just dumbfounded. My husband said, "I don't believe it."'

What had happened?

It was shrouded in secrecy, and it was, in the judgement of John Marshall, 'an appalling thing'.

With the original commission dispersed, Cardinal Ottaviani had had the Pope to himself. Paul had already shown his Hamlet-like tendency to prevaricate in the debate on religious liberty at the Council, and there was a hint of the way in which his mind was moving in his treatment of Cardinal Suenens after his Galileo speech. Cardinal Ottaviani went to work.

Three days after *Responsible Parenthood* had been presented to Paul, Cardinal Ottaviani gave him the minority report, which had been produced by the small group of theologians on the commission who dissented from its call for change. Their case was not really about birth control, it was about authority. The argument was simple. For centuries the Church had taught that the purpose of sex was procreation; the Holy Spirit protects the Church from error, and therefore could not have allowed the Church to be wrong for so long. It was Father Ford's existential angst elevated into a theological formula.

It was an argument that held special force for Paul. The cruellest irony of the whole affair was that he took his decision not as a stern and arrogant authoritarian but through an excess of modesty about his own powers as pope. He did not believe himself competent to change a teaching the Church had sustained for so long. We tend to think of *Humanae Vitae* as an illustration of the dangers of investing too much power in the hands of one man, who can then ignore the opinions of others. In fact, Paul felt that the weight of institutional history rendered his own views of no value.

The Crowleys had presented Pope Paul with copies of all the letters they had received in their survey. There is no record of whether or not he read them. Cardinal König was of sufficiently senior standing in the hierarchy to talk to the Pope frankly about the issue, and says that Paul did not appreciate the pain of the faithful: 'My impression was that he did not really understand or did not realize that the result would be so many, many problems for families and for the Church.' Others argue that he understood the implications of his decision all too well, and he certainly agonized long and hard before taking it.

A new commission was set up with the express intention of undoing everything the original commission had achieved. It was not just the conclusions that were rejected: the method of working established during the months of debate at the Spanish College was unceremoniously abandoned. All the members of the new commission were priests, and had been handpicked for their enthusiasm for the traditional line. 'The great advance of bringing in the lay people to get a wider view of the whole Church, not just the clerical Church,' says Marshall, 'was completely reversed by a commission composed entirely of clerics.'

Cardinal Ottaviani built his team around the four theologians who had held out for the traditional teaching on the original commission. This time, secrecy was sustained. Working steadily through 1967 the new group created the basis for the encyclical *Humanae Vitae*. In the autumn of that year, once he was confident that the Pope would support the conservative plan, Cardinal Ottaviani retired. Paul's biographer, Peter Hebblethwaite, describes *Humanae Vitae* as 'Ottaviani's I-told-you-so revenge' for the Council.

At the heart of the encyclical lies the Church's claim to a papal monopoly on the Truth. 'Jesus Christ, when He communicated His divine power to Peter and the other Apostles and sent them to teach all nations His commandments, constituted them as the authentic guardians and interpreters of the whole moral law,' the encyclical argues. The Church's teaching on sex was an interpretation of a moral law given by God, and could not therefore be changed. Contraception had always been, and therefore would always remain, 'intrinsically evil'.

Some of the theologians who had driven the reforms of Vatican II felt the blow especially heavily. Hans Küng had been a *peritus*, or theological adviser, at the Council. Swiss-born, but now established as a teacher at Tübingen University in southern Germany, he was seen as one of its intellectual stars. By 1968 he was already in trouble with the Church authorities. His book *The Church*, first published in German the year before *Humanae Vitae*, argued for a more democratic Church: 'It is very clear that in the early Church there were no absolutist rulers – even Peter,' he said in an interview at the time. He even hinted at the possibility of popes being chosen by some kind of general election. One of Cardinal Ottaviani's final acts before retirement was to issue a *monitum* (an official warning or instruction) banning translation of Kung's book into other languages.

Humanae Vitae gave a new edge to his questioning of the way authority is exercised within the Church. As a ground-swell of rebellion grew across Europe and America, Küng took on the doctrine at the heart of the Church's claim to preach absolute truth: Infallibility. Papal Infallibility had been introduced by Pius IX at the First Vatican Council in 1870. It applies only to a limited set of core Catholic beliefs, such as the Divinity of Christ and the Resurrection, and the circumstances in which the Pope is judged to be speaking infallibly are rare. It does not mean, for example, that if he says a black dog is a white sheep, Catholics are required to believe him. But Küng argued that the reasoning behind *Humanae Vitae* suggested the existence of a wider, creeping doctrine of Infallibility that existed even though the Church did not acknowledge it. The teaching on contraception had not been changed because the Pope did not believe he could challenge what the Church had taught in the past; in other words, the centuries of Church pronouncements on contraception had a kind of Infallible status of their own. Since this supposedly Infallible body of teachings was, as represented in *Humanae Vitae*, not just fallible but – in Küng's judgement and that of vast numbers of the Catholic faithful – plain wrong, the Church's claim to Infallibility was itself called into question. It is the kind of circular argument that makes you dizzy if you think about it for too long, but most people got the basic point: a respected Catholic theologian was arguing that a Church dumb enough to try banning contraception could not go on claiming it was always right.

Küng's 1970 book *Infallible?* was published to mark the centenary of the promulgation of the doctrine and set him on a collision course with Rome. He fought a dogged battle with the Sacred Congregation for the Doctrine of the Faith – as the old Holy Office was now called – over the orthodoxy of his views throughout the 1970s, and in 1979 the Church withdrew his right to teach as an approved Catholic theologian.

The offence caused by Küng's rebellious views was compounded by the manner in which he conducted his campaign. Instead of meekly accepting correction from Rome, he behaved as if the Second Vatican Council really had turned the Church into an open society and a democracy. He demanded the civil rights that democratic citizens have come to expect. 'The problem,' he told me, 'was that I asked for fair procedure, and especially to see my files. There is no criminal in the world who is not allowed to see his files. What are the accusations? Where are the witnesses and so on? But that was always declined.'

It set a pattern that has been repeated many times since. And, in the end, it was the Church as much as Hans Küng that had to face a painful lesson. When his licence to teach was withdrawn, Tübingen University moved his chair out of the Catholic theology faculty and gave it an autonomous status so that he could continue to work. The Church might not be an open society, but its discipline is ineffective in societies that are.

It was not just progressive theologians who were reflecting on the impact of the encyclical on the authority of the Church and the Pope. The world's bishops were being asked to promulgate a teaching that most of them knew would be almost impossible to sell to the faithful. During the two years that had elapsed since the end of the commission's deliberations, many Catholics had taken matters into their own hands, unwilling to go through any further marital misery while they awaited a decision most believed was a foregone conclusion. Often, they had done so with the encouragement of a parish priest, and it was scarcely likely that they would revert to the old ways.

Some priests challenged the Church publicly. On 20 October 1968 a group of fifty-five wrote a letter of protest to *The Times*. John Marshall, who wrote separately to *The Times* to disassociate himself from certain specific points in the encyclical that he felt were scientifically wrong, had great sympathy for them: priests, he said, 'were involved in the personal situation of their parishioners and at the same time were supposed to be official representatives of the Church. That put them in an impossible position.'

On 24 September 1968 the bishops of England and Wales issued a statement designed to meet the tide of rebellion that was sweeping through Britain's Catholics. 'In the heat of the controversy,' they state sternly, 'some writers appear to have forgotten that the Pope is the Vicar of Christ. It is for him to issue encyclical letters whenever he thinks it is his duty to do so.' But the tone of the statement suggests that the bishops rather wished he had not thought it his duty to issue this particular encyclical:

It was widely believed that a change in the Church's attitude would be announced. Understandably, many wives and husbands, anticipating the promised statement of the Pope, have come to rely on contraception. In this they have acted conscientiously and often after seeking pastoral advice. They may now be unable to see that, at least in their personal circumstances, the use of contraception is wrong. A particular difficulty faces those who after serious thought and prayer cannot as yet understand or be fully convinced of the doctrines as laid down.

The bishops' instructions to such people are so tentative that they can hardly be described as instructions:

They should pray for light to understand the doctrine taught by the encyclical. It is not unreasonable to ask all to practise the Christian virtue of humility and acknowledge the duty of every Catholic to listen with respect to the voice of the Vicar of Christ.

This was not the voice of thunder in which the Church of old was accustomed to hurl its anathemas of condemnation against the modern world. It is not surprising that so many people were so confused. First, the Council had torn up and thrown away many of the certainties with which they had grown up, and they had gradually come round to the idea of participating more fully in the life of the Church and exercising their consciences more freely. Now the Pope had issued an instruction that seemed to take Church teaching back to the Middle Ages. It almost made things worse that their bishops tried to impose this thoroughly unreasonable ruling in the reasoned language of the modern Church.

It led to something entirely new in the history of Catholicism: a wave of conscientious dissent from a major Church teaching. For the first time ever, a great mass of Catholics, while continuing to regard themselves as faithful members of the Church, chose to disobey a clear papal instruction. 'I think it is tragic,' says Archbishop Hurley of Durban, 'that there can be such a gap between official teaching and the great majority of people.' Denis Hurley has retired, and is able to speak frankly about *Humanae Vitae* in a way those still holding senior positions cannot. But even serving archbishops acknowledge that the impact of the encyclical went far beyond the matter at issue. 'It did call into question the authority of the Church,' says Cardinal Hume, 'and I think that has been a bit the pattern subsequently. People have often said, "Well, that's what the Church used to say but we aren't certain it's right."' With the revolt over *Humanae Vitae* the subjective approach to moral choice entered the Catholic Church. Cardinal König describes its impact like this: 'Nowadays everyone feels, "I don't need a general rule, I need no law to organize society and Church life, I make the rules myself."'

I met Patty Crowley in her eighty-eighth floor apartment in a tower overlooking Lake Michigan; the lake-front glistened into infinity in both directions, and swimming-pools on top of less majestic skyscrapers looked like little blue puddles below. Her husband Pat died in 1974, but the walls are crammed with photos of smiling children getting married, and grandchildren graduating. The drawing room was hung with good modern paintings and religious art, and in the dining room stood a wonderful beaten-silver relief of the Last Supper. But amid the abundant evidence of well-financed good taste, energetic intelligence and wholesome happiness, there was still a wound from the way in which she had been treated by the Church.

Once the commission had finished its work no one wrote to the Crowleys or spoke to them. No one thanked them or explained why their advice had been ignored. 'It hurt us,' she said. 'We didn't ask for this, they gave it to us. They asked us to come to Rome. We listened, and we tried to understand both sides and we just felt after we read the letters and we talked to couples that the Church had to change.'

When Cardinal Bernadin became Archbishop of Chicago he asked for letters from people who had been hurt by the Church and Patty wrote to him about her experience on the commission. There was silence for a year and then she received a standard letter. The Cardinal's tenure in Chicago was cut short by illness, and not long before he died he telephoned Patty out of the blue and asked if he could come to see her. Somewhat taken aback, Patty agreed, and he walked over immediately.

They sat together in her drawing room for an hour during which she poured out her feelings about what had happened. He kissed her as he left and asked for her prayers. She took it as a kind of apology. A month later he was dead.

That kind of unspoken admission of error is symptomatic of the way in which the Church in America has coped with *Humanae Vitae*. Charles Curran, a prominent professor of theology at the Catholic University of America in Washington DC, was driven, like Hans Küng, into open dissent by the encyclical. He held a press conference to denounce it at the Mayflower Hotel on Washington's Connecticut Avenue – just a stone's throw from the White House and about as high-profile a location for a protest as it is possible to find anywhere. As a result, again like Hans Küng, he found himself embroiled in a long battle with the guardians of orthodoxy in Rome. But today he is relaxed about the double standards at the heart of Catholic life that have resulted from the birth-control encyclical: 'Can one dissent and still be a Roman Catholic? That's the view of the folks,' he says succinctly. And he regards it as 'a positive sign', evidence of a mature Church.

The overwhelming majority of married American Catholics use artificial birth control when it suits them. Yet the American Church remains one of the healthiest in the world. The three years I spent living in America taught me what it is to belong to a living Church. Instead of the rather gaunt and empty Victorian building in South London to which I would drag myself more out of duty than devotion, I found a church bursting at the seams with people and enthusiasm.

In London what I did on Sunday mornings was regarded as a little eccentric; at the Blessed Sacrament Church in Chevy Chase, Maryland, so many people turned up for Mass that car-parking was a real problem.

Father Andrew Greeley, chronicler of the contemporary Church and tireless interpreter of its statistical profile, believes 'the American Catholic Church down in the grass-roots, down in the parishes, is very strong. Where there is a pastoral leadership that is sensitive and secure, the typical American neighbourhood parish has more generosity working probably than at any time since we got out of Jerusalem.' He says the level of defections in the American Church – those who were born Catholic and leave the Church – is running at about 15 per cent, roughly the same level as it was in 1960. American Catholics seem to have shrugged off the rupture between the Church's teaching and their own experience.

But not all Catholics were able to adjust so easily to the lie they were required to live. And in Europe, where secularism in society as a whole was more advanced and the national Churches were older and less vigorous, the impact of the encyclical was especially destructive. When you have been brought up to believe that every moral choice you make carries with it the possibility of eternal damnation, it is difficult to treat a matter of such moment in a cavalier fashion. The new 'pick-your-own' Catholicism identified by Cardinal Hume did not square with many people's understanding of what religion should be.

Thousands of Catholics left the Church over *Humanae Vitae*, and often it was the most committed who led the way. That rigid Catholic belief in the unity of Truth, which had once kept them to the Church's teaching on birth control, now drove them away. One woman who abandoned her faith because of the encyclical put it to me like this: 'It became rather like going into a supermarket and you pick up your basket and go round the shelves picking up the bits of moral theology that appeal to you. It is a sort of self-access form of religion, and we felt it should be a seamless garment where our experience in the world was not at odds with our experience of the Church.'

Paul VI went into a state of intellectual shell-shock after the reaction to *Humanae Vitae*. He never wrote another encyclical: it was as if his capacity to offer decisive moral guidance had been exhausted.

After the creative explosion of the Council, the Church seemed to go into a holding pattern. For a decade between the encyclical and the death of Pope Paul VI all its energies were consumed in adjusting to the aftermath of revolution and counter-revolution. Grumpy old Catholics muttered about the new Mass and gradually got used to it. Enthusiastic young priests tried guitars and tambourines, then realized they could not abandon the past altogether. Everyone wondered what to do about *Humanae Vitae*, and most concluded that a decent silence was the appropriate response. The subjective morality ushered in by the way Catholics had reacted to the encyclical brought with it terrifying questions that threatened the foundations of the Church's authority: perhaps the Church did not matter quite so much as we had all thought; perhaps it did not hold the keys to Paradise, after all; perhaps we could defy its teaching without automatic condemnation to eternal damnation. The churches and seminaries emptied steadily.

That at least was the way it looked from Western Europe. The Church in the sixties was about bells, smells and sex, and the Vatican had told us we could not enjoy any of them.

Only now do I appreciate the energies released in the rest of the Church by the events of the sixties. While we were agonizing about incense and condoms, the rest of the Church was locked in a struggle for Freedom and Food.

5

Only God Before Their Eyes

The apartment block attached to the Ursuline Convent at 2 Wiślana Street in Warsaw is as ugly as any built in the brutalist style so beloved of Eastern Europe's Communists. But the nuns have softened its edges. In the summer, there are flowers on the balconies surrounding the courtyard, and a statue of the Madonna, her halo composed of electric candles, looks down over an immaculately behaved Virginia creeper that covers the grey walls.

The nuns wear long grey habits and heavy leather belts round often comfortable waists, a few short hairs poking out beneath their black caps the only concession to the more relaxed dress codes allowed for religious orders introduced by Vatican II. They do not so much walk as bustle, with all the sense of purpose and old-fashioned cheerfulness that word implies, and their convent has a well-swept and cared-for appearance that contrasts sharply with the grubbiness of the streets outside. The chapel is a cleanly built, white-painted room dominated by a vast modern crucifix above the altar, with windows giving on to a small park.

To walk from the squalor of a medieval city into one of Europe's great cathedrals gave our ancestors a physical sense of the presence of the Kingdom of God in their world. To walk from the grime of Communist Poland into almost any of its carefully tended churches and convents was to understand that Catholicism offered an alternative reality. All those well-swept corridors and flowered altars evoked the possibility of a different way of ordering things.

A nun carrying a huge, enticing plate of cabbage disappeared round a corner as I was taken to see the room where Cardinal Karol Wojtyła used to stay on his trips to Warsaw. His visit here in October 1978 was occasioned by one of the oddest episodes of the Church's history this century: the thirty-three-day pontificate of John Paul I. 'Only a month earlier,' recalls the Mother Superior, 'he stayed here on his way back from the conclave in high spirits, declaring, "We have chosen a good Pope."' Now he was returning to Rome for a second conclave.

The election of John Paul I on 27 August inspired a wave of optimism in the Church: he had established a reputation as a pastoral bishop, and after the tumult stirred by *Humanae Vitae*, the Church desperately needed a leader who cared about people. And then there was that smile: from the moment he stepped on to the balcony of St Peter's to accept the crowd's applause, it became his trademark; it seemed a symbol of the openness of the Council spirit, which had been forgotten during Paul's last dark decade.

The smile was about the only thing for which Albino Luciani had time to become famous. On the morning of 29 September he was found dead in his bed. It was one of those news events like President Kennedy's assassination or the death of Diana, Princess of Wales: a thunderbolt so unexpected that everyone can remember what they were doing when it struck. Cardinal Hume was praying in his chapel in Archbishop's House in Westminster: 'My secretary came along and he said, "The Pope is dead." I said, "I know the Pope is dead. We've got a new pope now." He said, "The Pope is dead." I said, "What – you mean *this* pope?" I just couldn't believe it. I had to go out and preach that morning at a convent. To this day I can't remember a word of what I said.'

For Franz König it meant shouldering the burden of leadership in the Sacred College of Cardinals for a second time. His reputation as one of the giants of the Church had been established at the Council; he had participated in the conclave that chose Paul VI fifteen years earlier so he knew how the system of discreet campaigning works in a papal election. Too old to be a candidate himself, in October 1978 he found himself playing a part carved out centuries earlier by the Borgia and Medici cardinals: that of a 'great elector' with the clout to play a decisive role.

The great electors of the Renaissance had been concerned with the exercise of influence on European governments, but their stage was confined to the powers of the age like Spain, France, England and the

Italian states. Cardinal König painted on an altogether grander canvas. His role during the Council had been rewarded with a job that could only have existed in the post-Conciliar Church: since 1965 he had run the Secretariat for Non-believers, created by Paul VI in his endless quest for engagement with the modern world. When he had asked Paul what he should do with this curious invention, the Pope had replied, '*Usus docebit*,' which translates loosely as 'Work it out as you go along.'

König insisted he should be allowed to run his secretariat from Vienna, not Rome, so that he could escape the claustrophobic atmosphere of the Curia. In the Austrian capital, favoured city of Cold War intriguers, he used his new position to indulge his passion for East European culture and explore the areas where Communist and Catholic ideologies confronted one another. He flourished in the Cold War world: according to Oleg Kalugin, the KGB's head of counter-espionage, the Soviets paid him the ultimate compliment of consideration as a prime candidate for 'turning', and actively studied the possibility of recruiting him as an agent. It was König's background in Eastern Europe that prompted him to think the unthinkable.

Walking one evening in Rome before the October conclave with his old friend Cardinal Stefan Wyszyński, König floated the idea of 'a pope from Poland'. The Polish primate, well established by then as a figure of international standing because of his dogged resistance to Communism, misunderstood: 'I could never leave Poland,' he said. 'Too much is expected of me there.'

'But what of Wojtyła?' asked König.

'Too young. He'll never get elected,' came the reply.

In London Cardinal Basil Hume, usually the most sure-footed public performer, found himself at a loss in the face of questioning about the sudden death of John Paul I. He had returned from the August conclave relieved that the predictions that he might become the first English pope since Nicholas Breakspear in the twelfth century had not been fulfilled. 'I really felt,' he told an ITN reporter, 'that the Holy Spirit was working among us. We have a pope to take us into the next century.'

'Did the Holy Spirit get it wrong?' the same reporter asked, as a month later the Cardinal left for Rome again.

By tradition no autopsy may be performed on the body of a pope, which added to the conspiracy theories spawned by the death of John Paul I. His nearest rival in the voting had been the arch-conservative Cardinal Siri of Genoa, and plenty of people were willing to believe he had been despatched by a Curia bent on avenging the defeat of its favoured candidate. Some even whispered that the new Pope had been preparing to reverse his predecessor's ban on birth control, and was killed to stop it happening.

Some time later a detail emerged that suggested the Vatican had not entirely shaken off the baroque ways of a past in which such things were possible. John Magee, secretary to Pope Paul and both John Pauls, now a bishop in his native Ireland, admitted that the Vatican made up the story that he had found the Pope's body. Each morning a nun left a cup of coffee outside the Pope's bedroom; one day when she returned to find it undrunk she opened the door to find him dead in bed. But the idea that a woman had been the first person to see the body was considered so shocking that the John Magee story was put out instead. It is characteristic of Vatican thinking at its worst that a female presence in a dead pope's bedroom should have been thought less acceptable than a public lie.

A troubled Sacred College reassembled in Rome, and the ITN reporter's question must have been on some of the cardinals' minds. It raises an issue that worries any Catholic who looks honestly at the Church's history. Before the cardinals are left alone to their deliberations in a conclave, they are given a sermon on the gravity of the task they face by a preacher they have themselves selected. He instructs them to make their choice 'solum Deum prae oculis habentes' – having only God before their eyes. The history of papal conclaves includes all too many stories which suggest that for many cardinals God has been lost in the misty distance, obscured by more secular concerns.

In 1585 Cardinal Ferdinand de Medici needed the support of Cardinal San Sisto, nephew of the late Pope and therefore a figure to be reckoned with, to secure the election of his preferred candidate. San Sisto, wrote de Medici, 'would have elected the devil himself to get out of the conclave and return to the arms of his mistress'. So de Medici promised him a quick result and, through an intermediary, assured him that his paramour's awkward husband would be disposed of in the traditional Medici manner. Whatever was before San Sisto's eyes as he marked his ballot, it seems unlikely that it was God. The annals of Rome offer plenty of similar tales of venality.

The belief that the Holy Spirit guides the cardinals in their choice is entirely in keeping with the way Catholics view the world. If God is present in history, and if the actions of men reflect His purpose – however difficult it may sometimes be to discern – then it would be odd if He did not involve himself in the choice of the leader of His Church.

But John Paul I was not the only Pope whose short reign has made the Holy Spirit's intentions appear eccentric: Pius III and Marcellus II both lasted twenty-five days, and Urban VII was dead within ten days of his election – even before being enthroned. And the list of popes who survived to reign for decades includes so many who were corrupt, lecherous, avaricious, sadistic and even atheistic that it calls the Holy Spirit's wisdom seriously into question. The Church's answer to this apparent contradiction is perfectly logical: man, being imperfect, misunderstands the Spirit. The curse of being a Catholic in the more sceptical post-Conciliar age is that that kind of logic is more difficult to accept. In October 1978 the cardinals were to elect a man who had no doubt about the working of Divine Providence in history, or about his place in the fulfilment of its purposes.

Cardinal König described a conclave to me as 'a very ordinary meeting', and told me that 'there is nothing mysterious' about it. That is disingenuous, to say the least. Of course, great events can seem banal to those directly involved, while those of us who watch them from afar endow them with a heightened significance. But through history there has been no other political process with quite the mix of mystery, intrigue and faith in divine inspiration that comes together when the Sacred College of Cardinals meets to choose a successor to St Peter.

The origins of the conclave reflect the combination of faith in divine inspiration and recognition of the power of human appetites that has marked the history of papal elections. In 1271 the people of Viterbo walled up the episcopal palace to encourage the seventeen cardinals meeting inside to make up their minds – they had been trying to decide on a new pope for two years. After a few further weeks of indecision they turned up the pressure by limiting Their Eminences' rations to bread and water – and removed the roof to allow the Holy Spirit better access. The tradition of discomfort survives in the conclaves of the twentieth century: Cardinal Hume describes the living conditions as 'very rough'. Lots are drawn to decide who sleeps where, and in the first of the two conclaves in 1978 he did badly: 'We were four cardinals sharing one tap' – this in the heat of a Roman August – 'and I was sleeping in an office with a bed which I am quite sure came from a seminary for very short people.'

A conclave has been defined as 'a congregation of cardinals forming the Sacred College, assembled within enclosed premises with the object of electing a pope'. It need not necessarily be held in the Sistine Chapel, although that has now become established practice. When Pius VI died in 1799 as a prisoner of Napoleon, the Sacred College was forced to find a meeting place outside Rome, and chose the Palladian Benedictine monastery of St Giorgio Maggiore in Venice.

Although the incense of mysterious tradition now floats around the business of choosing a new pope, the practice has existed for less than half the Church's history and was not fully formalized until the Council of Constance, a mere 550 years ago. In the very early days of the Church it seems likely that each successor of St Peter chose his own successor. That was followed by an experiment in Church democracy: from the third century, the senate, clergy and people of Rome took part in their bishop's election just as the faithful elected their bishops in other dioceses. In choosing its leader, as in so many other areas, the Church was most radical in its earliest days. But as it grew, and the power of the papacy increased, democracy proved dangerous: different factions sometimes turned to mob violence in their efforts to influence the outcome of elections. Over the centuries the system for choosing a pope changed to reflect the demands of the times. Until the beginning of the twentieth century, the great powers of Europe enjoyed a right of veto: the monarchs of France, Spain and Austria could exclude a candidate – which, as one historian of the papacy has observed, gave them precedence over the Holy Spirit. The most recent reform of the system was in 1996; since then, the method of choosing a candidate has been restricted to 'scrutiny' or election by secret ballot by cardinals of the Church.

When the conclave of October 1978 opened, few outside observers appreciated how great an influence the revolution initiated by the Second Vatican Council would have on the election of a new pope. No one seriously questioned the conventional wisdom that the Pope must be Italian, and when the doors of the Sistine Chapel closed on 14 October public interest focused on two Italians, Cardinals Benelli and Siri. But as Cardinal Hume succinctly remarked, 'Anyone who is tipped to be pope, won't be.'

In theory, the system gives a pope a powerful voice in choosing his own successor because he alone creates cardinals. The longer a pope holds office, the greater his capacity to put his own stamp on the College of Cardinals by making new appointments. John Paul I had been pope for only a month, but Paul VI's reign had lasted fifteen years, and he had presided over a quiet revolution in the Sacred College: it had changed to reflect the way in which the Church's centre of gravity had shifted away from Rome and its historic European heartland. In the conclave that had elected him 65 per cent of the cardinals were from Europe, more than a third from Italy. By 1978 the Italian contingent was down to less than a quarter, and for the first time Italy and Western Europe together accounted for less than half the total electorate. The Italians and Europeans were still over-represented – Latin America, the world's most populous region, had only 16 per cent of the cardinals – but the election of the first non-Italian pope for close to half a millennium can be explained in part by the demographic change in the electorate.

Also, in the years since Vatican II, the non-European Churches had acquired a new self-confidence, and a conclave provided a perfect opportunity for them to flex their muscles. One of the leaders of the Latin-American Church, Cardinal Arns, told me that he went to Rome determined to elect a pope from anywhere but Western Europe. His archdiocese was sixteen million strong; the fact that the millions represented in his vote carried the same weight as the view of a curial cardinal, more civil servant than pastor, must have rankled.

Cardinal Giuseppe Siri, Archbishop of Genoa, was again the favoured candidate of the Italian conservatives. He had been one of Cardinal Ottaviani's closest allies during Vatican II, a leader of the right. Even though he had been under sixty when Pope John XXIII died he ran Paul VI close in the conclave of 1963, and ever since had done his best to fight attempts to modernize the Church. He had the support of the most organized group in the conclave: the curial cardinals. Because they are permanently resident in Rome and talk to each other regularly in the course of running Church business, they are able to marshal their forces around a candidate much more effectively than cardinals from outside their charmed circle. And despite Paul's attempts to bring in fresh blood, the Curia in 1978 remained stubbornly Italian-dominated.

But in the eyes of many cardinals a Siri papacy would have been a betrayal of Vatican II. The very factors that attracted to him the support of the conservatives made moderates and progressives look elsewhere. It was not until the evening of the first full day of the conclave, Sunday, 15 October, that Karol Wojtyła's name emerged for serious consideration. In retrospect it seems blindingly obvious that he had almost all the qualities required by the progressive, liberal majority. He was young – and after the sudden death of John Paul I that was a big advantage. He was non-Italian, which pleased the leaders of the new Church like Cardinal Arns of Brazil. He came from outside the tight curial circle, and was acceptable therefore to all those who resented curial power. Critically he was seen as a man of Vatican II. Although he was almost unknown to the world at large, his fellow cardinals knew Karol Wojtyła as a man of powerful intellect who had played a significant part in the Council debates. He had been a prominent voice in support of the Declaration on Religious Liberty, and one cardinal who voted for him in the conclave described him as 'one of the main fathers' of *Gaudium et Spes*, the document on the Church in the Modern World.

At one level, those who supported Karol Wojtyła as the torchbearer of the spirit of Vatican II got it wrong: he has been so conservative on social issues, and so ferociously authoritarian on matters of religious discipline, that he is often accused of trying to reverse the Council's reforms in a manner that would have made the defeated Cardinal Siri proud. Yet at another level they were right. According to Cardinal Ratzinger – Cardinal Archbishop of Munich at the time of the conclave – the electors wanted someone who 'would give new impetus to the Council'. Karol Wojtyła was seen as 'a man in touch with today's culture and in a position to take up the dialogue with today's cultural movements, which was an important mandate of the Council'. If the cardinals wanted someone who would fulfil the Council's ambition to engage with the world, they got that with a vengeance.

Did they grasp the implications of electing a pope from the Soviet empire? Franz König, who was leading the Wojtyła campaign, certainly did: 'He was non-Italian, from a Communist country, with new ideas. That was my motivation,' he says. Joseph Ratzinger says: 'He was a man who had personal experience of a region all Western bishops knew little about, but which was extremely important to the Church because the socialist world was one bloc of mankind, and exerted considerable influence in the Third World.' But none of them can have anticipated the impact he would have in Eastern Europe. If the death of John Paul I made some doubt the influence of the Holy Spirit, the early years of the papacy of John Paul II must have restored their faith. The choice they made belonged to the next decade.

A gulf separates the world of today from the world of 1978. John Paul II was elected under the shadow of the great wars of this century. There seemed no escape then from the momentum of history that had carried mankind from the First World War to the Second and on to the Cold War. No one in Washington, Moscow or the capitals of Western Europe could offer even the glimpse of a way to halt the train of events that began with the murder of the Archduke Ferdinand in Sarajevo in 1914.

If the 1960s were marked by a spirit of optimism, the late 1970s were a time of uncertainty and confusion about right and wrong in public policy. In Washington Jimmy Carter's presidency seemed crippled by self-doubt about America's world role; as the cardinals met for their conclave, riots in Teheran threatened the Shah, and the seeds of American humiliation in Iran were being sown. In London, Britain's experiment with the left was drawing to a bitter close as the Callaghan government limped towards the Winter of Discontent, which proved its undoing. And in Africa, that autumn was one of the bloodiest in the long civil war being fought for Rhodesia.

The state of the world invited humility and agnosticism, not certainty. The Cold War was the only certain fact of political life: the day before John Paul I died, police in London announced that the Bulgarian secret service had murdered Georgi Markov, a Bulgarian dissident and BBC broadcaster, by stabbing him with a poisoned umbrella tip.

The cardinals did what the electorates of Britain and the United States were about to do when they chose Margaret Thatcher and Ronald Reagan: they fixed on a leader of adamantine convictions untroubled by self-doubt. The contrast between John Paul II and

Paul VI was the contrast between Fortinbras and Hamlet. With the accession of Karol Wojtyła to the throne of St Peter, conviction not doubt became the mark of modernity.

Much of the campaigning in a papal election is done before the conclave actually meets. The cardinals gather in Rome for the funeral of the dead Pope, after which nine days of mourning follow before the formal conclave begins. During that period the cardinals run the Church collectively: they meet every day and talk informally too. The lobbying that goes on within the conclave is discreet: Cardinal König's description evokes the atmosphere of an academic conference at an ancient university. 'The cardinals walk up and down in the gardens and in the rooms and you see talking two, three, four, perhaps sometimes even five. But there are no big meetings, no big discussions.'

When they enter the Sistine Chapel to vote, the campaigning stops. Even the ballot papers in a papal election have a certain distinction about them; each is printed with the sonorous Latin phrase '*Eligo in summum pontificem . . .*' (I elect as Supreme Pontiff). Thomas Reese, the Jesuit author of *Inside the Vatican*, gives this account of the process of voting:

One at a time, in order of precedence, the cardinals approach the altar with their folded ballot held up so that it can be seen. On the altar there is a receptacle (traditionally a large chalice) covered by a plate (a paten). After kneeling in prayer for a short time, the cardinal rises and swears, 'I call as my witness Christ the Lord, who will be my judge, that my vote is given to the one who before God I think should be elected.' He then places the ballot on the plate. Finally he picks up the plate and uses it to drop the ballot into the receptacle.

The Church relies on the Holy Spirit to guide its leaders, but it does not necessarily trust them to eschew all worldly temptations. The system is designed to make it difficult to cheat by dropping in two ballots, and the totals are carefully checked by three scrutineers to ensure that they tally with the number of cardinals present. The ballots are then burned – the 'rickety old fire', as Cardinal Hume calls it, is in a corner – and the colour of the smoke tells the crowd in St Peter's Square and the world beyond whether or not they have produced a result. A chemical mix is added to make the smoke black, for a non-decisive vote, or white, for a successful one. In 1978, on the

Sunday morning of the conclave, the mix was wrong: first black then white smoke puffed out. Cardinal Hume observed that they were the colours of his favourite football team, Newcastle United.

It had taken two days and eight votes to elect a Pole, the first non-Italian pope since 1522.

In St Peter's Square there was a collective intake of breath from the crowd.

In Washington, Zbigniew Brzeziński, President Carter's national security adviser, was chairing a meeting in the White House situation room when the duty officer handed him a slip of paper bearing the news. He had met the Archbishop of Kraków once before, when the Cardinal had been giving a lecture at Harvard, and had been impressed by 'the scope of his intellectual interests and also by his directness'. So when Brzeziński telephoned President Carter at Camp David he gave the new Pope a good review: 'A philosopher, a worker priest, a theologian, a thespian, a proselytizer.' He was horrified to hear the President describe John Paul on television that night as 'the closest personal friend of Dr Brzeziński'.

In Poland Tadeusz Mazowiecki, then an opposition activist and one day to become Poland's first post-war Catholic prime minister, called it 'the smile of history'. Some of his fellow dissidents expressed disappointment – because they knew Karol Wojtyła and realized what they were losing. Jacek Kuroń, one of the intellectual fathers of the Polish revolution and a founding member of the workers' Defence Committee KOR, recalls hearing the result in a telephone call from a BBC correspondent: '"Oh, bad news," I said. "I had the feeling he understood us, and that he could give us support in certain situations. And suddenly he goes to Rome."'

But the overwhelming feeling was of national pride – even among Communists. Mieczysław Rakowski was a senior party official and served as General Jaruzelski's right-hand man throughout the upheavals of the 1980s: 'Regardless of Party membership, the whole society, including the leadership of the Communist Party, were proud that a Pole had become pope.'

In Moscow the news took time to sink in. The gerontocracy that ruled the Soviet Union had never taken the Vatican seriously as a force in world politics. 'They didn't draw any far-reaching conclusions,' Mikhail Gorbachev told me. 'I didn't feel the impact in Stavropol' –

where he was the local Party boss – 'or when I found myself here in Moscow.'

But it was not long before the KGB took notice. President Carter's remark about the new Pope's friendship with his national security adviser fed a paranoid theory that soon began to do the rounds in Moscow. Mikhail Kowalski, a Soviet Vaticanologist since attending Vatican II as an accredited member of the press corps, told me that some in the Kremlin believed that John Paul's election had been the work of Dr Brzeziński and his friends in the CIA. However absurd the idea of a plot to subvert the cardinals' choice may seem today, Oleg Kalugin, a former head of the KGB's counter-espionage division, says that at the time, 'Russian propaganda always painted all events which ran contrary to Russian political interests as machinations of the CIA or other Western special services,' and that the KGB had begun to believe its own propaganda. 'The CIA's behind it' was, Kalugin says, the KGB explanation for almost any Russian failing, and the Politburo was heavily influenced by KGB reports. 'When they saw the CIA name they would take it for granted. For them there was no doubt that there was CIA involvement.' Perhaps it is no odder than believing it was the Holy Spirit's idea.

The Pope soon became aware of the theories. Brzeziński recalls having supper with him some years later: 'As I was leaving he said to me, "Do come again." I answered, "I won't abuse the privilege." And he laughed, wagged his finger at me and said, "Well, you elected me, you've got to come and see me."'

Popes often astonish the world by the way in which they change once in office, and the history of the Church is replete with examples of pontiffs who have acted in a manner their sponsors never anticipated. When Sixtus V won the Triple Crown in the election of 1585, he was chosen as a puppet of the Medicis. He was a Franciscan friar, who had begun his life as a swineherd and was valued chiefly for his subservience and humility. On his election he startled everyone when he 'burst into a vibrant and sonorous hymn of thanksgiving'. He became the most forceful of pontiffs, famous for restoring law and financial stability to the Papal States and, in almost equal measure, for the ferocity of his punishments: he once ordered that a wit who satirized his sister should have his hands cut off and his tongue slit. The transformation of John XXIII from caretaker into revolutionary is a more recent and benevolent example of the same principle.

For Cardinal König, the election of John Paul I I remains an inspiring example of what the Holy Spirit can achieve, and the unique role the Church can play when God takes a hand. It is difficult to imagine any other state or institution that could have produced a leader so little known to the world at large who was to have such a profound impact on its affairs.

6

Queen Jadwiga's Footprint

God's bell the Conclave's petty strife has stilled;
Its mighty tone
The harbinger of Slavic hopes fulfilled–
The Papal Throne!
A Pope who'll not – Italian-like – take fright
At sabre-thrust
But brave as God Himself, advance to fight . . .

Juliusz Słowacki's prophetic poem – it was written in 1848, when the idea of a non-Italian pope seemed unthinkable – goes on to describe 'Our Slavic Pope's' triumphant transformation of the Church and the world. It hints at a muscularity and mysticism in Polish Catholicism that the cardinals meeting in Rome 130 years later may not have fully appreciated.

In the Western Church, one of the most readily accepted of the Second Vatican Council's reforms has been the taking of communion in the hand rather than the mouth; in retrospect the old practice of sticking your tongue out at the priest seems somewhat undignified. Yet when I put my hands forward for communion at Mass in Poland, I was greeted with a look of startled incomprehension – more than thirty years after the Council had ended.

Karol Wojtyła may have been a powerful advocate on the floor of St Peter's during Vatican II, but in many areas of its life the Church from which he sprang still behaves as if the Council had never happened. And John Paul is very much a child of the Polish Church. The Nobel prizewinning author Czesław Miłosz told me that 'to understand the Pope you must first understand the city of Kraków', the 'strange, beautiful, medieval city', as he called it, where 'the most durable Polish tradition is really located'.

Like Miłosz, who still keeps a flat in Kraków, where he lives when he is not teaching and writing in America, Karol Wojtyła is a true son of Poland's ancient capital. He was born thirty miles away in the small industrial town of Wadowice, but it was Kraków that schooled him, and it was here that the future pope and history met for the first time: the nineteen-year-old student was serving at Mass in the city's cathedral when the first German bombers struck in 1939. It was here, too, that he had his first experience of resistance to authority when he joined the secret seminary run by Cardinal Prince Adam Sapieha, the aristocratic archbishop who was to have such a powerful influence on his development. It was to Kraków that he returned in 1948 after his studies in Rome, to serve as curate, parish priest, theology teacher, assistant bishop – all at the remarkably young age of thirty-eight – and finally, from 1964, as archbishop.

It is a magical place, one of those jewels of European civilization that were hidden from the West by the Iron Curtain. For most of the generation that grew up during the Cold War, 'Europe' stopped at Checkpoint Charlie, the crossing point between the free West and Communist East Berlin. Our imagination held no map of the lands beyond. On my first visit to Kraków I found it a shock to discover a place that combined the qualities of all my favourite cities: Kraków is as intimate as Cambridge; it has York's atmosphere of undisturbed antiquity; and Venice's flair for public spaces.

In the wall of the Carmelite church in the city's old town a stone panel is embedded carrying the imprint of a tiny foot. It is said to have been left there by the fourteenth-century Queen Jadwiga. It seems that the Queen and her ladies-in-waiting liked to stop here on their way back from riding in the country while the church was being built – no one has suggested anything but the purest religious motives in the pleasure the Queen took in watching the bricklayers raise the walls higher and higher. During one visit she was distressed to find one of the labourers weeping because his wife had fallen ill; he could no longer afford the doctors' bills and his children were going uncared-for. The gracious Queen placed her foot on the block of stone he was working, removed the gold buckle and gave it to him. The act of kindness was recorded in a miraculous imprint. In the city where John

Paul spent so much of the life that prepared him for the papacy, there is a ready acceptance of the presence of the supernatural in history, and also of the idea that history leaves an imprint – on the minds of men as well as on the stones of the city.

Kraków is a symbol of Polish nationhood, a city of faith, but first and foremost an intellectual city, and John Paul has been the most intellectual of popes. The Jagiellonian University, where he studied Polish literature, is second only to Prague in antiquity among the universities of Central Europe, and boasts among its old boys the fifteenth-century astronomer Nicolaus Copernicus. Today the medieval and baroque buildings gathered around the city's vast central market-square are home to a seemingly endless proliferation of 'institutes' where colloquies and seminars are held, and books are written. Where Washington has its Carnegie Endowments and its Brookings Institutes, devoted to the study of geopolitics and macro-economics, Kraków has its Tertio Millennio Institute and its International Cultural Centre devoted to religion and art, while in the offices of *Tygodnik Powszechny* – the intellectual Catholic weekly that began to publish Karol Wojtyła's articles in 1949 – earnest young men are still studying obscure-looking tracts amid tottering piles of dusty back numbers. Karol Wojtyła belongs to a city imbued with the belief that ideas matter, and that thought can change life.

Father Józef Tischner, now editor of *Tygodnik Powszechny*, tells an engaging anecdote about Karol Wojtyła when he was Archbishop of Kraków. When ticking off a priest who was talking too freely, he admonished him with the words 'For this tongue of yours, you will suffer purgatory, Father.' 'I know, and I even know my penance,' came the tart reply. 'I shall have to read all Father Cardinal's books.' Words have been pouring from Karol Wojtyła's pen since the 1930s, cascades of poetry, plays, books, articles and, as pope, encyclicals. Much of it is sufficiently impenetrable to justify the loose-tongued priest's gibe: Wojtyła's doctoral thesis was devoted to phenomenology – not the most accessible of the philosophical disciplines – and boasted the gloriously intimidating title *An Assessment of the Possibility of Erecting a Christian Ethic on the Principles of Max Scheler*. 'He is difficult as a teacher,' concedes Halina Bortnowska, who studied under him at the University of Lublin. 'He has the university teacher's belief that people listen from the beginning to the end, and not just to one lecture but to lecture after lecture.'

Father Mieczysław Maliński was one of Karol Wojtyła's closest confidants in the war years in Kraków and a fellow student at Cardinal Sapieha's secret seminary, and he says that drama and poetry were every bit as important to the future pope as philosophy and theology. 'Polish literature,' he said, 'was his daily bread in Wadowice and in Kraków. It was in his acting, writing, studying, playing, everything he did. It gave him his sense of humanity.' The theatrical group Wojtyła joined as a young student had a special interest in Polish romanticism, and the ideas he absorbed there had a direct impact on the sense of mission he took to Rome forty years later. There can be very few priests, let alone bishops, who have devoted themselves so strenuously to poetry in their early years. Karol Wojtyła saw art as 'a companion of religion and a guide on the road to God; it has the dimension of a romantic rainbow – from the earth and heart of man to infinity'.

Polish romantic literature is the well-spring of a streak of messianism that runs deep in Polish culture, popular as well as intellectual. It gave rise to the idea of Poland as the Christ of Nations, which would redeem the world through its suffering, rising from its history of partition and oppression to offer the hope of a new world to all mankind. It is rooted specifically in Poland's historical experience. Adam Mickiewicz is the high priest of the romantic genre, an admirer of Byron and a tireless campaigner for Polish independence and democracy who occupies a position in Polish national affections analogous to Shakespeare's in our own. His *Books of the Polish Pilgrims*, published in 1832, provides an example of the kind of sentiments that would have worked their way into the young Wojtyła's soul. Poland, the poet writes, has been given 'the heritage of the future freedom of the world'. It has the power of resurrection, a 'Lazarus among nations'. It is the nation loved by Christ, peopled by those who 'believe, who love and who have hope'. Eternal spiritual ideals and contemporary politics are jumbled together in a bewildering and promiscuous manner: 'Raise our country from the dead,' beseeches the poet in 'Litany of the Pilgrim', and then adds, moving from sublime aspiration to particular political objective without so much as a nod to the possibility of bathos, 'From Russian, Austrian and Prussian bondage,/ Deliver us, O Lord.'

During the 1980 Solidarity strike in the Gdańsk shipyards, poetry was daubed on the walls like graffiti, and the edition of Mickiewicz's poems I secured from the Polish Centre in London yielded up a yellowing Solidarity leaflet. There cannot be many industrial movements that have used verse to encourage striking workers. Polish poetry is part of Polish political discourse.

If the Pope believed that Poland was the 'Christ among Nations' it would, of course, be heretical as well as eccentric. There was and is only one Christ, and no nation can be the Son of God. But the idea that Poland's suffering served some larger purpose must have exerted a powerful influence on his mind. Adam Mickiewicz grew up in a Poland partitioned between Russia, Prussia and Austria. Karol Wojtyła first read his words in a Poland under German occupation, followed shortly by Soviet domination.

Halina Bortnowska – who, as a theologian as well as a papal confidant, may be one of the few people who really has 'read all Father Cardinal's books' – says there is nothing in his texts to justify the claim that he is fired by crude Polish messianism, but she believes he has a sophisticated and complex idea of the role of nations in history: 'For him the existence of nations, of peoples with ethnic identities, is important. It is somehow involved in the history of salvation – that's true, that's his theory. But it doesn't mean that Poland is more called to give God to the world than other nations. All nations are called to it.' That may be true in theory, but many of those I spoke to in the wider Church who had crossed swords with John Paul argued that he found it difficult to free himself from his Polish background so that he could appreciate the distinctive contributions of other Catholic traditions.

Czesław Miłosz remembers attending a seminar of historians and writers assembled at Castelgandolfo – the Pope's summer residence – to discuss the future of Europe. The Pope listened carefully to what was said and rounded it off with a crisp reflection on St Peter's decision to come to Rome: 'You see what happened as a result of that decision of one man: a Europe.' Karol Wojtyła believes passionately in the providential interpretation of history and the importance of individual acts in deciding destiny. The ideas come from traditional Catholic theology, but Polish poetry supplied the passion.

Kraków became the city of Polish nationhood with the crowning of King Władisław the Short in 1320. It was the first capital of the united Poland, and even when the court and government moved to

Warsaw three hundred years later, it was to Kraków that Polish kings came to be crowned and were brought to be buried. The Gothic cathedral where Karol Wojtyła presided as archbishop for seventeen years, with its tombs of kings, queens and poets, has the same status as a national church as Westminster Abbey in Britain.

The political upheavals of the eighteenth century entrenched Kraków's special place in the nation's heart still further. Tadeusz Kościuszko, the champion of Polish unity and independence, took his 'oath to the nation' in the Kraków market-place in 1794. His uprising failed, and the Russian, Prussian and Austrian partition followed. But during the years of national division and foreign domination, this ancient capital of the Piast and Jagiellon dynasties became a place of pilgrimage for Poles, the one visible symbol of their nationhood. The ideal of Polish nationhood is intimately bound up with the country's Catholicism. Norman Davies, the most exhaustive of modern historians of Poland, writes that the baptism of the tenth-century Prince Mieszko, a founding father of the Piast dynasty which established the Polish nation, and the adoption of Catholicism as the national religion in 965 was 'the most momentous event of Polish history', and describes the Church's position in medieval Polish society like this:

It provided the ideology which explained the links not only of the king to his Crown, but also of every man and woman to the universe. It was the fount of all knowledge . . . Its prelates combined the powers of barons, ministers and diplomats. Its friars and nuns were the teachers and social workers. Its faithful, who accepted Faith with a finality inconceivable in the present age, comprised the overwhelming mass of Poland's population.

That picture would have held true for many medieval societies, but what distinguishes Poland is that it survived for so much longer. During the painful history of partition in the eighteenth and nineteenth centuries, Catholicism became the focus for Poland's resistance to outside rulers, and the sole means of maintaining its jealously guarded links with Western European civilization and culture. The upheavals of the twentieth century, which brought so much misery to Poland and made some of its towns bywords for mass murder, had the perverse effect of strengthening its Catholic identity. In the late seventeenth century, at the time of the first partition, around half of Poland's population was Catholic. After the Holocaust and the expulsion of Germans and Ukrainians in the post–Second World War settlement, 96 per cent of Poles owed allegiance to Rome. Traces of the 'finality' of medieval faith are still readily discernible in Poland today. Sit in a café for an hour or so and a religious pageant will pass before you: gaggles of young seminarians idling their way along the pavement – good-looking young men laughing and joking like any of their age – a brace of nuns in fantastic pre–Vatican II headgear, perhaps a military chaplain with a dog-collar beneath a smartly pressed uniform.

Karol Wojtyła showed how well he understood that heritage with a characteristically flamboyant symbolic gesture at his inauguration as Kraków's archbishop. He entered the cathedral wearing a chasuble donated by the medieval Queen Anna Jagiellon, a palium given by Queen Jadwiga in the sixteenth century, the mitre of a seventeenth-century predecessor and a crozier that dated from the reign of King Jan Sobieski, seventeenth-century victor over the Ottomans. As Carl Bernstein and Marco Politi remark in their biography *His Holiness*, 'This wasn't mere respect for tradition: it was a way of reminding the faithful and the "infidels" in power that the Church in Poland was the nation, that without the Church the history of Poland did not exist.'

For the Polish pope the great figures of Poland's past are much more than symbols, more even than ghosts that stalk its present. Czesław Miłosz believes he shares one salient Polish characteristic, 'an extremely strong sense of the communion of saints, namely of the link between the living and the dead . . . If you go to a cemetery on All Saints' Day,' he says, 'you will realize that it is the greatest feast in Poland.' Kraków's cathedral houses the giant silver sarcophagus holding the remains of St Stanisław, patron saint of Poland. He was an eleventh-century bishop of Kraków who stood up to his monarch, Bolesław the Bold. Stanisław disapproved of Bolesław's taste for pillage and sensual pleasure, and said so in his sermons. Increasingly irritated by being preached at, the King sent a posse of knights to kill the Bishop while he was saying Mass, but 'some supernatural force held back their swords', and the King was forced to ride into the Bishop's church himself to strike a deadly blow to the prelate's head from behind as he stood at the altar. Then he had the Bishop's body dismembered and thrown into a nearby pond.

According to legend, four white eagles appeared from heaven, fished out the bits and put Stanisław back together so that he could be properly buried. He has been a powerful focus for myth-making ever since. In a Communist Poland nine centuries after his martyrdom Stanisław stood as a symbol of the Church's duty to defy oppressive and unjust rulers, a still resonant reminder of its role as a force of resistance.

This pope has canonized more saints than all his predecessors combined. Almost all of them have – and are intended to have – a relevance in the contemporary life of the Church or the political arena. For John Paul the saints are not dead, they are living companions.

Kraków also holds the key to understanding Karol Wojtyła's devotion to popular mysticism. That can seem puzzling when set beside his high intellectualism. To non-Catholics, suspicious of weeping Madonnas and dubious apparitions, the idea that a man of this pope's formidable intellectual gifts could be fooled by peasant superstitions must be impossible to grasp. It is one of those areas where the secular and the Catholic mind can never meet. To anyone brought up a Catholic, even those of us who grew up in the enlightened post-Vatican II Church of Western Europe – the idea of everyday miracles and sacred places seems entirely natural.

Next to its cathedral, the Church of Our Lady in Kraków's market-square, where Karol Wojtyła attended and celebrated Mass as priest and bishop, is Kraków's most famous. It was begun in the early years of the thirteenth century and completed in the fourteenth. It is a medieval masterpiece. Its dark interior is dominated by a vast altarpiece, thirteen metres high and eleven across. Created by the master craftsman Veit Stob and his apprentices, it depicts the life, death and Assumption of the Virgin Mary. She and some of the figures around her stand nearly three metres tall, and if you kneel before them their sheer size underscores the impression that they belong to a different dimension. Saints Adalbert and Stanisław are present at her Assumption in the upper panel – allegorical truth was judged more important than historical accuracy when this inspiring artefact was created. The atmosphere in St Mary's recalls an earlier age of faith, a time when belief was a simple fact, not a system structured by theologians. The church is an expression of a sense of the divine in human life at its most mystical, and the carved figures evoke that uncertain world where folklore and religion merge.

Bishop Pieronek, former secretary of the Polish Bishops' Conference, defends the popular mysticism of the Polish Catholic Church against the charge that it slips into superstition and folklore. It is a question of 'seeing one's life in the perspective of the faith which exists in all, even the most minute manifestations of human life in Poland. Life begins with God and ends with Him. I think this religiosity is truly deep, though some reproach it for its shallowness or folkishness. But these were the values that formed a human being to his very depths.' John Paul has never shown the least embarrassment about his attachment to the mystical, and his affection for and understanding of popular piety. In the late twentieth century, the Catholic Church chose a leader who combined some of the most sophisticated political and media skills of any on the world stage with a faith that drew its inspiration from the earliest medieval roots of the Slavic Church.

Finally it was in Kraków that John Paul learned and practised his form of resistance. To study as he did while doing forced labour in a quarry for the Nazis, and to join an underground religious movement – the Living Rosary – in wartime Kraków must have required great courage. Father Mieczysław Maliński gives this account of his own recruitment to the Rosary group: 'I was in the habit of going to morning Mass during the German occupation . . . Such were the times we lived in that leaving your house in the morning you never knew whether you would be back in the evening. You could get shot in the street or be taken to Auschwitz. That was how it was. Outside the Church there was a man waiting for me, wearing a black raincoat, his wavy blond hair brushed back. "May I accompany you?" he asked. My immediate impression was that he was from the Gestapo and had come to arrest me. When I agreed to his company he said he too was going to Madalinskiego Street. How did he know I lived there? On the way I asked, "What is it about?" He said, "I would like you to join a human rosary I want to organize." You can imagine my relief. At that moment I would have joined anything. I was so relieved that my life was not going to end then and there.'

Father Maliński met Karol Wojtyła that same evening: 'This is Karol, who wants to be an actor,' was his introduction to the future pope. And together they began the clandestine prayer meetings that eventually led them both to ordination.

It was a form of resistance to the godless Nazi authority under which they both lived. But it was a curiously passive form of resistance, especially if it is compared to the way in which millions of other young men were living across Europe. Cardinal Sapieha's secret seminary began to function in October 1942, when all over the world youth was offering itself up in one of the few wars in which good really did confront evil. A place that can claim to be the epicentre of that evil was on Karol Wojtyła's doorstep: Auschwitz is around an hour's drive from the centre of Kraków. In France, which, like Wojtyła's Poland, was under occupation, young men and women inspired by General de Gaulle were blowing up trains and slitting Nazi throats while the future pope studied his Aquinas. As his countrymen and -women died heroically in the Warsaw uprising in 1944, Karol Wojtyła was preparing for his 'tonsure ceremony', the shaving of the head that symbolized attainment of the priestly state.

It is striking that a man with such an intense appreciation of the difference between good and evil, with such a strong sense of both God and the devil at work in the world, should have chosen a path so distinct from that of most of his contemporaries. It was the first indication of a commitment to non-violence that borders on pacifism.

Although John Paul was to have a profound political impact, his original concept of resistance was centred in religion, not political activism. The Karol Wojtyła of the war years, who joined the Living Rosary group and trained secretly for the priesthood, saw resistance as a question of clearing a space in which his relationship with God could develop. It was something quite distinct from the more pro-active and overtly political response of taking up arms.

It re-emerged in his early days as Archbishop of Kraków. His primary objective when he took on the job was to secure freedom for his priests to do their pastoral work in their parishes and for the catechism to be taught to the young. Jacek Woźniakowski, a fellow member of one of those 'intellectual circles' that seem to have proliferated in Kraków, says that when Karol Wojtyła first became archbishop he believed that secular politics could be left to Cardinal Wyszyński, the Archbishop of Warsaw. The Primate of Poland had already established himself as a colossus of Polish politics, and according to Woźniakowski, Wojtyła hoped that he could 'perform only his pastoral duties, not being diverted from his main tasks by difficult everyday relations with the government'. Rather than playing politics, he wanted to 'fix up a very difficult situation concerning teaching and the possibilities for priests to operate properly in their parishes, pastoral letters to be read in churches, everything concerning the normal functioning of the church'. It was only when he realized that the state left him no room to work as a purely religious leader that he became fully engaged in Poland's political life.

The American journalist and papal biographer Tad Szulc unearthed an intriguing 'position paper' from the Polish secret police, which offers the Party leadership a strategy for dealing with the Polish Church. It is dated 5 August 1967, soon after Archbishop Wojtyła became Cardinal Wojtyła, and confirms that in those days he was not regarded by the regime as a political threat. The document carefully analyses the differences between the new Cardinal and the established figure of Cardinal Wyszyński in Warsaw, and recommends that everything be done to encourage what the authors see as an incipient rivalry between them. Wojtyła, it says, 'rose in the Church hierarchy not thanks to an anti-Communist stance, but thanks to intellectual values (his works on Catholic morality and ethics, such as Love and Responsibility, have been translated into many languages) . . . It can be safely said that he is one of the few intellectuals in the Polish episcopate . . . He has not, so far, engaged in open state political activity. It seems that politics are his weaker suit; he is over-intellectualized.' It was a perceptive analysis, but also a portent of the fatal error that Communist intelligence services made in the 1980s: their failure to understand that 'intellectual values' may have a profound impact on day-to-day politics.

Despite its beauty there is a certain sadness about Kraków, a sense of resentment that it was forgotten for so long. It is a city on the extreme edge of the civilization to which it owes allegiance. It is Latin and Catholic, but it is physically much closer to the world of Cyrillic script and Orthodox belief than it is to Rome. Its market-square and baroque buildings may recall Vienna or Amsterdam, but there is more than a hint of the icon-jewelled darkness of Russia's monasteries about the interior of its churches. It lies close to Europe's great fault-line, which existed long before the Iron Curtain, that divides the Orthodox East from the Catholic West.

At his meeting with Mikhail Gorbachev in 1989, John Paul II told the Soviet leader that Europe must 'breathe with two lungs'. The first and greatest task of his papacy was to make that vision a reality, and the city of Kraków had served as a uniquely effective teacher to prepare him for the task.

7

The Church and Communism

The former Soviet leader Mikhail Gorbachev told me that Catholicism and Communism were 'competitors in the battle for the soul'. For most of this century the Vatican saw the Communist world as the most serious threat to the Church's future, politically and ideologically.

Both belief systems conceive of human history as a progress towards a clearly defined end: for Catholics, it is a preparation for the Second Coming and the Day of Judgement, and is driven by God's presence in history; for Communists, it is an inevitable march towards the perfect society, which will be achieved with the withering away of the state. As the Kremlin's veteran Vaticanologist Mikhail Kowalski puts it, 'Marxist Leninism has its roots in Christianity – the only real difference is that Marxist Leninists conceive of the possibility of building the Kingdom of Justice on Earth.'

In both cases the goal offers hope to men and women. The Catholic paradise may seem a richer place because it has been adorned by the imaginations of great artists over the past two thousand years and endlessly reworked by great minds, and because it is necessarily unknowable it allows endless scope for individual hopes and dreams. But the millions who have flocked to Communist flags are equally a tribute to the power of the Communist ideal of a perfect society: Chinese peasants and Russian workers chose to follow their revolutionary leaders because they were offered a New Jerusalem. Critically, both systems claimed to have all the answers. That meant there could, in the end, be no accommodation between them. George Weigel, an American Catholic academic of the right, put it to me like this: 'They were locked in a battle in which there could be no negotiated settlement. Somebody was right and somebody was wrong in their reading of the human condition here. This was going to be a struggle in which one view was vindicated historically.'

Cardinal Agostino Casaroli, the wily Vatican diplomat who became one of the most enduring players on the international stage during the Cold War years, said the struggle was fought with the zeal of a crusade: 'The first Communists were sincere in their conviction that they had to fight against religion to create a new world of justice. That made things very difficult because it meant the ideology was almost a religion itself. And religious wars were always the worst in history.' Alexander Tsepko was on the other side of the battle-lines during those years, but his judgement is similar. He was an adviser to the Central Committee of the Soviet Communist Party during the Brezhnev era, and says its leaders were 'educated in the traditions of so-called militant socialism. It wasn't even atheism, it was an animal hatred of religion and everything connected with religion.'

Catholicism and Communism see forces greater than humanity at work in history – providence for Catholics; the iron Hegelian laws of thesis, antithesis and synthesis for Communists – but each gives a central place to a human agency that can interpret and facilitate the operation of those forces, the Church on one hand, the Party on the other. The bureaucratic armies that met on this ideological battlefield had much in common too: they were based on the idea of absolute authority that flowed from the top down. The structures built around a Communist Party general secretary and a pope were equally founded on the belief that the leaders have a special access to the truth: in the days before the fall of the Berlin Wall Party officials had the mysterious inaccessibility of the pre-Vatican II priesthood.

The human emotions of ambition, envy and pettiness drive any big institution where power is to be had for the taking. They were present in the old Kremlin and are present today in the Curia. In both they were given direction by service to an ideal. A curial monsignor had more in common with a Kremlin commissar than with 'Sir Humphrey' in Whitehall. Even the most cynical Catholic or Communist function-ary is, at some level, dedicated to advancing the cause of what he or she believes to be the truth, while the Whitehall civil servant is concerned with efficiency in the service of someone else's ideas about the national interest.

It took more than a century to establish what was really at stake in the battle between Communism and Catholicism. Marxism was one among the many -isms lumped together for condemnation by Pius IX in his sweeping rejection of the modern world and all its workings in the nineteenth century. When he retreated into the physical isolation of the Vatican and the dogmatic certainties of the Doctrine of Infallibility and the Syllabus of Errors, he set the Church against the good as well as the bad that the intellectual revolutions of the nineteenth century had to offer. Liberalism, pluralism, tolerance, and engagement with new ideas were caught up in the great net of heresy and cast over the side of St Peter's barque.

The first signs of Catholic social radicalism began to emerge towards the end of the last century. The English primate Cardinal Manning denounced capitalism as 'tyranny', and during the London dockers' strike of 1889 he sided with the workforce, helping to push the employers into a compromise over pay and conditions. Two years later, Pope Leo XIII published his encyclical *Rerum Novarum*, On the Condition of Labour, which denounced the exploitation of workers, and inspired the social ideas developed later during Vatican II and by John Paul II. But as the century turned, Catholicism remained a force of reaction, and Marxism was a force for revolution. The Church stood for the established order and against change.

In the 1930s the Church deployed the full majesty of its vituperative powers in its anti-Communist rhetoric. Pius XI's 1937 *Divini Redemptoris* described Communism as 'contrary to Western civilization' and condemned it, in a phrase to become so notorious when it was later applied to contraception, as 'intrinsically evil'. Anti-Communist zeal sent young Catholic intellectuals to fight for Franco on the unfashionable side in the Spanish Civil War, which was being cast as one of those decisive battles for the soul of Europe. And in 1942 *Divini Redemptoris* was enthusiastically reprinted by Mussolini's propagandist Roberto Farinacci to justify Italian participation with Germany on the Russian front.

In the late 1940s the future Pope Paul VI was up to his neck in machinations to keep the Communists out of power in Italy. As the Soviet empire tightened its control over the nations of Eastern Europe, the Vatican confronted the possibility that Italy's Communists might win power at the ballot box. So widespread were the fears of Communist success at the polls – or a *coup d'état* and civil war if they failed

– that the Irish ambassador offered Pius XII safe haven in Dublin. The Pope turned him down: 'My place is in Rome and, if it be the will of the Divine Master, I am ready to be martyred for Him in Rome,' he said, as he reflected gloomily on 'the imminent danger to the Church in Italy and the whole of Western Europe'.

According to Paul VI's biographer Peter Hebblethwaite, the future pope – then an up-and-coming curial official – met this danger by arranging financing for an organization of Catholic civic committees dedicated to countering Communist influence and campaigning for the Christian Democrats at the 1948 elections. He provided a start-up fund of a hundred million lira through the Vatican Bank, and financed it through the sale of surplus United States war material. The Christian Democrats emerged from the election as leaders of a coalition government, and civilization was spared.

That fierce anti-Communist fervour lingered on in the Church right up to the opening of the Second Vatican Council. Archbishop Hannan, arriving in Rome in 1962 as a newly consecrated auxiliary bishop of Washington, remembers being preoccupied with the question of whether the Communist nations would allow any of their bishops to attend. He describes the opening of the Council, when bishops and patriarchs of the Eastern Churches processed with their Roman brothers, as 'a great revelation of the entirety of the Church and at the same time a great reminder that Christendom was faced with a tremendous evil. The evil was Communism.'

Pope John XXIII inaugurated a new phase in relations between Communism and Catholicism with his encyclical *Pacem in Terris*, or Peace on Earth, published in 1963. His insight was simple but revolutionary in its implications. The Church would continue to condemn the 'error' of Communism but would no longer condemn those who erred: Communists might be mistaken, but they remained human persons with all the dignity that that status demands. The distinction – between the error and the misguided, the sin and the sinners – allowed the Church to adopt a new negotiating position towards the Soviet and Eastern European governments.

On 7 March 1963 Pope John told a group of journalists that the Church occupied a position of 'supra-national neutrality'. They included the son-in-law of the Soviet leader Nikita Khrushchev, and later that day, in a clear sign that the Vatican wanted to improve relations with the Kremlin, he and his wife were granted a papal audience. That October when the Cuban missile crisis blew up in the first weeks of the Council, America and the Soviet Union seemed on the brink of a nuclear war and John called for negotiation: 'We appeal to all rulers not to remain deaf to the cry of mankind. Let them do everything in their power to save peace.' In his Christmas message that year, as the world breathed a sigh of relief at the passing of the crisis, John was able to claim that his 'words were not wasted on the air'.

The changed relationship with the Soviet empire was a critical part of John's legacy to Paul VI – and he also bequeathed his successor the man who could use it best. Agostino Casaroli began his curial career in 1937. Delicate health kept him burrowing away in the offices and archives of the Secretariat of State until 1963, when he had his first encounter with Communist officials at a meeting on consular relations in Vienna. It was the beginning of a long diplomatic career with a specialist interest in Eastern Europe and the Communist world; by the time Cardinal Casaroli retired in 1990 he had served four popes and outlasted the system that had engaged his energies for so many years. The Cardinal died in the summer of 1998, not long after giving me an interview for this book.

Pope John instructed him at the outset with the words, 'The Church may have many enemies but it is no one's enemy.' Like skilled diplomats the world over Casaroli took his master's vision and turned it to good practical use. The Cardinal defined the first task of the Vatican diplomatic service as 'to occupy ourselves with the concrete problems of the Catholic Church, to assure the rights of our Church', in other words, the pursuit of what in a conventional diplomatic service would be called the national interest. He told me that the second task was 'to favour peace and good understanding among nations', but left me in no doubt that that is the *second* task.

In the Communist world, 'the rights of our Church' were under serious threat. Some seventy million Catholics lived behind the Iron Curtain. Their conditions varied significantly from one country to another: to be part of the Catholic majority in Poland was a very different experience from that of living and worshipping as one of the persecuted minority in a Lithuania that was still part of the Soviet Union, but everywhere they lived under regimes committed to an atheist ideology. And all the Churches, to a greater or lesser degree, were subjected to state harassment. In Czechoslovakia, for example, by the end of Paul VI's pontificate there was only one episcopal see in the entire country with a resident bishop. The Vatican judged that without priests to administer the sacraments and bishops to ordain the priests, the Church behind the Iron Curtain would simply wither and die. It was in the interests of this Church – 'common people, workers, young people' as well as priests and bishops – that Casaroli believed he should exercise his diplomatic skills: 'We felt the moral duty to try to assure them of the religious assistance they needed, of the possibility of attending a Catholic Mass in a church, of confession, of religious instruction.'

In practical terms that meant reaching accommodation with Communist regimes in the hope of preserving at least a skeleton of Church life. It meant toning down the anti-Communist rhetoric in the hope of winning concessions for the Church in return. The policy became known as 'Ostpolitik'; it was a minimalist strategy, designed for survival not victory.

It also brought the Church into the mainstream of East–West diplomatic relations. In his elegant apartment just behind St Peter's, Cardinal Casaroli proudly showed me a photograph of himself posing with the leaders of both the Communist East and the free West at the signing of the Helsinki Final Act in 1975. It was, he explained, the first time the Holy See had been represented at an international conference of that kind since the Congress of Vienna in 1815.

The Final Act, agreed during two years of negotiations between thirty-five European countries, the United States and Canada, confirmed Europe's post-Second World War borders, and committed the signatories to work towards a clearly defined set of human-rights objectives. It was one of the high points of what was known as *détente*, the policy of defusing East–West tensions. The Soviets saw it as a recognition of the status quo in Europe, confirmation that the West accepted the existence of the Iron Curtain that divided the continent. In fact, its provisions for the monitoring of human rights and the review conferences that followed it became powerful weapons for putting pressure on Communist regimes to live up to their promises. It allowed the Church to focus attention on the moral dimension of what was happening in Eastern Europe, so that, as George Weigel, the right-wing Catholic apologist, puts it, the Soviet Union could be 'put in the dock of international public opinion for its failure to recognize the human rights which it had obliged itself to recognize'.

But the diplomatic strategy adopted by Casaroli and Paul VI laid them open to the charge of appeasement. The triumphalist interpretation of the final battle of the Cold War, which credits Western victory to a triumvirate of conviction leaders – John Paul II, Margaret Thatcher and Ronald Reagan – tends to blame those who sought accommodation with Communism – whether they be Cardinal Casaroli or the Social Democrat German Chancellor Willy Brandt – for a failure of nerve which caused them to compromise their principles. Casaroli was criticized for a style like that of the Italian statesman Aldo Moro who 'believed there was absolutely no non-negotiable position'.

And at the heart of the Church's Ostpolitik lay the assumption that the Yalta settlement of 1945 was permanent or, at the very least, would survive for a long time. When Winston Churchill, the American President Franklin Roosevelt and the Soviet leader Josef Stalin met at the Black Sea resort of Yalta, they agreed the post-war shape of Europe. Churchill was aware that the resources of Britain and its empire had been exhausted, and Roosevelt was a sick man. They fell in with Stalin's determination to swallow large tracts of Europe into the Soviet sphere of influence, and drew what became the map of the Cold War.

Cardinal Casaroli told me that he had to base his policies on what the American State Department would call a 'worst case scenario', an acceptance that the lines drawn at Yalta would endure. 'At the beginning I was really impressed by the strength of Communism,' he said. 'It seemed settled in for centuries, maybe even millennia . . . You had to arrange a new strategy and a new tactic with this vision in mind.'

The orthodoxy of Ostpolitik changed radically the moment John Paul II took office in 1978. He regarded the division of Europe as unnatural and unjust – and had ever since he had first heard of the Yalta agreement. In 1944, the future pope was studying in the secret seminary in Kraków. His friend and fellow seminarian of those days, Father Mieczysław Maliński, recalls their conversations as they walked to the tiny flat in Tyniecka Street that Karol Wojtyła shared with his father during the war years. 'It was becoming more and more clear to us what the future held for us. We both had a feeling of betrayal. Both Britain and the United States sold Poland to Russia. We felt very bitter about it.'

The Second Vatican Council had promoted the idea that the Church should engage with the world. It had also furnished the ideological weapon the new pope needed to fight his Last Battle with Communism: the Document on Religious Liberty, with its resonant title *Dignitatis Humanae*, On Human Dignity, which neatly reversed the old relationship between Communism and Catholicism.

As George Weigel puts it, the document 'freed the Church at last from any enthralment to political power. This would no longer be a Church whose evangelical message had the corrosive power of the state behind it.' Communism, by contrast, had acquired all the sclerotic trappings of a state religion, so that its message of liberation was hopelessly compromised by its association with the privilege and power of a few. The similarities between the Vatican and the Kremlin became more apposite than ever, except that those on the barricades were now likely to see the first as the people's friend, the second as the enemy. Catholicism had become the force of revolution, Marxism of entrenched interests and power.

The change allowed John Paul II to focus on the real issue at stake in the battle between Catholicism and Communism. Both take the human person as their starting point, but for John Paul, the humanism behind Communism is false because it fails to take into account human spirituality. Communism believes that the human condition can be explained entirely in terms of material need; John Paul believes that that is an inadequate understanding of what it is to be human.

The dignity of each human being is the mainspring of his pronouncements on almost everything, whether it be his deeply conservative views on contraception and abortion, his protests against human-rights abuses by totalitarian regimes from Cuba to Nigeria, or the social radicalism of his judgements on the value of work in some of his encyclicals. His view is, critically, distinct from the humanist view of humankind because it sees the religious dimension as an essential part of that dignity. Without it, in John Paul's world view, the individual is stunted, their humanity unfulfilled. 'We believed,' says Professor Swierzawski, who supervised the future pope's philosophy dissertation, 'that without metaphysics philosophy is lame, that it is deformed.'

On the archive recordings of Pope John Paul's inauguration, the new pontiff can be seen sneaking a glance at his watch during the dying moments of the ceremony. George Weigel relates that when

John Paul heard that the Polish authorities were going to broadcast the service live for three hours, he was determined not to leave any dead airtime for the Communist spin-doctors to put their own interpretation on the event. 'He was going to make sure,' Weigel says, 'that the last picture in the broadcast was him with that crozier standing there in front of this massive crowd.' So the Pope instructed his Master of Ceremonies that the service had to last three hours and not a moment less, and he chatted with every single one of the cardinals who came to pay him homage until he was sure it had run its full length.

John Paul's faith had been formed by an Eastern Church with its medieval roots still strong, but his appreciation of the power of the media was thoroughly Western and modern. Nothing in the papacy's past had prepared the world for a pope who could seize its attention in the way John Paul did. He was an ex-actor, and he had been given one of the most theatrical parts there is on the world stage. He played it for all it was worth, and used television as skilfully as any image-maker in an American presidential campaign. He deployed those skills to turn the spotlight on his homeland.

In the early days of his papacy, John Paul effectively invited himself back to Poland. The threat this posed to the Polish leadership was made especially pointed by the occasion the new pope planned to mark: the nine hundredth anniversary of the martyrdom of St Stanisław. Both the government and Poland's dissidents understood the message intended by remembering such a powerful symbol of the Church's resistance in the face of an unjust state. The Polish Communist Party's general secretary, Edward Gierek, was faced with an impossible choice.

Gierek's appointment in 1971 made him one of the first so-called 'reformist' Communists who later came to power elsewhere in the Soviet bloc. As a child Gierek had emigrated to France and Belgium, and had worked in the coal mines there during the Nazi occupation. He was chosen to lead Poland in the hope that he could heal the wounds left after one of the most serious outbreaks of unrest in its post-war history: the riots provoked by an increase in food prices in December 1970 had culminated in Polish troops firing on Polish workers, leaving, according to the government's own figures, forty-five people dead and more than a thousand injured. He tried to forge good relations with the West in the hope of attracting foreign investment, but he was still forced to look to Moscow as the seat of imperial power.

I visited him in the country home he built during his Party days: full of airy spaces and constructed of glass, concrete and steel, it must once have been the apogee of modernist chic, but the low-grade materials used all over the Eastern bloc have given it that ineradicable mustiness that is the hallmark of Communist-era buildings everywhere. From the cellar, his wife produced an enormous oil painting of Gierek with Leonid Brezhnev at the latter's retreat in the Crimea. Both are in suits, but the official portrait painter has reflected the holiday mood by giving them a softer look than those usually expected of Party general secretaries – even the hint of a smile. Edward Gierek regarded Leonid Brezhnev as his friend.

That was to change when Brezhnev telephoned to tell 'Edek' to prevent the Pope returning to Poland in 1979. Gierek protested that that was impossible: 'It would go against the enormous enthusiasm which gripped the country following Wojtyła's election,' he told the Soviet leader. 'How could I tell the people I was closing the border against him?' Brezhnev advised Gierek to 'tell the Pope that he should declare publicly that he could not come due to illness'.

If the leader of the Soviet empire really believed matters could be arranged like that, he had failed to judge the character of the Pope, the political climate in Poland, and the true condition of his empire. Indeed, it suggests that his grip on any kind of reality was tenuous. If Western analysts had been privy to the conversation they might have been less surprised when the Soviet power structure began to unravel.

Gierek's account of the conversation and his own heroic defiance of Soviet bullying may have been coloured by the self-serving tricks memory can play: 'He [the Pope] is a Pole and I'm a Pole,' he told his former Black Sea buddy. 'We were not going to change the decision we had made because it was a collective decision, a sovereign decision, our Polish decision.' That telephone call was the last 'Edek' Gierek received from Leonid Brezhnev. 'It was the end of my personal friendship with Brezhnev. That was how our ways parted.' But there was nothing heroic about the Polish leader's decision to agree to a papal visit: it was a simple recognition of political reality. 'They could not say no to us,' says Cardinal Casaroli. 'It would have been impossible for them to face the reaction of the Polish people.'

The Church's unique historical role in Polish society had blossomed into a modern political force, which made Poland equally unique among the nations of the Eastern bloc. Catholicism was, as Mikhail Gorbachev puts it, the 'core of resistance' to Communism, and it was powerful enough to offer institutional protection. In no other country of the Soviet empire could dissidents look to a similar force for help. Jacek Kuroń, who formed the Workers' Defence Committee, K O R, in 1976 and was one of the founding fathers of the opposition movement, says, 'The Church was a space of freedom . . . One could expect that people within the Church, who sought the space to be free, were potential allies and would come to us.' Jan Szydlak, one of Gierek's most loyal party aides, put it more brutally: 'The opposition without the Roman Catholic Church was a small group of people wandering around Poland making speeches to other small groups of people. But the opposition supported by the Church, sustained by its organizational power, found a great source of strength it could draw on.'

In 1979 Alexander Tsepko was attached to the Institute of Philosophy and Sociology in Warsaw, and as an adviser on Polish affairs to the Central Committee of the Communist Party in Moscow, he was expected to 'write a report' on what he saw in the Polish capital. He was, in other words, a kind of academic spy. On the afternoon of 2 June he joined the crowds gathered to welcome home the Polish pope. He found a place on the corner of Uizdowski Allee and watched the offices of the Polish Communist Party across the way. His memories of what he saw, as the papal procession moved past, are still vivid. It was a moment of insight that explained everything that followed; a realization that even members of the Polish Communist Party were Poles and Catholics first, Communists second. 'Suddenly the windows of the PZPR [the Communist Party offices] opened. All the Party workers sat right on the window-sills – all of them from the third and fourth floors. And it was as if they merged with the crowd. The people were singing "Ave Maria", and it sounded like a great anti-Communist hymn. A fellow academic who was standing next to me said, "Sasha, this is the end of socialism in Poland." It happened in a matter of seconds, while the Polish Party workers hung out of the windows, merging with the crowds. During those seconds, and the hours that followed, power passed to the Church. Nothing, not even martial law, could change that, and that was the end of socialism.'

In a formal sense, all that happened during the visit was that the Church took over the running of practical areas like security and crowd control for its duration. That in itself was remarkable in a society where the state habitually intruded in every area of daily life. And since the visit was a bigger event than almost anything that had happened in Poland since the Second World War it effectively meant the Church taking over the running of the country.

And it worked. There were no riots, no breakdowns in law and order. Communism had survived in part because even many of those who did not believe in it as an ideology saw it as the only force capable of running the country. But for nine days in June 1979 Poland experienced the reality of life under a non-Communist regime.

Jacek Kuroń says the significance of what was happening struck him as he walked through Warsaw the night before John Paul's Mass for the young: 'There was extraordinary order on the streets, and it was supervised by the Church militia, young people in Catholic organizations. It was amazing, because it was a self-organizing society. One of those church militiamen would give a sign – this way or that – and people immediately obeyed. The fact that people organized themselves and were aware of the fact gave them in turn the feeling of freedom.'

Jacek Woźniakowski – who had been one of Wojtyła's intellectual sparring partners in his Kraków days – recalls the experience of attending the papal Mass there in 1979. 'Everything went so smoothly, without the help of the police or the authorities, and with such goodwill and peacefulness towards each other, that this gave many people the feeling that so much could be achieved by such simple means. In every totalitarian system fear is the elementary weapon. This fear was overcome, vanquished simply by the fact of people being together with a common voice.'

The keynote of the Pope's inaugural address in Rome had been the ringing invocation, 'Be not afraid.' His visit taught Poles what that meant: the experience of joining one of those million-strong crowds made them realize that they were not alone. The idea of social solidarity – soon to bear political fruit in the formation of the trade union Solidarity – was born. Lech Wałęsa, who as leader of Solidarity was to act as midwife for the transformation, puts it like this: 'He made us realize that we were a great force, that faith can move mountains, and we came to believe this. "There are many of you, be not afraid." That was his message.'

Jimmy Carter's national security adviser, Zbigniew Brzeziński, watched events from the unique and privileged perspective of an exiled Pole at the heart of the world's most powerful government. His judgement on the long-term impact of the Pope's first Polish pilgrimage is characteristically brisk and to the point: 'The dominant mood till then was the inevitability of the existing system. After he left the dominant mood was the non-inevitability of the existing system. I think that was a fundamental transformation.' A decade later, in 1989, the people of Hungary, Czechoslovakia and East Germany learned what could be achieved when 'fear was overcome'.

The Soviet leadership saw the Pope as a threat, and a former senior KGB officer told me they took active steps to undermine his influence. If the Kremlin leaders did not appreciate the full importance of the papal visit to Poland in 1979 they do have some excuse for their myopia: the Orthodox Church in Russia had been first emasculated by the Soviet authorities and then enslaved by them. Most of its leaders were deeply compromised by their closeness to the regime, and the idea of an independent Church was simply outside the experience of the men in the Kremlin. Alexander Tsepko believes Moscow's failure to understand the significance of the Pope's first visit to Poland can also be explained by the poor quality of Soviet diplomats and intelligence agents at the Warsaw embassy. 'When the dramatic events started there, there wasn't a single person in the embassy in Poland who could give an accurate explanation of what was happening,' he said, and told two stories to illustrate the 'stupidity and dogmatism' that prevailed. He says he was used to pass on a message from the Vatican to the Kremlin via the Soviet embassy in Warsaw. The Pope wanted to offer Moscow a token of his good intentions, and promised that he would bow to the monument to the Soviet soldiers who died in the battle for Poland and acknowledge the USSR's role in ousting Fascism. Tsepko made sure the message reached the right ears but it produced no response: 'The stupidity, the damn stupidity, of the Party apparatus at that time! They didn't even send the ambassador to meet the Pope in Warsaw, so they immediately adopted the most antagonistic attitude.'

On another occasion, he says, he was approached by a group of

Catholic intellectuals looking for direct contact with the Soviet embassy in the hope of opening some kind of dialogue. Again, he passed on the message – this time to a KGB officer – and, again, ran up against a brick wall: 'If I get involved with the Polish Catholic Church,' said his contact, 'they'll rip off my stars and I'll lose my job.' That reflects the atrophy of a career structure in which advancement was built on ideological rectitude instead of initiative, but it also touches on a deeper problem for the Communist system when confronted with the Catholic challenge. Mikhail Kowalski, the Soviet academic who specialized in studying Church affairs, says the Kremlin had never treated the Vatican as a political enemy, but had always thought of it as an ideological enemy. 'That's the only viewpoint from which it was studied,' he says. 'It was a big mistake of our rulers, because they underestimated the political force of the Vatican.' The Kremlin could not grasp the possibility that the Church's ideas could become a factor in day-to-day political life, that it could build that bridge between the world of ideology and the world of political power. After all, as Stalin himself had observed, 'How many divisions has the Pope?'

Polish Communist leaders were more sensitive to the realities of the power of the Church than their comrades in Moscow, but they, too, were enslaved by their ideological prejudices; there was something about the materialistic mindset that made it difficult to comprehend a revolution with a powerful spiritual dimension. When I talked to the key players in the events of that time, I found that a profound fissure in perception persisted. Protagonists from both sides agree on the basic facts of what happened and which events had made a difference – on the wheres, whens and whos. But there is a fundamental difference of approach to the whys.

George Weigel's judgement on the significance of that first visit is so breathtaking it might make the Pope himself blush: 'I think everyone now recognizes that the Holy Father's visit to Poland in June 1979 was a period of nine days on which the history of the twentieth century pivoted in a fundamental way. Indeed, one might say it is the second pivot of the twentieth century.' The first, according to Weigel, was the week of the Archduke Ferdinand's assassination in Sarajevo, which led to the First World War, which in turn led to the Second, which itself gave birth to the Cold War.

According to the Weigel analysis, the first papal visit to Poland began the unravelling of that process: 'The people of that country had their first experience of self-government for forty years . . . They understood they could be subjects of their own history, not just objects of some regime-driven historical process.' He believes there was a 'spontaneous combustion' that 'led in fourteen short months to the founding of Solidarity in Gdańsk in August 1980 – and the rest, as they say, is history'.

The road that led from the epiphany of the first papal visit to Poland to the country's first free elections and the collapse of Communism in Eastern Europe a decade later was rough. In the 1980s no one knew its direction, and even the most enthusiastic apologists for John Paul would accept the importance of other players on the world stage and the political and economic factors that combined to destroy Communism. But in retrospect it is apparent that 1979 marked a turning-point in the relationship between Catholicism and Communism. Until then Communism had seemed to have the force of history behind it, while Catholicism was fighting vainly to stop history's tide. Afterwards, the positions were reversed. The two players who became the chief antagonists in the next stage of the struggle were powerful symbols of the transformation.

When General Wojciech Jaruzelski emerged from the shadows into the world's consciousness with his declaration of martial law in 1981, he seemed the epitome of the Stalinist strongman. The face never betrayed emotion, and the ever-present dark glasses gave him a menacing, Mafia-like air. The unnaturally straight, ramrod bearing added to the impression that he was a man beyond feeling. He stood before us as a Party boss who would take any order from Moscow and inflict it on his people with iron determination. In fact Jaruzelski's appearance tells a much more complex story about the Poland of the twentieth century. He was born into Poland's Catholic aristocracy – a 'deeply Catholic family', in his own words – and for six years in the 1930s he was educated by Marian priests. In 1939 his family fled the ancestral home in the face of the German advance, leaving the family silver buried in the grounds. In 1941 they were caught by the Soviet invasion of Lithuania and deported to Siberia, condemned as wealthy landlords, a 'socially dangerous element'. The glare of the snow was so fierce that it cracked the young Jaruzelski's eyelids; his dark glasses are the legacy of Stalin's gulags, not an affectation. And his stiff bearing is the result of an injury he sustained while cutting wood during his Siberian exile. He came home as part of an invading Soviet force. He was an officer in the Polish contingent that marched into Poland with Stalin's troops in 1944. That army has a special place in Polish folklore of Russian infamy: it sat across the Vistula river doing nothing while the Nazis suppressed the August Warsaw uprising less than a mile away, leaving a quarter of a million Poles dead.

By the time I met him, General Jaruzelski had apparently gone through yet another transformation. The elegant manners of his childhood world had reasserted themselves, and he kissed the hand of our Polish producer with elaborate courtesy. But he remained a Communist at heart. Our interview about the Pope was revealing not so much for what he said as for the way he said it. Of the 1979 visit he offered the view that it 'undeniably created a new quality in the situation in which opposition elements could find certain incentives and support for undertaking the actions which followed in 1980, in the form of strikes and, accompanying them, further events'. The syntax was so strangled that it was almost as if he wanted to stifle all meaning in the sentence because he still could not quite bring himself to face its truth.

Wojciech Jaruzelski's nemesis seems to care nothing for the impression he makes. Lech Wałęsa relishes the role of buffoon: after his brief stint as Poland's President he set up offices in a students' union building in Gdańsk which had a reputation for housing groups of cabaret artists. His performance for us put him firmly in the cabaret tradition. The camera team moved his furniture around to position him for the interview, and our producer was forced to lean tightly against a wall to translate during the interview. She picked up some plaster dust on her back and Wałęsa noticed it as we left: 'Not only do you move the furniture around,' he said, 'you try to steal the paintwork.' He also made a great show of not remembering the name of Harvard University, where he had recently lectured. It was like being in the presence of an anarchic post-modernist comic – I am not surprised the Communist authorities found him so difficult to deal with.

But there can be no doubting his roots: if Jaruzelski is an aristocrat at heart, Lech Wałęsa is truly a man of the working classes. There is no doubt either of the sincerity of the faith that keeps the badge of the Black Madonna of Częstochowa, one of Poland's most cherished objects of devotion, pinned to his lapel. When I asked him why he is a Catholic his answer was quite without affectation: 'Without faith I am nobody.' Against the tortured intellectual Communist aristocrat, history placed an instinctive, cunning working man of deep and unquestioning faith.

On 9 August 1980, a forklift-truck operator in her early fifties was fired from her job at the Lenin shipyard. Anna Walentynowicz had been caught taking the remains of candles from a graveyard; she wanted to use the wax to make new candles for a memorial to the victims of the unrest in 1970. The strikes sparked by her sacking quickly became much more than a demand for her reinstatement. Under Lech Wałęsa's leadership the strikers drew up a list of objectives ranging from pay increases to more general political demands, like access to the media. By the end of the month they had won most of them. Wałęsa and the government signed the Gdańsk accords, and Solidarity was established as Eastern Europe's first free trade union. At the signing ceremony Wałęsa wielded an enormous souvenir pen adorned with the Pope's picture. He describes the Pope as the 'instigator' of his movement, and says flatly, 'Without him, the changes we are now going through would not have happened.' John Paul had provided Solidarity with a name and an ideological foundation. In March 1979, not long before his visit to Poland, the Pope published his first encyclical, *Redemptor Hominis*, Redeemer of Man. Drawing on Vatican II's ideas about freedom of religion and his own long reflections on the dignity of the human person, he introduced the concept of 'solidarity'. It meant acting together through choice, not compulsion, and it was intended to chart a middle way between individualism and collectivism.

The way in which Solidarity developed reflected those ideas. It was much more than a trade union: it was an alternative society that ran in parallel to the society directed by the Communist state. Ten million people, a quarter of all Poles, became members. One million combined membership of Solidarity with membership of the Communist Party. Even forty thousand members of the police force joined. It was an invigorating experience, a social experiment unlike anything that had been seen in the Communist world. Tina Rosenberg records in *The Haunted Land*, her anatomy of the fall of Communism, that during Solidarity's first phase suicide attempts fell by a third and Poland's legendary alcohol consumption by a quarter.

Halina Bortnowska threw herself enthusiastically into the Solidarity experiment, and paints a benign picture of the influence John Paul exerted on the movement: 'It was not that he incited us to do things – to form a trade union or to revolt against Communism. I think people who see it now in this light are interpreting the past in the light of much later experiences. It was mainly existential, and existential things have an impact on politics in the ordinary sense of the word ... The first thing he did was change people's lives. People did experience something like a triumph, and that made them more likely to say no to further humiliations.'

But the Church provided more to the opposition than inspiration in Poland during this period. When I asked Lech Wałęsa what practical help and advice the Church had given to Solidarity he snapped back accusingly, 'Of course, a lot of people, particularly non-believers, try to find some conspiracy here, a plot, as far as this "help" is concerned. Nothing of the sort, in the physical sense, took place.' He likes to cast John Paul's impact in Poland in the highest philosophical terms: 'The system of deceit had to lose to the system of faith,' he says. The fact that the Church played a direct, practical role in the politics of the 1980s is still sensitive in modern Poland, and partisans of the Catholic Church's part in the revolution there shy away from it. To former Communists it is evidence that the Church acted simply as another institution, and that events can be explained by the normal laws of politics without recourse to high-sounding talk about moral leadership or Divine Providence.

General Jaruzelski declared martial law in a six a.m. broadcast on 13 December 1981. He told me that making the decision had been a 'nightmare' and gave him 'sleepless nights', but he had concluded that it was the only way to ward off the threat of a Soviet invasion. 'Citizens and Lady Citizens of the Polish People's Republic!' he began his televised address. 'I turn to you as a soldier and chief of government! Our motherland is on the verge of an abyss.'

The debate over whether his action was justified hangs on that last sentence. Was the 'abyss' really there? Would the Soviet Union have invaded to crush the Polish experiment with democracy, which Solidarity had introduced, if the General had not taken matters into his own hands? For what it is worth, Mikhail Gorbachev says that Jaruzelski was right to act as he did. 'Poles were lucky that at that

Pope John XXIII   Pope Paul VI

The opening of the Second Vatican Council, October 1962

Polish piety: a Corpus Christi procession

Martyrdom: Sister Lucita shows where Archbishop Romero of
San Salvador fell

A giant of the Church: Cardinal Franz König

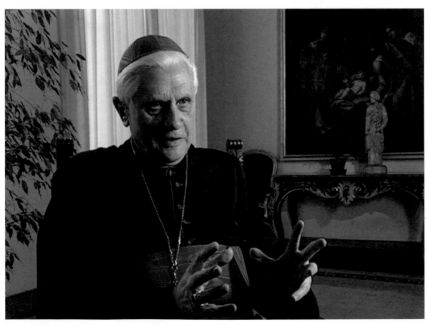

The Prefect of the Sacred Congregation for the Doctrine of the Faith:
Cardinal Joseph Ratzinger

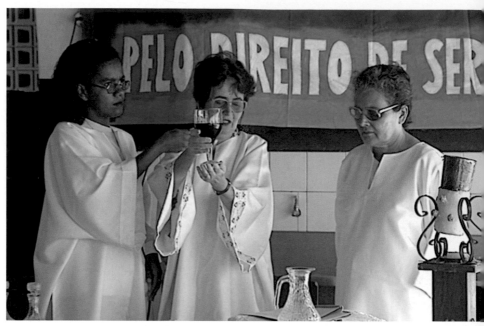

The Liberation Church: a rebel mass in Brazil

Father Tony Terry has lost his parish but still works with the street
children in Recife

The priest as guru: Father Amildev at an ashram in Varanasi

Where Doubting Thomas preached: confession in Kerala

Sister Leonia with an Aids patient in the Freedom Compound

The growing Church: a confirmation service in Zambia

Casting out devils: Archbishop Milingo in Northern Italy

A new way of worshipping: the offertory, Zambian-style

Coming home: Poland, 1997

moment General Jaruzelski was at the leadership of the country. God must have taken into consideration the Polish people's religious devotion and given them the General as their leader at such a time,' he told me, apparently unaware of the irony of casting his praise in those terms.

At the time, the Church hierarchy in Poland thought so too. A new and more timid Archbishop of Warsaw, Józef Glemp, had become primate of the Polish Church on the death of Cardinal Wyszyński. His first response to the declaration of martial law was to plead for calm. That decision, too, has been hotly debated but, right or wrong, it was a reminder of the active institutional role the Church was playing in the politics of the period. Mieczysław Rakowski was deputy prime minister and had been the chief government negotiator with Solidarity during the tense days of the 1980 strike. He recalls the episcopate being involved in the day-to-day micro-management of the martial law crisis, usually as a moderating force on the more extreme elements in Solidarity. He counted no less than eighteen substantive meetings between Cardinal Glemp and General Jaruzelski.

Rakowski's emphasis on the institutional as opposed to spiritual role of the Church is in line with his continued conviction that what happened in Poland was not a victory for one ideology over another. It was, for him, more a matter of economics: 'Communism,' he says, 'exhausted itself because its creative power had long become a thing of the past, and from the economic point of view it was completely inefficient . . . If the system had been more economically efficient and the people had been satisfied, then he [the Pope] would have achieved nothing. And so I treat the role of John Paul II in what has happened in this part of Europe as one of the roles but not the main one.' It is an analysis shared by his ex-boss General Jaruzelski, who sees the Pope as the catalyst for change rather than its instigator. Jaruzelski believes that John Paul only had the impact he did because 'certain social and political conditions were ripe' – the habits of the Marxist vocabulary die hard – and that his part in events in Poland needs to be 'seen in a sober and rational light'.

The Pope's second direct and public intervention in Poland's affairs suggests that spiritual leadership was combined with a deft political touch. When he arrived for his next visit, in June 1983, Poland had already endured a year and a half under martial law, and Solidarity had been banned. John Paul built into his programme a meeting with Lech Wałęsa. It was a way of signalling his continued public support of Solidarity's ideals. 'What was important was the fact of the meeting itself, because the Holy Father confirmed that he agreed with our values and that he identified with them,' says Wałęsa. The content, he adds, was less significant than the symbol: 'The talk itself was not as important because we knew the meeting was being bugged.'

But John Paul also held two meetings with General Jaruzelski during that visit, and took some of the pressure off the beleaguered regime by doing so. By then the threat of Soviet invasion had evaporated, and the West's economic sanctions were beginning to bite. Jaruzelski was looking desperately for a way out, and the meetings with Poland's national hero gave him the cover he needed. 'The Pope,' says Jaruzelski, 'kept assuring me that he was undertaking efforts to lift economic sanctions.' He says that the meetings 'justified the actions of the Polish authorities'. The following month martial law was lifted.

But the struggle was far from over. In October 1984 the body of Father Jerzy Popiełuszko was dragged out of a reservoir near Warsaw. Since the beginning of 1982, just after the imposition of martial law, he had held a monthly Mass for the Fatherland at his Church in Warsaw, and the message of resistance he preached in his sermons attracted congregations ten to fifteen thousand strong. It made him the priest most hated by Communist hard-liners, and he paid for it with his life. The three men who had dragged him from his car were quickly identified as state security police. They were arrested eventually, together with a superior officer, but there was no inquiry to establish how far complicity extended up the chain of Communist command.

It was one of those critical moments when the tensions in Poland could have erupted into bloodshed. Several hundred thousand people attended Father Popiełuszko's funeral – indeed, some estimates put the figure as high as a million. Halina Bortnowska was among them, and still marvels at the way it passed off peacefully. 'In how many other countries,' she asks, with quiet passion, 'does the funeral of a leader who was killed by the security police not produce more victims? And where a million people stay quiet while looking at the very same police who killed the leader they are now mourning? And they somehow resist the temptation to produce more violence.' She believes it was evidence of the Pope's greatest contribution to the way the revolution in Poland was conducted: his consistent advocacy of non-violent means. 'I think one of his main messages, perhaps the main one, did come through,' she says, 'and this was not to fight evil with evil. The message of non-violent forgiveness has come through.' The opposition to Communism John Paul promoted was pacific, and the Church he led was sometimes criticized for erring too far towards moderation during the period of martial law in Poland. It was consistent with his past: Karol Wojtyła's resistance during the Nazi occupation had been non-violent, at a time when millions believed that the evil of Nazism demanded a violent response. It was also to be one of the determining factors in his troubled relationship with the Latin-American Church as pope.

Was the Pope's part in the collapse of Communism the work of Divine Providence? I asked Czesław Miłosz, who had given me the clearest exposition of John Paul's idea of the providential interpretation of history, whether or not he believed it himself. 'I would like to,' he replied, 'but it is very difficult because I have seen and heard of such horrors in the history of the twentieth century. My problem is to combine providential lines of history with the millions of people who died. That's a permanent problem of history which may work towards good – but what about the suffering, the hell created by history on its way?' We were speaking in a place that gave the world the papacy of John Paul but will always be remembered for the concentration camp at Auschwitz.

The formal apotheosis of the Pope's relations with the Communist world came in December 1989, more than a decade after his first visit to Poland, with Mikhail Gorbachev's visit to the Vatican, the first time a Soviet leader and a Roman pontiff had met. The groundwork for the meeting had been done by the ever assiduous Cardinal Casaroli. When he had visited Russia during the previous summer's celebration of a thousand years of Christianity among the Eastern Slavs, he came armed with a letter to the Soviet leader. But like the Vatican, the Kremlin knew how to use its mystique to impress visitors. Although he was playing a central part in the formal celebrations in Leningrad, the Cardinal was given no opportunity to fulfil his diplomatic task, and began to suspect that he would have to return to Rome with the Pope's letter unopened in his pocket. At the last moment, as everyone was dispersing, he was summoned to the Kremlin and this consummate diplomat, who had spent so many years and so much intellectual energy wrestling with the Communist monster, finally sat down with a Soviet president in the heart of the Evil Empire. 'A conversation between two highly enlightened people,' is the way Mikhail Gorbachev describes the meeting.

As he looked back at the tortuous path that had brought him there, Casaroli may have reflected on some of the difficulties he had had to overcome. Four years earlier he had taken the almost unprecedented step of disagreeing publicly with one of his most senior colleagues. When Cardinal Ratzinger, Prefect of the Sacred Congregation for the Doctrine of the Faith, issued his condemnation of the new Liberation Theology that was emerging from Latin America, Cardinal Casaroli feared that its stridently anti-Communist rhetoric might damage his diplomatic efforts in Eastern Europe, and said so.

In the 1980s, therefore, the Church was fighting on two fronts.

8

Option for the Poor

At the chapel of the Hospital de la Divina Providencia in San Salvador, a small tear has been made in the skin of the physical world so that a ray of the transcendent shines through. The chapel is rather larger than the name suggests, certainly bigger than most English parish churches. It is modern but basically traditional in design, with transepts and a large crucifix above the altar. The European style has been adapted to suit the sub-tropical conditions of El Salvador, which must have been in the architect's mind when he gave it such wide doors and the long, slatted windows along each side of the nave. From the hospital driveway you look towards the altar down a long, polished marble floor beneath a white vaulted ceiling; if you stand there on a hot evening the coolness tempts you inside.

On Sunday 23 March 1980, Monsignor Oscar Romero, Archbishop of San Salvador, preached a Lenten sermon remarkable for the urgency of its tone and the audacity of its message. The Archbishop was inciting mutiny in the name of God, and his words were broadcast to the nation by the Church's own radio station: 'I would like to make an appeal in a special way to the men of the Army, and in particular to the ranks of the Guardia Nacional, of the police, to those in the barracks. Brothers, you are part of our own people. You kill your own *campesino* brothers and sisters. And before an order to kill that a man may give, the law of God must prevail that says: "Thou shalt not kill!" No soldier is obliged to obey an order against the law of God. No one has to fulfil an immoral law. It is time to recover your consciences and to obey your consciences rather than the orders of sin. The Church, defender of the rights of God, of the law of God, of human dignity, the dignity of the human person, cannot remain silent before such abomination . . . In the name of God, and in the name of this suffering people whose laments rise to heaven each day more tumultuous, I beg you, I ask you, I order you. In the name of God: stop the repression!'

The following morning Major Roberto d'Aubuisson, a former intelligence officer turned champion of the right, convened a meeting with a group of like-minded conspirators at a house in San Salvador. Another former officer, Captain Alvaro Saravia, was among them. The United Nations Commission on the Truth, which was set up to investigate crimes committed during El Salvador's civil war, gives a clinical and straightforward account of the gathering:

Captain Eduardo Avila arrived, and told them that Archbishop Romero would be celebrating a Mass that day. Captain Avila said this would be a good opportunity to assassinate Archbishop Romero. D'Aubuisson ordered that this be done and put Saravia in charge of the operation. When it was pointed out that a sniper would be needed, Captain Avila said he would contact one through Mario Molina. Amado Garay was assigned to drive the assassin to the chapel.

A red four-door Volkswagen was provided for the driver, and the car park of the Camino Real Hotel was chosen for his rendezvous with the hired marksman. This man has never been identified, and is described in the Commission's report simply as 'the bearded gunman'. It is a short drive from the Camino Real to the grounds of the Hospital de la Divina Providencia, which Archbishop Romero had made his home. He regularly celebrated Mass in the chapel there, and on the evening of 24 March was doing so at the request of a friend to mark the anniversary of his mother's death. Although it was intended only for her family and close friends, the Mass had been announced in the newspapers, despite the concern of some of those close to the Archbishop about the recent threats to his life.

The red VW must have turned round before parking, because the driver gave evidence that the gun was fired from the right-hand rear window. Those wide chapel doors and that bright, cool marble interior leading up to the altar afforded the bearded gunman a clear view of his target. He told the driver to bend down and pretend to be mending something, fired a single shot from his high-velocity .22 rifle, then instructed the other man to 'drive slowly, take it easy'.

Sister Lucita was sitting close to the front of the south transept during the Archbishop's homily. She says that the shot came as Romero finished his address and moved to the altar; he looked down for a moment so would not have seen the gun being raised. She remembers the sound as so loud that it was like a bomb exploding. By the time Sister Lucita had covered the few steps to the altar where the Archbishop lay, 'He was haemorrhaging through his eyes, nose and ears. I couldn't do anything so I ran to a telephone to find a doctor.'

Like Pope John Paul's patron, St Stanisław, murdered by King Boleslaw at the altar of Kraków Cathedral in the eleventh century, Oscar Romero fell while saying Mass. And, like the Polish saint, he became a focus for myth-making: martyrdom made St Stanisław a symbol of Poland's struggle for nationhood, still potent in the late twentieth century, and it made Oscar Romero a symbol of the Church's struggle for social justice in Latin America. Far from silencing this turbulent priest, Roberto d'Aubuisson and his co-conspirators ensured that his influence has lasted far longer than if he had lived out his life and endured the failing powers that accompany old age. The unassuming bungalow across the driveway where the Archbishop lived has become a shrine. In the modest sitting room, a glass case contains the bloodied surplice and vestments he was wearing when he was shot together with an assortment of cufflinks, photographs and episcopal skullcaps. There is a battered typewriter on the plain table in his bedroom where he wrote his sermons and his diary. Dozens of small marble tablets have been inset in the wall just outside the front door inscribed 'with thanks to Monsignor Romero for a miracle granted' – the nun who showed me round said they had been placed there by people from all over the Americas who felt their prayers had been answered through his intercession. A plaque next to his bust describes him as 'Martyr and Prophet'. Strictly speaking, the inscription is inaccurate: 'Martyr' is a term the Church uses to honour those saints who willingly submit to death rather than renounce their faith. The Vatican has not granted the status of saint to Oscar Romero, but he has been canonized by popular devotion.

He remained such a powerful presence in Salvadorian politics that when one of the most notorious massacres of the country's civil war took place nearly a decade later it seemed a grim tribute to Romero's influence. On the evening of 15 November 1989, six Jesuits were murdered at the University of Central America in San Salvador. Their cook, Julia, and her fifteen-year-old daughter, Celina, were killed with them. The seventh member of the Jesuit community at the university, Father Jon Sobrino, was in Hua Hin, in Thailand, 'giving a short course on Christology'. He learned what had happened to his fellow priests – which would have happened to him, had he been there – from a friend, an Irish priest in London, who passed on the details by telephone: 'The killers were about thirty men dressed in military uniform. He told me they had taken three of the Jesuits out into the garden and tortured and machine-gunned them there. The other three and the two women they had machine-gunned in their beds. My friend could hardly go on speaking. Like many during those days he had no words to express what had happened.'

The block where the Jesuits lived had been named the Oscar Romero Centre, and the radical theology they studied and taught there was inspired by his memory. 'For them, for me, and so many others,' writes Jon Sobrino, in his tribute to his six dead confrères, 'Archbishop Romero was a Christ for our time, and, like Christ, a sacrament of God. Meeting Archbishop Romero was like coming into contact with God. Trying to follow Archbishop Romero was like following Jesus today in El Salvador.'

As the Jesuits' killers left the University of Central America in the small hours, their work done, they trashed the Romero Centre and sprayed the Archbishop's portrait with bullets – 'to kill him again', in the words of the man who led the Commission on the Truth's investigation into the violence in El Salvador. It was an act of deliberate sacrilege, which quickly became part of the Romero myth, and only added to its power.

In Thailand, one of Jon Sobrino's hosts asked him, 'Are there really Catholics who murder priests in El Salvador?' The martyrdom of Catholics by their co-religionists is new in the history of Christianity; in the early Church, death was often the price of evangelization in the Roman Empire. The centuries-long conflict with Islam produced plenty of martyrs on both sides. In Reformation England, men like St Thomas More were executed by fellow Christians because they refused to abandon their allegiance to the Roman Catholic faith. The 'isms' of the twentieth century have produced a fair crop of martyrs too: some, like Maksymilian Kolbe, who died at Auschwitz at the hands of Fascists, others, like Father Jerzy Popiełuszko, under Communists. But there was no precedent for the phenomenon of Catholics being killed by fellow Catholics in an overwhelmingly Catholic continent.

Archbishop Romero's death and all the other martyrdoms of that terrible time in Latin America's history were a direct result of the revolution in the Church that John XXIII had set in motion. In both his climactic sermon the day before his death and the homily he had just finished when the assassin struck, Oscar Romero made it explicitly clear that the sense of mission which had led him to take on the government and the armed forces had been directly inspired by Vatican II. In his dramatic call for mutiny against murder, the Council's language and spirit echoed through his appeal for 'human dignity, the dignity of the human person'. He was of a generation of bishops and priests transformed by applying the Council's ideas to the realities around them. The story of the Church in Latin America is the story of conversion, not from one faith to another but from one kind of faith to another.

The impact of the Council was felt more dramatically in Latin America than anywhere else in the world. In Europe, the revolution touched people's personal lives, and altered the way they understood their relationship with God. In Latin America it was the Church's role in the public sphere that changed. It led to an earthquake that convulsed both the politics of the region and those of the universal Church, and the aftershocks of what happened are still being felt. The way the landscape looks when they finally subside is critical because in terms of numbers the Church's heart is now in Latin America, not Europe. After five hundred years on the continent, and despite a challenge from a vigorous rash of Protestant Pentecostalist churches, many of them originating in the United States, Catholicism still commands the allegiance of the vast majority of Latin-Americans. Brazil alone, with its 150 million people, is by far the largest Catholic nation in the world. When I remarked to the Archbishop of Recife that it seemed unfair that Brazil should have five cardinals while England has only one he pointed out that his archdiocese alone numbered almost as many Catholics as the whole of the English Roman Catholic Church. Parishes of eighty or ninety thousand souls are not uncommon.

Even at the time of the Council, Latin America's bishops were beginning to make their numbers felt; including the bishops of the Caribbean, the block from the southern Americas made up nearly a quarter of all the bishops at the Council. They were well organized: the Latin American Bishops Conference, or CELAM, had been formed in 1955 and was well ahead of the rest of the Church in the practice of collegiality, which emerged from the Council. And the bishops came from a continent that was beginning to feel the breath of revolution: in the month that John XXIII called the Council, Castro expelled the Batista government from Cuba.

Leonardo Boff, a Franciscan friar who was one of the leading lights of the specifically Latin-American theology that emerged in the aftermath of the Council, says that Vatican II 'helped our Church to stop being medieval' by advancing the idea of engagement with the wider world. Jon Sobrino, who has become rector of the University of Central America since the murders took place, expands that idea: 'From the fourth century onwards,' he says, 'the Church saw itself as the centre of the world and the world turned around the Church so the world showed servitude to the Church. The Council turned that on its head.'

The European Church had plenty of its own intellectual baggage to shed before it could focus on the needs of the Church in what were seen in the early 1960s as far-flung provinces, and despite their numbers, the Latin-American bishops produced no real stars at the Council debates – there was no König or Suenens among them. Leonardo Boff says that the Council was fundamentally 'Eurocentric', and that it understood the world in a rationalist, European way. But it provided the intellectual springboard that in the 1970s allowed the Latin-American Church to make the great leap which transformed it.

In Western Europe the concept of the Church as the servant rather than the master of the world has meant engaging with atheism and secularism. In Eastern Europe it enabled Cardinal Wojtyła to combat Communism. In Latin America 'the world' outside the Church was dominated by one problem: poverty.

Judged in absolute terms Latin America has had a raw economic deal. In 1970 gross domestic product (GDP) in the region was 1,435 American dollars *per capita*. That looks grim next to the industrialized world's figure of 9,546 dollars for the same year, and was well below the world average, although it seems positively healthy when set alongside Africa's 1970 *per capita* GDP of 598 dollars. In the past quarter of a century Latin America has worked its way steadily up the rankings in most economic and development indices, but the overall figures conceal an inequality in the division of wealth more extreme than almost anywhere else in the world. Even in the 1990s the World Bank estimated that 110 million people in the region – a quarter of its population – get by on less than a dollar a day, and more than twenty million Brazilians are judged to be living below the poverty line. In Latin America the First and Third Worlds rub shoulders in almost every city. The experience of poverty and the daily reminders of inequality provided the framework within which the Council's teaching came to be understood.

Cardinal Paolo Arns, who as Archbishop of São Paulo, Brazil, was the leader of the world's largest diocese, was appointed bishop just as the Council was ending. He says, 'We were very satisfied with Vatican II, but we didn't really understand what it meant for us.' That changed in 1968 with the Medellín Conference in Colombia. Medellín was the Latin-American Church's Declaration of Independence. Indeed, because the Church is such a dominant and unifying force across the region it was a political Declaration of Independence by Latin America itself. 'Until Medellín we were a colony, and had been since 1500,' says Cardinal Arns. His analysis of the conference's impact echoes Lech Wałęsa's remarks about the Pope's visit to Poland; 'From Medellin onwards, people came to have the idea that history could be made by themselves and not imposed by other people.' The development of a distinctively Latin-American theology was inspired in part by the drive to forge a sense of Latin-American identity. Catholicism had come to the region with Spanish and Portuguese colonial expansion, but after half a millennium it had been there long enough for the people to see it as part of their own heritage. The Church became a means whereby they reclaimed their history and their destiny, and that is one of the reasons why Latin America's theological battles have been fought with such passion.

It was a Declaration of Independence initially blessed by the capital of the empire. Pope Paul VI travelled to Colombia to open the conference, and encouraged its avowed purpose of interpreting the teachings of the Council in a local context. It was the month following the publication of the birth-control encyclical *Humanae Vitae*, and at home Paul was being demonized as an arch-conservative. In Latin America he was heralded as a revolutionary. His encyclical *Populorum Progressio*, published the previous year, contained a passage that seemed crafted to reflect the inequalities in Latin-American societies:

If certain landed estates impede the general prosperity because they are extensive, unused or poorly used, or because they bring hardship to peoples or are detrimental to the interests of the country, the common good sometimes demands their expropriation . . . It is unacceptable that citizens with abundant incomes from the resources and activity of their country should transfer a considerable part of this income abroad purely for their own advantage.

In a foretaste of conflict to come, the *Wall Street Journal* condemned the encyclical as 'warmed-up Marxism'.

The intellectual inspiration for the conference was the work of the Peruvian theologian Gustavo Gutierrez. His originality lay in the way he used the language of Christianity to preach a message of social revolution. From his experience of working as a priest in the slums of Lima, he developed the new theology that came to be identified with the phrase 'the option for the poor'. Liberation Theology does not accept the idea that Christians can simply wait for the Kingdom of Heaven in the next life: it argues that liberation from poverty is a legitimate goal for Christians striving in this life – and to priests all over Latin America, working in the kind of conditions Gutierrez had experienced in Lima, that message rang true. Its analysis of the causes of poverty draws heavily on Marxism, and a strong streak of anti-Americanism runs through the writings of most of its adherents, but it expresses the idea of liberation in Christian terms: liberation will come, it teaches, not through Marxist revolution but through the Good News of the Gospel.

Gutierrez argued that unjust societies could be defined as 'structures of sin'. 'Sin,' he writes, 'takes place in oppressive structures, in the exploitation of man by man, in the domination and slavery of peoples, races and social classes. Sin emerges, then, as the fundamental alienation, as the root of a situation and exploitation.'

As Penny Lernoux puts it in her study of Liberation Theology, *People of God*:

Gutierrez also reinterpreted the classic doctrines of sin to include the sins of societies as, for example, US behaviour towards Latin-America and that of the Peruvian oligarchy towards the country's peasants. It was not enough to seek liberation from personal sin, he argued, since faith also meant a commitment to work for social justice. Conversion demanded society's transformation, not just a change of heart.

The idea that sin could be found in a social structure rather than in an individual soul has hugely important consequences. The search for personal salvation and the threat of personal damnation are at the heart of the way most European and North-American Catholics think about their faith: they provide the framework within which, for good or evil, we make our choices.

But if the real sin is not in ourselves but in the society around us, and real salvation lies in the transformation of that society, then the choices we make in our personal lives become much less critical. Liberation Theology's redefinition of sin explains why the sexual issues that have caused such agony in the European Church have troubled the Church in Latin America much less. In the years following the publication of *Humanae Vitae*, most priests and bishops in the region were too busy managing a revolution against what they saw as sinful societies to worry about what people were doing in their bedrooms. Cardinal Arns of São Paulo said he went along with the encyclical – with which he clearly disagrees and which the vast majority of his flock ignore – because he believed that at that time the unity of the Church in the face of political oppression was more important than anything else. It was a convenient way round an issue that might have caused bitter divisions in a culture that is anything but sympathetic to the ideals of chastity and sexual continence. If you mention sin in Europe, most Catholics would think of sex; if you mention it in Brazil, they think of society.

The idea of sinful social structures inevitably propels the priest into the world of politics: it is a priest's job to root out sin, and if sin is in politics then into politics he must go. It must also lead to a re-evaluation of the Church's teaching on violence: along with the idea of sinful structures comes the concept of social systems that are inherently violent because of their oppressive nature – 'institutionalized violence' was the bishops' phrase at Medellín. It is easy to understand how that notion led some to the conviction that it was not just a priest's right but his duty to pick up a gun.

Only a minority of the bishops at Medelín may have understood the full implications of what they signed when they put their names to the documents that endorsed Liberation Theology. The need to address the problem of the poor was being brought home to them every day in their pastoral work, and there was almost universal agreement that the Church must transform itself from a Church of the haves to one of the have-nots. Jon Sobrino summed up the conference's conclusions: 'Medellín said the world is not just a planet with typical European problems like secularization and agnosticism. It is a planet of poverty where the main issue for human beings is to live and to survive . . . If we are Christians we cannot believe in God any longer without trying to save God's creation. And the problem in the world is not, as they say in Europe or the United States, that there are pockets of poverty: in the world there are pockets of abundance, and the rest is poverty.'

Liberation Theology was rooted in the day-to-day experience of most priests and bishops; it moved from the parish to the seminaries and universities – not, like traditional theologies, the other way round. It was the empirical method of theological inquiry, pioneered by the Pontifical Commission for Population, Family and Births, writ large, and this time it was embraced, not strangled, by the Church leadership. That guaranteed Medellín an immediately enthusiastic reception among the clergy. And the way the new ideas were expressed in the traditional language of Christianity made them immediately accessible in this most Catholic of continents. 'Here,' says Jon Sobrino, 'people know what sin is. Of course, many years ago we used to reduce sin to the Commandments in the arena of sexuality. But when priests and bishops start saying, "This country is in a state of sin because the economic structure produces poverty and death," people know what they mean. Sin is a very powerful word on this continent.'

It was an extraordinary transformation of the Church's role in Latin America. In the past, it had always been identified with the ruling classes, the established order. The Jesuits were an honourable exception: during the eighteenth century they had been suppressed by the King of Portugal after suggesting, rather tiresomely, that the slaves in Brazil had souls. But Catholicism came to Latin America with colonial conquests, and it had traditionally seen its interests as lying on the side of the oppressors, not with the oppressed. Robert White, who was

Jimmy Carter's ambassador to El Salvador and an acute observer of the Latin-American scene, says, 'The traditional Latin-American societies rest on a tripod: there's the rich, there's the military, and then there's the Catholic Church.'

The revolution in Cuba defined the political backdrop against which the Medellin Conference took place. Jon Sobrino says that he saw Castro's successful revolt against the American-backed Batista regime as an example of Divine Providence at work because it showed that it was possible to stand up to the United States, and gave hope to others in the region. I had to suppress a smile when he put forward that idea: Pope John Paul believes in Divine Providence too, but he certainly would not have seen a successful Communist revolution as an example of God's hand in human history.

Cuba turned the whole of Latin America into a playground for Cold Warriors for three decades. For most of its history the region had been a side-show: its revolutions, wars and addiction to violence may have been a source of interest to the politically curious, but they carried little weight in the scales of serious international politics. The revolution in Cuba and the Cuban missile crisis – which brought the world as close to nuclear conflagration as it has ever been – transformed Latin America's politics from a joke in rather poor taste into one of the most serious fronts of the Cold War.

North American anxiety about the advance of Communism in its 'backyard' became acute – often slipping into paranoia – for the Soviets gave what help they reasonably could to regimes and movements that they saw might make their rival superpower uncomfortable. The battle-lines allowed no room for subtle distinctions between right and wrong: as Washington viewed it, the Free World and Democracy stood on one side, Communism and Oppression on the other, and every politician or political movement defined itself by which side they chose. It meant that the United States became associated with all sorts of unsavoury regimes simply because they were deemed to be on the right – in both senses – side of the world struggle with Communism: Pinochet in Chile, Galtieri in Argentina, the generals in Brazil, and Somoza in Nicaragua (until he was undone by a combination of popular outrage and Jimmy Carter's sense of decency). Oppression, it seemed, could be justified as long as it was carried out in the name of free markets.

Of course, America's spies had a field day. I was in the White House on the day that Ronald Reagan's attorney-general, Edwin Meese, called the Washington press corps together to announce that Oliver North had been selling arms to Iran and channelling the funds he raised to the right-wing Contras, who were trying to overthrow the Nicaraguan government. At the time, Iran was one of America's arch-enemies, and it was illegal for the American government to give money to the Contras. I had to check with colleagues that I had heard correctly before I could bring myself to report it on television. And even today I find it so preposterous, such a caricature of security policy from the world's most powerful nation, as to be almost beyond belief.

Richard Allen, national security adviser during the early days of Ronald Reagan's first term, had the grace to concede that American policy may have been over-zealous during that period. 'At the time Ronald Reagan took office, it can be argued the Soviets were on a roll,' he told me. 'They had put American thinking into retreat, almost into reverse. We were very concerned about Cuba . . . El Salvador, Nicaragua and other parts of Latin America, Central America particularly. They were, we thought, in danger of going under, and we simply could not allow that in our vital national interest – next door, in our front yard. Our first line of defence had to be to create order and stability.' But he also confessed, 'That came at a price we were to learn later.'

The Cold War rhetoric added a new layer of passion and ideology to a political culture of violence that was already well established. The mix was deadly. The 'death squad' is a peculiarly Latin-American phenomenon. Its origins long pre-date the Cold War, and it survived that war's end, reappearing in the armies of the drug barons in Colombia, and in the extermination units – often made up of off-duty police officers – that have killed thousands of street children in Brazil because they are regarded as a social nuisance. In investigating the war in El Salvador the Truth Commission built up a picture of the way the death squads there permeated the social structures at every level. 'The death squads, in which members of State structures were actively involved or to which they turned a blind eye, gained such control that they ceased to be a marginal or isolated phenomenon and became an instrument of terror used systematically for the physical elimination of political opponents.'

The state in El Salvador had been using violence to control the population for so long that it had become part of the common currency of the country's politics. 'In the past 150 years,' the Truth Commission notes, 'a number of uprisings by peasants and indigenous groups have been violently suppressed by the State and by civilian groups armed by landowners.' Violent repression in Communist Eastern Europe was the work of government security forces, which at least preserved the illusion that someone could be held responsible for what was done. In El Salvador, and much of Latin America, the line between the security forces and freelance enforcers was blurred, so that accountability became a mirage. El Salvador's National Guard was founded in 1910, and from its earliest days it was common practice for local commanders to hire out their men to local landowners. The most notorious use of violence by the unholy alliance of landlords and the security forces was the massacre in 1932 known as La Matanza. Some ten thousand people were killed in the western part of El Salvador – a country roughly the size of Wales – during the suppression of a peasant insurrection.

Roberto d'Aubuisson, the man who ordered the assassination of Archbishop Romero, saw himself as an anti-Communist crusader, a front-line soldier in the great ideological battle being fought out between the United States and the Soviet Union. But the way he operated his death squads owed much to the older tradition of semi-officially sanctioned violence in El Salvador. He was able to attract substantial funding from the country's landowners and businessmen, and was elected to serve as the president of the National Assembly, although his activities were almost an open secret.

From this volatile mix of a new, radical theology, a deeply rooted addiction to violence in Latin-American state culture, poverty and Cold War rhetoric, there arose some truly heroic figures.

9

Seeking Justice

The fifth of thirteen children, Cardinal Paolo Evaristo Arns was born in 1921 to German immigrants in Santa Katerina state in southern Brazil. Even in old age a trace of his German antecedents remains in his accent. Cardinal Arns is a short, stocky man with the mildest manner. But his integrity and the strength of his moral conviction give his words monumental power. During the years of military rule in Brazil he made a habit of visiting the local commander once a week to lecture him on the regime's latest iniquities. I spent an hour as the object of the Cardinal's piercing gaze, which was enough to convince me that it must have been a demanding weekly appointment for the general in question.

'Dom Paolo', as he became known universally in Brazil, was appointed archbishop when the military regime had been in power for six years and repression was at its most brutal. During the 1970s a plague of right-wing repressive military dictatorships spread through-out the region: Chile, Uruguay, Paraguay, Argentina and Bolivia were all ruled by such regimes. Unlike some of their neighbours – such as General Stroessner in Paraguay and Pinochet in Chile – Brazil's generals at least stuck to notional terms in office, and succeeded one another to power, but they imprisoned and tortured thousands of people for their beliefs. In 1995 a democratically elected government admitted some of the crimes committed during the twenty-one-year military dictatorship, when it published the names of 136 prisoners who had 'disappeared' in custody. Human-rights groups have said that more than two hundred people died after being arrested.

'During the dictatorship in Brazil,' the Cardinal told me, 'I saw my principal task as the defence of the people.' This remarkable statement touches on one of the main sources of the conflict to come between the Latin-American Church and the Vatican. Yet, in many ways, Cardinal Arns was doing in São Paulo in the 1970s what Karol Wojtyła was doing in Kraków during the same period. Like the Church in Poland, the Church in Brazil occupied a place in the hearts of the people that gave it a degree of immunity against repression. 'The people of Brazil are a very religious people, and the Bishop could speak in their name,' he says. 'They [the government] imprisoned priests, and there were thirteen imprisoned when I began as archbishop. But they could never touch or take a bishop, because of how the people would react.'

Cardinal Arns exploited his relative immunity. He has great respect for the power of the press, and likes to regard himself as something of a journalist: with forty-eight books and hundreds of articles and radio talks to his credit, he has more than earned the right to do so. His most unclerical belief that the press can be an ally rather than an enemy is one of the many ways in which he has shown himself to be a true heir to the spirit of the Second Vatican Council. He came up with imaginative ways to circumvent government censorship: in 1971, soon after he took office, an Italian priest and a social worker were arrested and tortured; Arns ordered that an account of what had happened should be posted on the door of every church. An Irish missionary priest who worked in the archdiocese at the time recalled that if the Cardinal wanted an especially contentious message broadcast from the pulpit he would circulate the text to individual parishes on Saturday evening; that meant there was no time for the authorities to get wind of it before it was read out at Mass on Sunday morning. 'The political police couldn't take us all into prison,' the priest pointed out. 'There were more than a thousand of us, so we were relatively safe.' But there was always a government spy at the back of each church during Mass, and a firm discipline imposed by the Archbishop ensured that individual priests never became vulnerable by going further than he had in his own statements.

Arns also believes in the importance of a written record of past wrongs as a means of preventing their repetition and, like Karol Wojtyła in Kraków, he exercised the institutional powers at his disposal to pursue an agenda of his own. During the dictatorship years, he assembled a team of twenty-four lawyers and investigators to gather evidence of torture and human-rights abuses carried out by the regime. They collected court records and testimony relating to hundreds of political prisoners, concealing much of the material in Church buildings. One million pages of court proceedings were reproduced and smuggled out of the country. When the military finally left, the evidence was edited and published. Its title *Brazil – Nunc Mais* – Brazil, never again – speaks for itself.

There is an intensity in the way witnesses describe some of Cardinal Arns' services, inspired by the awesome creative power unleashed when true religious feeling is turned to a political end. One of his most striking lessons in the power of a religious service as a political weapon was prompted by the death in 1975 of the journalist Vladimir Hertzog. Hertzog was well known for his opposition to the regime, and when he was taken into custody some of his fellow journalists alerted the Archbishop. Arns and his staff spent a whole day trying to get through to the chief of police to find out what had happened to him. In the evening they managed to establish that he was dead; he had been tortured, but the official announcement said he had committed suicide.

Arns' proposal for a service in the cathedral to commemorate Hertzog prompted the state President to plead with him to abandon his plan. The authorities argued that there should be no service because the dead man had been Jewish. Arns responded that that did not make him any less of a victim, and he secured the support of the Jewish community for a service that could embrace both faiths. Fifty thousand people turned up outside the cathedral in one of the biggest anti-government demonstrations to that date. The Cardinal believes, 'That was the beginning of a real reaction against the regime and the regime began to realize that they couldn't do what they wanted to.'

It would be wrong to conclude that this was secular political activism disguised as religion. Arns' actions were deeply rooted in his faith, and it was the way in which they drew on the Christian message that made them so powerful. Following the torture and murder of a prominent student leader, Arns conducted a service that has entered the mythology of the Latin-American Church. The security services had refused to give the young man's body to his mother for burial, which inflamed the angry students at São Paulo University even further. Such was Arns' reputation that he was the first person to whom the student leadership turned: a delegation came to tell him that if he went to the university campus he would find some twenty thousand students awaiting his instructions. He refused to visit the campus – he was concerned that things might turn ugly – but suggested a special memorial service in São Paulo's cathedral.

Almost every priest in the archdiocese came to concelebrate with the Archbishop, who had just returned from Rome where he had been given his Cardinal's red hat, so he spoke with the authority and weight of the Vatican behind him. Several thousand students packed the cathedral and the streets around it. The Army turned out with tanks. One of the priests at the altar that day has a vivid memory of what happened: 'When we came to the gospel I was surprised to see it was only three or four lines long. It was from St John and it was the account of the disciples going to Pontius Pilate and asking for Christ's body. "After this Joseph of Arimathea, who was a disciple of Jesus, but secretly, for fear of the Jews, asked Pilate that he might take away the body of Jesus, and Pilate gave him leave. So he came and took away His body." So Dom Paolo says, "We have just read the gospel, which shows a pagan governor acceding to the desire of a bereaved mother and he gave the body of her only son back to her. So we are here today denouncing the fact that a so-called Christian government has refused to give the body of an only son to his bereaved mother." There was complete silence in the cathedral – you could have heard a pin drop . . . Dom Paolo's preaching showed the power when you place a page of the gospel next to a page of real life.'

The Latin American Church produced a network of remarkable leaders in the aftermath of Medellín and two of Arns' fellow Brazilians were prominent among them: Cardinal Aloisio Lorscheider of Forta-leza was a candidate for pope in 1978, and Archbishop Helder Câmara in Recife was a thinker and Church statesman of international standing. There was an enviable certainty in the way Arns reminisced about the events of the 1970s and early 1980s: he had faced a stark moral choice, he had made the right decision and he had lived to see his courage vindicated. Archbishop Romero was another giant of the Arns genera-tion, but the story that led to his martyrdom was painted in much more complex colours, and even now there is a revealing ambiguity in the way he is regarded both at home and in Rome.

The story of the Church in Latin America in the 1970s and 1980s is far from simple. Vatican II liberated the Church in Latin America to become dynamically engaged with the world, but as a consequence it was plunged into politics, and tainted by revolution, repression and violence. Oscar Romero has become an emblematic figure because he inspired such contradictory emotions: he was loved and hated in almost equal measure. The case for his canonization is now before the Vatican, yet when he was alive he was regarded with deep suspicion by many in the Curia. And despite all that has been written and said about him – there are not many recent archbishops whose lives have been recorded as a feature film – he remains curiously enigmatic: the rather owlish figure, more middle manager than crusader, who smiles out of the black-and-white photographs preserved at his house in the Hospital de la Divina Providencia sits uneasily alongside the uncompromising power of the recorded voice of the sermons that speak to us from beyond the grave and the heroic stature history has assigned to him.

When he was chosen to succeed Archbishop Luis Chavez y Gonzalez, who had presided over the Church in San Salvador for thirty-eight years, San Salvador's ruling élite – the so-called Fourteen Families in whose hands both its wealth and its power were concentrated – were delighted with Rome's choice. 'My mother supported him,' one indignant landowner told me, as if that should have guaranteed faithful service to the interests of the rich; she had, after all, hired a private plane with several other matrons of the moneyed class and flown to Guatemala to lobby the Cardinal Archbishop there on Romero's behalf. Oscar Romero had served as auxiliary bishop of San Salvador and had been bishop of Santiago de Maria for two years when he became El Salvador's leading prelate. He had preached against the 'new Christologies' – which, for those who knew how to read the code in which theological debates were conducted, put him on the side of the conservatives. In a newspaper interview just before taking on his new job he said, 'We must keep to the centre, watchfully, in the traditional way, but seeking justice.' He described the mission of a priest as 'eminently religious and transcendent', which reassured those who felt that priests were becoming too involved in the nation's politics.

Romero became archbishop two days after El Salvador's general elections of 20 February 1977. During the week that followed the ballot, it became apparent that the government had engaged in massive fraud to secure the success of its candidate – also, confusingly, called Romero – a former general, and defence minister, who stood for the interests of the rich. While the political temperature rose in the capital with a series of strikes and rallies, the new archbishop left for Santiago de Maria to tidy things up in his old diocese. It was the last time he acted as if he could conduct his own business in his own time without taking into account the events going on around him.

On 26 February General Romero was declared the winner in the election and the following day, a Sunday, more than forty thousand people turned out in San Salvador's main square. A Mass was said and most of the crowd dispersed in the evening, but some remained. The Jesuit Father James Brockman, in his biography of Oscar Romero, gives this account of how the Archbishop first encountered the realities of Salvadorian politics.

'After midnight, troops with armoured cars cordoned off the square, and gave the remaining 6,000 ten minutes to disperse. Many left, but the troops opened fire on the 1,500 to 2,000 who remained. The crowd fled to El Rosario Church on one side of the plaza. There they remained until about 4.00 a.m. when Bishop Rivera, Archbishop Chavez and the Red Cross arranged a truce.

'The weary Rivera was returning to the seminary when he unexpectedly met Archbishop Romero, who explained, "They called me in Santiago at midnight, and here I am."' And there, at the centre of the crisis, Romero remained for the rest of his life. He responded to the aftermath of the elections with a refusal to compromise his principles, quickly dispelling the doubts of the more radical priests in his archdiocese. And within a month of his appointment the violence that haunted El Salvador struck home to him personally.

Father Rutilo Grande was shot dead while travelling from his parish to the village where he had grown up a few miles away. An old man and a boy of fifteen were with him and were also killed. Rutilo Grande was a national figure, and an intellectual child of Medellín. A radical Jesuit who denounced injustice in his sermons, he led a team of younger members of the Society of Jesus working among the *campesinos*, encouraging them to organize themselves, which angered the local landowners. Father Grande was also a close friend of Romero. For a while he had been prefect of discipline at the Jesuit seminary where

Romero had lived, and when Romero was appointed bishop in 1970 he chose Rutilo Grande to act as master of ceremonies at his ordination. In his eulogy at Grande's funeral Romero recalled that 'At peak moments of my life he was very close to me, and those gestures are never forgotten.' With Rutilo Grande's murder El Salvador's struggle became Romero's struggle.

Romero had such a powerful impact that it is easy to forget how little time he was allowed as archbishop: three years to the month after Rutilo Grande's assassination, Romero, too, was dead, but in that short time he established an extraordinary rapport with El Salvador's *campesinos* and slum-dwellers. His weekly sermons were broadcast to the nation on the archdiocese's radio station, YSAX, and despite their sometimes heroic length, they became cult listening. Indeed, their audience extended beyond the country's borders: Robert White, the American ambassador in El Salvador, recalls that 'Those sermons were broadcast throughout Central America. You could be in the remotest village of El Salvador or Nicaragua, and you could walk through those villages and you wouldn't miss a word. Because every radio was tuned in to hear him.'

Letters poured into the archdiocese from all over the country. Many were only half literate. Sometimes they came from a whole community, signed by a collection of thumb-prints to indicate the support of those who could not write. They were a daily reminder to the Archbishop of the suffering in the lives he touched with his words.

Jon Sobrino, whose radical theology had made him a target for Romero's criticism before the Archbishop's political conversion, paints a picture of a man on an uncomfortable journey: 'He was a traditional theological thinker, but when he saw the suffering of the people, it changed him. Then he became a prophet. But I do not think his temperament prepared him to become a prophet. By temperament he was rather quiet, subdued. But the suffering made him change.'

Non-Catholics are some of Oscar Romero's most enthusiastic supporters. Westminster Abbey has chosen him as one of the modern martyrs to fill the niches on the West Front. Thomas Buergenthal, the chairman of the UN Commission on the Truth, who is Jewish, speaks of Romero with religious reverence as 'a very courageous, humble, modest man ... very much a priest of the people, not an archbishop of the Church in the way one thinks of the princes of the

Church, but a local parish priest who felt he had an obligation to protect his flock'.

Within the Vatican, though, mention of his name provokes an uneasy response. Cardinal Alfonso Lopez Trujillo, one of the few prominent conservatives in the Latin-American Church and now based in Rome as president of the Pontifical Council on the Family, described Romero as a friend but gave him the faintest of praise: Romero, he said, 'like many bishops and many other people wanted to pursue the holy way. But to say whether he succeeded in that or not, this is God's ultimate judgement or the Church's through its ordinary ways.' Cardinal Edward Cassidy, another curial insider, knew Romero well when he was posted to El Salvador as a junior diplomat in the nunciature – the Vatican embassy. He remembers going to barbecues and swimming parties with the young priest, and about once a month they would meet with a group of priests to discuss documents that had come out of Vatican II. He seemed perplexed somehow by the change 'from the Monsignor that I knew to the Archbishop who was assassinated', but even he said he did not 'know the whole story' and 'never had a chance to really understand the development that took place, or be able to judge it'. His last memory of Romero, however, is telling. They bumped into each other in St Peter's Square in 1979, just before Cassidy took up a posting in South Africa and not long before Romero's assassination: 'I found him very depressed and concerned that he wasn't trusted any more by the Holy See . . . He said, "You know me and you know how I think and my love for the Church" . . . He seemed deeply hurt.'

The aura of sanctity that surrounds Archbishop Romero's memory should not be allowed to obscure the fact that he was a highly controversial figure. Those on the political right who hated him – including those implicated in his murder – were sincere in their belief that he was on the wrong side of the front-line in the war against Communism. Maria Luisa d'Aubuisson, Roberto's sister, sometimes discussed the Archbishop with her brother and tried to persuade him to confess the sin of ordering the murder. But he could not be brought to repent: 'He thought the Monsignor was a great hindrance and that he had entered very dangerous political ground,' she said. 'He thought he had deserved a violent death for having taken a clear stand.'

General Adolfo Blandon served with d'Aubuisson in the National

Guard, and the two were in the same unit during El Salvador's war with Honduras. Blandon went on to become El Salvador's senior military officer during some of the worst years of the civil war, and he remembers that at the military academy they both attended 'fierce anti-Communism' was drummed into them as rigorously as drill and military tactics. They were indoctrinated with the idea that Communism represented a threat to 'religion and private property', the two things they held most dear. 'The officers in El Salvador considered that any person who favoured the poor or the working class was a Communist, and those who had ideas in favour of private enterprise were classified as right-wing,' the General told me. 'Archbishop Romero, by being on the side of the poor, was identified with the left.' It was as simple as that. Thomas Buergenthal, of the Truth Commission, puts it like this: 'Each side of the conflict was convinced it was totally right . . . and if you were totally right you could justify anything – killing, murder, torture – in order to support your side.' The political signals from the resident superpower, the United States, gave an added twist by the way in which they represented the struggle against Communism in Latin America as part of a wider world struggle between two competing ideologies. It was, says Buergenthal, seen as a 'world conflict between good and evil'.

During Ronald Reagan's first term Jeanne Kirkpatrick and Alexander Haig were two of the most powerful influences in the framing and implementation of American foreign policy. Both were ferociously anti-Communist, and both took a special interest in Latin America. Both were questioned about the killing of four American nuns in El Salvador not long after Romero's assassination. The Commission recorded that:

On 16 December 1980 United Nations Ambassador Jeane [sic] Kirkpatrick said, 'I don't think the government [of El Salvador] was responsible. The nuns were not just nuns; the nuns were political activists. We ought to be a little more clear-cut about this than we usually are. They were political activists on behalf of the Frente [the opposition front] and someone who is using violence to oppose the Frente killed them.'

Secretary of State Alexander Haig testified as follows before the foreign affairs committee of the House of Representatives:

I would like to suggest to you that some of the investigations would lead one to believe that perhaps the vehicle the nuns were riding in may have tried to run a roadblock or may accidentally have been perceived to have been doing so, and there may have been an exchange of fire.

The nuns were found to have been raped before they were killed; quite how they might have run a roadblock and exchanged fire after being violated General Haig did not explain.

Robert White was ambassador to El Salvador when the four nuns were killed. He was given a chilling insight into the nice distinctions the Salvadorian military made about members of the Church: 'When the four American women disappeared,' he said, 'I called Colonel Garcia, the Minister of Defence, and said, "Look, I'm very worried about these women. Do you know where they are?" He said, "Were they dressed in habits?" And right then I knew that they had killed them – that was his way of telling me that if they had been dressed properly they would have been respected.' He remembers a Salvadorian military training film: 'They'd show a priest with a biretta and a book in his hand, and they'd say, "This is a good priest." And then they'd show a man in a sports shirt and a pair of slacks, with a cross, and they'd say, "This is a bad priest." They'd show a nun in full traditional regalia, with rosary beads and the wimple, and they'd say, "This is a good nun." And then they'd show a sister with a short skirt and a blouse and just a little head-dress and they'd say, "This is a bad nun." '

He says of Jeanne Kirkpatrick's comments that what was 'just a hare-brained remark in the context of the United States, in the context of El Salvador could mean deaths'. In the light of the public statements she, General Haig and other senior officials in Washington were making, it is perhaps no surprise that the anti-Communist warriors of El Salvador considered they had *carte blanche* to do as they pleased. One described the battle he was fighting in terms that could have come from Ronald Reagan himself: 'We are part of Western civilization and we consider Communism the enemy. We had to defend the West, not only El Salvador. We had to defend the West and each country has its own methods of doing so.' The Truth Commission found no direct evidence of American support for the death squads, but Buergenthal says, 'If the United States didn't intentionally create the climate that made some of these acts possible, it certainly gave the impression to Salvadorians that they could get away with it.'

The continuing hatred felt for Romero by those he opposed is a kind of perverse compliment to his influence. He had enemies within the Church, too. He was not always an easy man to get on with – saints seldom are – and even his most ardent admirers cannot escape the fact that his outspoken sermons and his determination to challenge the government led to a deep and bitter rift among the bishops of El Salvador. At one point, the split within the Bishops Conference became so serious that the Vatican sent an 'Apostolic Visitor' to investigate. An apostolic visitation is roughly analogous to a failing school receiving an emergency visit from a 'hit squad' team of government inspectors. In this instance the visitor, Bishop Quarrancino of Argentina, recommended that an administrator be appointed to take on the day-to-day running of the archdiocese, leaving Romero as archbishop in name but without real power. Romero managed to fight off that suggestion, but there was no let-up in the assaults against him from some of his brother bishops. He was himself quite capable of tough bureaucratic infighting: within a month of John Paul II's election in October 1978, the Pope received a six-page letter from the turbulent Archbishop of San Salvador, presenting his side of the case. The first target of his attack was the Vatican's own nuncio, whom Romero accused of undermining him. The nuncio, he wrote, 'had shown himself influenced more by government, diplomatic and capitalist sectors than by the sufferings of the people'.

Father James Brockman records that at Romero's funeral a banner was hung above the cathedral entrance demanding that the papal nuncio, the four bishops who opposed Romero and the American ambassador should stay away – a visible sign of the dissent within the Church that accompanied his ministry. Strife was part of his legacy – and part of the legacy of the Second Vatican Council.

Throughout its history the unity of the Church has been threatened by the breadth of its ambition. Preserving the integrity of an institution that embraces all humanity is no easy task. The tension between the Church's 'Roman' and its 'Catholic' aspirations has always existed. One is centralizing, unifying and imperial: it lays down laws, makes the doctrinal trains run on time and forms the sometimes grubby political alliances necessary for God's earthly kingdom to survive. The other delights in diversity and the uniqueness of individuals. It loves freedom and experiment, and its politics are local. The Second Vatican

Council gave the sanction of Roman law to Catholic diversity. But the way in which the Church in Latin America developed threatened Roman control. When Paul VI opened the Medellin Conference in 1968, he believed that local revolution could be readily accommodated in the universal Church. By the time his successor, John Paul II, began his energetic pilgrimages to the region, the spectre of schism was haunting the corridors of the Curia.

Moving down a receiving line of local dignitaries in Honduras, Pope John Paul was brought up short by the unexpected sound of his mother tongue. Thomas Buergenthal had learned Polish as a prisoner in Auschwitz while the future pope was studying for the priesthood nearby in Kraków. He had been only a child and was one of the camp's youngest survivors. He emigrated to America where he studied law and became a lecturer at George Washington University in the American capital. Buergenthal believes that his early experiences gave him a moral compass that made him uniquely well qualified to undertake his task as chairman of the Truth Commission.

He is equally convinced that the Pope's formative years – especially those spent in fighting Communism – denied him the capacity to understand the great battle that his fellow bishops were fighting in Latin America while he fought his in Eastern Europe. Thomas Buergenthal believes that John Paul II could have protected Archbishop Romero, perhaps even saved his life, by offering him more public support. It is a cruel charge, but it gives an indication of the way this pope is viewed by the champions of the Church of the Poor in the world's most Catholic continent.

Pope John Paul's tempestuous relationship with the Church is shot through with ironies. Latin America occupied just as immediate a place on his agenda as Eastern Europe: he went to the second great gathering of the region's bishops, at Puebla, six months before his decisive first visit to Poland. When that meeting was convened, 850 priests and nuns had paid with their lives for their faith across Latin America, and the parallels between what the Church was doing there and in Communist Poland were striking. In both cases the Roman Catholic Church was a rallying point against injustice and sufficiently powerful as an institution to make its stand count in the world of real politics. Both the struggle in Poland and that in Latin America had produced martyrs. And in both areas the forces unleashed by the

Second Vatican Council had produced a dynamic effect no one could have anticipated when the Council Fathers gathered in St Peter's.

But for Pope John Paul the differences were more significant than the similarities. It was not a simple matter of politics – although it is perfectly true that while the United States was the Church's ally in Poland it was its enemy in Latin America. It was a battle of ideas, and it was fought with passion because the circumstances in which both John Paul and the Liberation Theologians had learned their faith had been such stern and influential teachers. The faith of both sides in this great intellectual debate of the 1980s had been stamped indelibly by their different historical experiences.

10

Deadly Errors

There was a hint of the clash to come in a meeting in Rome during the Second Vatican Council. One of the reasons the Council unleashed so much creative energy was that it provided the opportunity for cultural cross-pollination: cardinals from Chile met bishops who had grown up in the slums of Asia, while African princes sat down with fashionable Frenchmen and stern Slavs. They reflected on what united them and what divided them, and most came away satisfied that more of what mattered fell into the first category than the second. But when Karol Wojtyła sat down with Latin-American bishops in the autumn of 1964 he heard something guaranteed to make his hackles rise. Dom Helder Câmara, Archbishop of Recife and one of the founding fathers of the revolution in the Church in Brazil, suggested that all Catholic teachers should take a course in Marxism. Wojtyła's response is not difficult to imagine.

It would be unjust to Pope John Paul to claim that his dispute with Liberation Theology springs from a lack of concern for the poor. It is sometimes said of his chief ideologue, Cardinal Ratzinger, that he 'has never smelt a dead baby being carried in a shoe box through the *barrios*', but John Paul's own writings are deeply imbued with a sense of the pain of social injustice. Indeed, in an ironic twist to the epic struggle of the 1980s, he became in the 1990s rather a hero to old Communists like Gorbachev and Fidel Castro because of his stern critique of capitalism.

John Paul's lack of sympathy for Liberation Theology is a striking illustration of the way place and culture determine ideas. He believes deeply in the importance of the way in which religion, local culture and national identity are woven together, and he is himself a Catholic

European of a kind that perhaps only Poland could have produced. But São Paulo is a long way from Rome, and even further from Kraków. The link of the faith is there, but with the diversity in the Church released by Vatican II it has become a narrow bridge over a deep chasm, and Pope John Paul has never really managed to cross it. To mix the metaphor, the training that gave him perfect pitch in Eastern Europe made him – in the judgement of the champions of Liberation Theology – tone deaf in Latin America.

There is bound to be a dash of prejudice in any debate over labels. Father Jon Sobrino, still proud to call himself a Liberation Theologian in defiance of current intellectual fashion, says that being demonized as a 'Communist' in the Latin America of the 1980s was like being demonized as a 'Protestant' in sixteenth-century Spain or a 'Catholic' in the England of the same period. The close relationship between Marxism and Liberation Theology is beyond dispute, and Marxism, Sobrino explained, provided a useful analytical tool for understanding contemporary conditions in Latin America. Theologians there borrowed from Marx's ideas in just the way European theologians had been borrowing from classical and European philosophers for centuries: 'Liberation Theology was used in the same way that Aristotle was used and Plato and Heidegger,' Sobrino said. 'No theologian is attacked if she or he uses Heidegger's thinking to convey something, but if you use a Marxist critique . . . !' He allowed the sentence to trail off suggestively.

But that is somewhat disingenuous. Liberation Theology did more than use Marxism as a tool of analysis for understanding social problems. It allowed Marxist ideas to provide a blueprint for redesigning Christian teaching. Marxism promises a paradise in this world, Catholicism promises one after death; Marxism promises liberation from a certain condition of human life, Catholicism promises liberation from the human condition itself. Liberation Theology blurred those distinctions by elevating the struggle for an earthly paradise above the aspiration to transcendence.

The Vatican issued two 'instructions' on Liberation Theology in the 1980s. The first, published in 1984, was a ferocious condemnation of an approach that Rome said 'subordinates theology to the class struggle'. The second, which appeared eighteen months later, was milder, designed to quieten the rebellious outrage the first had provoked in the

Latin-American Church. But its language was still robust. The new theology, it argued, was 'contaminated by deadly errors about the human condition'. Real liberation, it insisted, meant liberation from 'the radical bondage of sin', not the building of 'a purely earthly plan of liberation', which 'would very soon be revealed as an illusion'.

Of course, there was a political overlay to that fundamental ideological anxiety, and there were important differences in the political circumstances in which the battle in Eastern Europe and the battle in Latin America were being fought. In Poland the Church stood against an atheist state, which, in theory at least, threatened it with extinction. The regimes in Latin America were essentially Catholic – or would at least have regarded themselves as such – and the battle was being fought within a Catholic world. And while the Church in Poland was united in its opposition to an unjust power, the Church in Latin America was often deeply divided over the right response to the injustice of the social order.

One of the most memorable images of the Pope's battle with the Church in Latin America came on his visit to Nicaragua in 1983. The left-wing Sandinista government, which had come to power in the aftermath of the defeat of the Somoza dictatorship, included four priests: the foreign minister and minister of social welfare, and two brothers, Father Fernando Cardenal, the minister for education, and Father Ernesto Cardenal, a well-known poet who held the appropriate job of culture minister. The four were in open warfare with their bishop, who had repeatedly told them that such an active and partisan participation in politics was incompatible with their priestly ministry. But they had refused to leave their government jobs, and Father Ernesto Cardenal found himself in the cabinet receiving line when Pope John Paul touched down at Managua airport. He was a venerable figure, very much the white-haired poet and prophet, wearing a distinctive white smock rather than clerical dress. When he knelt to kiss the Pope's ring John Paul yanked back his hand, wagged his finger angrily at the figure kneeling before him, and, in an unabashed display of papal authority, told him to 'regularize your situation with the Church'.

The image fuelled the prejudices of those who saw the Pope as a slavish follower of American interests. The Sandinistas were Washington's favourite bogeymen, feeding the nightmares of Middle America about Soviet tanks sweeping up through Central America and into Texas. American support for the Contra rebels who were fighting the Sandinista regime was to bring the American crusade against Communism in its 'backyard' to an apotheosis of absurdity in the Iran–Contra affair; Ronald Reagan presented the Contras as champions of democracy, but the evidence that many of them were little more than drug-dealers and bandits grows as their record is being examined. In berating a Sandinista priest, John Paul aligned himself firmly with the United States in the eyes of many in the Latin-American Church.

John Paul did draw a distinction between the behaviour of the American superpower in Latin America and the Soviet superpower in Eastern Europe, and some in the Latin-American Church did not. Many of those on the radical wing of the Church in Latin America saw the United States as the real heart of the evil they encountered in daily lives, the consumer of resources when so many around them were poor, and the provider of weapons to the military who used violence to uphold the established order. Father Jon Sobrino told me, 'The American government, the Pentagon, the Army, along with their allies in Europe, were an instrument of repression in Latin America.' That suggests a moral equivalence between the two super-powers that John Paul could not accept. It was a further source of tension between the Pope and the followers of Liberation Theology, and again its roots lay in their different experiences.

Rome and the Latin-American Church were also divided over the issue of violence. The leaders of the Latin-American Church were scrupulous in their attachment to non-violent means and to orthodox Church teaching on the subject. Cardinal Arns, for example, consist-ently tried to ensure that his vast congregations should not provoke violent clashes with the security forces. In El Salvador, where violence was part of the currency of daily life, Archbishop Romero had to define the line between legitimate opposition and violent insurgency even more carefully. But not all the Church's junior officers were so circumspect. One of the heroes of the Latin-American Church was Camilo Torres, a priest who had joined the guerrillas in Colombia in 1965; he had been killed by the army there the following year, and acquired the posthumous status of a clerical Ché Guevara.

Liberation Theology accepted the idea that violence was something built into the structure of society, and this inevitably blurred the

Church's traditional stand on the issue. Once violence is depersonalized in that way, individual decisions about violent acts are devalued and collective decisions become more important. Some priests came to see their struggle against injustice in the same terms as the Allies' struggle against Nazism; they believed that the social conditions of Latin America in the 1970s and 1980s laid a duty upon them to resort to violent means. That led to a suspicion in Rome that Liberation Theology meant being soft on terrorism.

There was another dimension to Rome's dispute with the Latin-American Church. In keeping with a pattern established during most of the Church's internal arguments over the past thirty years, the issue of authority was at stake.

Leonardo Boff lives in the jungle above Rio de Janeiro. His apartment block curves around the side of a hill like the upper tier of an amphitheatre. He has a fiercely protective and devoted partner, who also acts as his appointments secretary, a study jumbled with books and religious artefacts, a diary crammed with academic engagements all over the world, and a breeze blowing through his picture windows to cool him as he works at his word-processor – all the accoutrements of the world-class intellectual. It is a long way from the austere life he embarked upon when he became a Franciscan friar, and he owes his changed circumstances to Pope John Paul and the Vatican's chief ideologue, Cardinal Joseph Ratzinger (the 'Panzer Cardinal' as he is irreverently known in Latin America), who inadvertently transformed him from a relatively obscure Brazilian theologian into an icon of the left the world over.

Boff's 1983 book *Church, Charism and Power* turned the searchlight of the new ideas he and his fellow Liberation Theologians had used to illuminate the vices of Latin America's rulers on to the Church itself. 'Normally,' he told me, 'the "theory of liberation" is applied within society, on behalf of the poor. The theory is not applied within the Church itself. My book was an attempt to show that the Church is only deserving of being called liberating if the Church itself is a church of liberty.' The Church fails the test, he argued, because 'it does not respect human rights in terms of differing opinions. It also does not recognize the importance of women' and it 'does not have a mechanism for general participation in the process of decision-making'. Boff uses the image of a pyramid to describe the way authority is exercised in the Church, flowing from the Pope through his Curia and his cardinals, on down through his bishops and clergy to the laity who make up the pyramid's base.

It was as if the Council prophets of doom had returned to say, 'I told you so.' With the Declaration on Religious Liberty, which had been so fiercely fought over in 1965, the Church had accepted the human right of each individual to decide his or her belief without coercion; now the Church was being judged by the moral standards it had set itself. Like Hans Küng before him, Leonardo Boff was questioning the Church's authority and, by implication, the Vatican's right to speak for God. His was another battle about power and the nature of truth.

Like John Paul, Leonardo Boff has a strong sense of theatre, and his account of his battle with the Vatican is told with relish and enthusiasm. In September 1984 he was summoned to Rome to account for himself. From the moment he arrived at Fiumicino airport it was apparent that the echoes of the Inquisition in a modern setting made this a gift for the media. The television cameras were there to meet him, and if Cardinal Ratzinger had planned a discreet interrogation and quiet but firm admonition it was not to be.

Boff describes the day of his appearance before the Cardinal as one of 'medieval scenes'. He recalls being thrown into a car and swept at high speed through the Vatican gardens and past 'an enormous iron gate with huge nails pointing outwards. I asked the official with me if this was the torture chambers,' he says, 'and he replied, "You politicize everything." We walked into a lift guarded by two Swiss Guards in official clothing . . . We crossed an enormous room, I guess it must have been eighty metres wide, with glamorous carpets and huge Renaissance paintings. Right at the very end of this room was a tiny room. It consisted of a small table and two chairs.' Boff teased his host by 'making a small reverence' to his chair, which, the Brazilian said, was the chair in which Galileo sat during his interrogation and condemnation.

When I visited Joseph Ratzinger, it was an altogether more mundane experience. I cannot think of any other public figure who arouses quite the same intensity of feeling in so many parts of the world: from El Salvador to Sri Lanka people utter his name with a mixture of fear, respect, awe and loathing.

The Council might have changed the title of the Cardinal's department from the old 'Holy Office of the Inquisition' to the less sinister 'Sacred Congregation for the Doctrine of the Faith', but that does not alter the fact that its function is very much what it was when Cardinal Ottaviani presided there in the 1960s. Ottaviani used to call himself 'the Church's policeman', and by an irony that has given his enemies much innocent merriment, Joseph Ratzinger is a German police officer's son. He is generally regarded as the second most powerful man in the Vatican, and he has a weekly audience with John Paul.

The close relationship he has established with the Pope allows him enormous freedom to pursue his own agenda. But he is also the beneficiary of a trend in the Church that has made his office steadily more important. In the days when the Church exercised secular power, its leaders could use secular means to consolidate their hold over its members; the promise of a remunerative diocese or the threat of a burning at the stake worked wonders. The institution is still strong enough and rich enough to use some secular means of pressure: a parish priest thrown out in his mid-fifties without support, for example, would find life extremely difficult in the world outside the Church, and withdrawing a theologian's licence to teach could deprive him or her of a livelihood (in theory, at least: in the Boff and Küng instances, it brought fame and fortune). But as the Church's secular influence diminishes, the way in which it uses ideas to exercise its authority becomes more important. And the Prefect of the Sacred Congregation for the Doctrine of the Faith is the man in charge of the ideas.

I was quite unprepared for the rather slight, hesitant figure who appeared in one of the reception rooms on the third floor of what is still referred to as the Palace of the Holy Office. Joseph Ratzinger has finely drawn features, piercing eyes and the manner of a genial grandfather. The moment I began interviewing him I realized that he is also endowed with a mind like a man-trap.

There had been a certain amount of spin-doctoring in the run-up to our meeting. The palace is in the heart of the Vatican, just behind St Peter's, and many of its rooms are decorated in Vatican baroque at its grandest. The two ornate gold chairs provided for visitors were considered inappropriate for a television interview, and the young American priest who served as one of the Cardinal's assistants insisted on something more 'austere'. Cardinal Ratzinger made a show of appearing taken aback when I told him about Leonardo Boff's colourful account of their meeting in 1985: 'It was in this room,' he said. 'He was very cheerful and very warm . . . Our conversation took place in a very relaxed atmosphere.' Boff's version must, the Cardinal offered mildly, be 'a subsequent distortion of memory'. He gave me a crisp account of what he believed to be the errors of Liberation Theology in general and the writings of Leonardo Boff in particular. The Church must not, he said, 'become a political institution itself; it has to inspire politics, but also respect the autonomy of politics'. Liberation Theology 'boiled down to a kind of theocracy, in which God Himself, however, hardly mattered any more, but the ideological rules of Marxism prevailed'. It was a 'transgression of faith, turning faith into politics, seeking to achieve the salvation of faith through political institutions'. As for Boff, he had indeed challenged the Church's authority with the idea that 'all churches were fragments of the one Church of Christ'. That 'leads to a situation in which no church can make authoritative statements any more, because they are all only fragments reflecting a part'.

When Leonardo Boff came to the Cardinal's lair, he was accompanied by two of the giants of the Brazilian Church, Cardinals Arns and Lorscheider. Like Boff, Arns was a Franciscan, and felt a special loyalty to the man he had taught for several years while Boff was a seminarian. He regarded Boff's work as a theologian as a complement to his own work as a bishop: 'We did the pastoral work and he did the ideological part,' he told me. 'He was the theologian and we were the practical men for the people.' Boff had taken care to don his Franciscan habit for the occasion – something he almost never did at home – and when he emerged before the cameras, a brace of cardinals at his side, he was every inch the virtuous priest. In public-relations terms, it was game, set and match to Boff, whatever the theological merits of his case. Cardinal Ratzinger may not have understood that being in the world meant taking account of the world's means of communication, but Leonardo Boff certainly had.

Leonardo Boff was punished for challenging a power that could not tolerate dissent from what it held to be Absolute Truth. Of course, the modern Church could not and would not inflict physical pain or imprisonment in the way the Church of the Inquisition once did – and the new absolutism of the Communist faith continued to do in the twentieth century. But it gave Boff precisely the kind of sentence human-rights activists complained about in the totalitarian regimes of the Communist world: it silenced him. He was told he could not speak publicly, teach or publish. When I asked Cardinal Ratzinger how he justified that, he seemed awkwardly caught between a genuine conviction that it was a perfectly legitimate form of discipline and an awareness that it did not look terribly good in the open societies of the late twentieth century. 'Of course it is not acceptable just to silence someone,' he said, 'but I think in a very talkative world, in which there is a temptation to remain in the public eye and take the floor even if there is nothing new to say, it might be a good thing if someone is invited in a friendly manner . . . to think more and speak less.' He made 'being invited in a friendly manner' sound like 'being made an offer you can't refuse'.

Cardinal Ratzinger has been widely criticized for his treatment of Leonardo Boff. But he was justified in his suspicion that Boff was – according to the traditional understanding of the nature of the Faith – a heretic. 'Christianity,' Boff told me, 'does not hold the monopoly of the truth . . . Jesus did not want a religion.' If the first of those statements is true, Cardinal Ratzinger, prefect of the Sacred Congregation for the Defence of the Faith, does not have a job. If the second is true, the Church he serves has been a gigantic two-thousand-year-long fraud. Boff has now left the priesthood, and writes extensively about ecology.

In the controversy with Boff, the Vatican challenged Liberation Theology on the field of ideas; but those ideas had wide support in the Latin-American hierarchy, as the presence of two senior cardinals during Boff's interrogation demonstrated, so the Vatican followed up the ideological attack with an administrative assault. Cardinal Arns was far too prominent a figure for the Curia to take on directly, so, with a stroke of administrative genius, Rome simply removed much of his power-base from under him. In 1989 his vast archdiocese of 16 million people was divided into five separate dioceses; he was left in control of the centre of the city, and new bishops were appointed around him.

Arns remains fiercely loyal to the Pope, and refuses to accept that he has had any hand in the machinations against him – 'The Pope is our father, he is always our friend and never did anything against us personally' – but 'as to the Curia, that is another thing'. He spits, rather than says, the word Curia, and the only stipulation he made before our interview was that I should not ask him about the division of his archdiocese.

In keeping with the pyramid model of the Church, the way the Vatican exercises power in the appointment of bishops is reflected in the way the bishops exercise their power over their priests. The Curia wanted nothing short of a counter-reformation in the Latin-American Church, and some of the bishops it chose to do the job went about their task with a determination that bordered on brutality. The most notorious instance followed the retirement of one of Liberation Theology's most famous prophets. Helder Câmara, like Oscar Romero, was one of those leaders whose personal conversion had played a pivotal role in the conversion of the Latin-American Church. By the time I met him, he was so frail and light in his old age it seemed that the essence of the man had already been drained away, leaving only a smile and kind eyes. With some prompting from a visiting priest he was able to say Mass in the fine sixteenth-century church that had provided his home for nearly forty years, and he spent a few minutes in the sacristy afterwards receiving admirers and blessing the odd rosary. But his grasp on the world around him was tenuous, and he was a shadow of the visionary leader he had once been.

Helder Câmara marched with the great movements of the century. He had been a Fascist sympathizer in his youth, a founder of a Brazilian movement called the October Legion inspired by the European dictators of the 1930s. In 1950 he made his first impact on the Church outside Brazil with an exploit that gave a hint of his extraordinary ability to fire others with his enthusiasm. 1950 was declared a Holy Year by Pius XII, and Helder Câmara was asked to lead a pilgrimage to Rome. This is Peter Hebblethwaite's account, in his biography of Paul VI, of what he did:

Helder Câmara scrounged a battered old troopship from his government, packed it to the gunwales with 1,350 people (it was meant to carry 800) and preached vigorous sermons on deck, which converted at least some of the prostitutes who had come on board thinking it the easiest way to get to Paris. It was the first time Helder Câmara and most of his shipmates had left Brazil.

Two years later he made his most significant contribution to the institutional life of the Church when he founded the National Conference of Brazilian Bishops. Bishops' conferences were a rarity in those days, and it was not until a decade later that Vatican II officially endorsed them. Helder Câmara's innovation gave the bishops of Brazil the unity to speak as a national bloc, and it bore further fruit when the Latin-American Bishops Conference (CELAM) provided an institutional voice for the region as a whole. Helder Câmara, in effect, invented a model for devolving power to the Church's provinces, and it was all the more significant because it sprang from the most populous of those provinces. If that suggests the mind of an energetic bureaucrat, the picture of life in his archdiocese of Olinda and Recife suggests a leadership style based on the principle of inspired chaos.

Father Tony Terry arrived in Brazil in 1962, fresh from seminary in Ireland; his missionary society, St Patrick's, had decided to respond to John XXIII's call to meet the needs of the Church in Latin America, and was diverting its resources from Africa. Father Terry worked for several years under Cardinal Arns in São Paulo and by 1979 had become superior of the St Patrick's community there. He decided to investigate whether he and his priests could help in Recife. 'We came up to meet Dom Helder, and said, "We are interested in coming to work in your diocese and would like to know your needs." We expected him to call in an assessor and give out the physical and statistical needs of the diocese. No. He simply said, "*Venite et vedete*," come and see. It was the answer that Christ gave to Andrew and the apostles when they asked him where he lived.'

When Father Terry took on the parish of Peixhinos in the archdiocese of Olinda and Recife, it had eighty thousand parishioners. It is worth pausing for a moment to reflect what the care of so many souls implies; he certainly could not expect them all at Mass on Sunday. The average income was estimated at around fifty American dollars a month. A demographic survey conducted in the parish in 1994 gives an idea of the kind of social problems it suffers from even today: more than half the homes are built of timber or mud, nearly 80 per cent are without sanitation, and the most common diseases are Aids and cholera.

The cities of Olinda and Recife sit side by side on the Atlantic. A reef – which lent Recife its name – snakes for miles along the coast some twenty yards from the shoreline. The climate on Brazil's north-eastern seaboard is kind – tropical sun mixed with cooling sea breezes – and the waters of the lagoon maintain the temperature of a comfortable bath. The Dutch settled the town for a while, and its centre is full of brightly coloured old houses, many recently restored to provide bars and restaurants for the tourist trade. But, as so often in Brazil, extreme poverty sits side by side with exotic beauty. The north-east of Brazil is one of the most feudal areas of the country.

Father Terry decided to live in the midst of the worst of it: in a breezeblock house by a dirt road with open guttering. There was a power supply, but the arrangement looked somewhat informal. It is one of the most densely populated areas of Brazil, and as you go deeper into the winding alleys, which are sometimes too narrow for more than one person to pass, the atmosphere becomes more desperate and threatening. Father Terry took me down a squalid side-street to meet what seemed to be an endlessly extended family whom he had once regarded as his neighbours. They were gathered around a game of dominoes. One of the teenagers was high – crack had just arrived in the area. The *paterfamilias* was drunk, and dropped his smallest child when he tried to show him off.

This was the kind of place where priests inspired by Liberation Theology tried to construct what became known as Comunidades Eclesiais de Base (CEB), 'base Christian communities': the building blocks of the new Church of Latin America. The work of priests in the CEBs was distinguished by two salient objectives: they encouraged the laity to take an active role in the life of the parish, and they tried to raise the consciousness of ordinary people about the injustice of the circumstances in which they found themselves. The first of those objectives was a more or less inevitable response to the problem of numbers; if a single priest was to give any kind of sacramental life to a parish of eighty thousand, he would have to rely on the assistance of the laity. But it was still controversial, because it had the effect of turning Leonardo Boff's 'pyramid' model of the Church on its head. Equally inevitably, the second of those objectives laid the priests open to the accusation that they were meddling in politics. If Cardinal Ratzinger should ever want to smell a dead baby being carried in a box through the slums, Father Terry's parish of Peixhinos would be a good place to do it. In the life of a parish priest like Father Terry, certain basic Christian ideals, such as love and charity, come into contact with an obvious reality and produce a response with which it is difficult to quarrel. 'When you look at the reality in Latin America,' he told me, 'you cannot not be shocked at the exploitation, at the fact that here in Brazil the richest one per cent earn more than the poorest fifty per cent of the people.'

I asked Cardinal Ratzinger about the charge that his lack of experience of poverty discredited his judgements on Liberation Theology. His answer was remarkable for its tone as much as its content: 'There was the objection that we did not know the empirical side of poverty. There was also a methodological objection, saying we proceeded by mere deduction from the Holy Scriptures and thereby neglected reality, whereas Liberation Theology proceeded by induction from the phenomenon of poverty . . .' And so on. His rebuttal of the charge was perfectly convincing in its logic. The language in which he made it suggests he had missed the point.

Dom José Cardoso became Archbishop of Olinda and Recife on Helder Câmara's retirement. He had spent twenty-five years in Rome, as a theology professor at the Carmelite College and then on his order's general council. He is in the vanguard of the counter-reformation against Liberation Theology. 'We cannot,' he told me firmly, 'reduce the Christian message to the temple of prosperity, as if once we have eliminated poverty or social injustice we have reached salvation.' Father Terry believes 'he came with a plan from the Vatican to dismantle the Church Dom Helder directed'.

I met him on his way to give a lecture on celibacy in a sixteenth-century seminary in the hills above Olinda. It had been built by the Jesuits in 1530, and the style of teaching was of roughly the same vintage. The classrooms were arranged around an arched courtyard, each with its regiment of neatly aligned chairs equipped with old-fashioned wooden writing boards attached to their arms. The Archbishop's students were all in their mid-twenties, most of them on the verge of ordination. But class began with a roll-call, and for an hour and a half he lectured them on the self-denial they would need to exercise to preserve the purity of their vocations.

This seminary was the centre for training all priests in the archdiocese; one of Dom José's first acts on his appointment as archbishop was to close down two others he considered dangerously liberal. The scandalous views of the seminarians were described to me by Dom

José's vicar-general, Miguel Cavalcanti: 'They wanted to build their own Church, a Church they called popular, a Church that grew from the people and was governed by the people.' Catholicism, like the Communist regimes it once feared, operates on the principle that control begins with the right kind of indoctrination.

Father Terry describes Dom José as 'the only bishop in the world who expels priests as most bishops are desperately looking for new ones'. Since the new regime took over, nearly twenty priests have resigned, been sacked or moved away. Father Terry was eased out by the simple device of allowing his missionary society's contract with the archdiocese to lapse; he had a series of disagreements with the new archbishop, including disputes over the way he embraced women during the kiss of peace, and his habit of having a drink in a local bar with some of his fellow Irish missionaries. In the most notorious clash, the archdiocese had to resort to force to take possession of a parish church.

In Morro da Conceiçao the intellectual battle of ideas in the Church became a physical battle for a piece of ground. This scruffy hilltop in north-east Brazil is a long way from Cardinal Ratzinger's elegant Roman *palazzo*, but the passions it aroused were the same as those that lay behind the Cardinal's duel with Leonardo Boff, and because it is a place of special devotion in the Brazilian Church, the struggle to control it was fought out in a very public manner. In 1908 a group of sailors caught in a storm swore to build a shrine to the Virgin if they were delivered from the waves. They returned safely and, true to their word, they erected a huge Madonna on the highest hill they could find. When the shrine was built it was in the countryside, but over the years the roughly built homes of the poor covered the hill like a spider's web. The community is now thirty-five thousand strong.

In keeping with the ideals of the base Christian communities, the people of this new parish themselves undertook the work of building a church. They scrounged materials where they could and brought them up the steep hill to the town square. Helena, the local primary-school principal who has lived in the parish for thirty-five years and is generally known as 'Santa Helena' because of her tireless devotion, describes the construction of the building like a story of Biblical heroism. She remembers a 'procession, like a pilgrimage' as the villagers carried the sand and cement up the hill.

When Dom José became archbishop, the parish priest of Morro da Conceiçao was among the most radical in his archdiocese. 'I don't see any sin,' Father Reginaldo told me, 'in a priest being viewed as a Marxist activist.' He established a popular following with his campaigns to bring sewage and paved roads to the community, and his parish was identified as a hotbed of dangerous ideas. On 11 December 1989 he was fired – and Dom José announced the decision on television without warning. Within a week two thousand people turned out to demonstrate in the centre of Recife. The priest nominated to take Father Reginaldo's place – who oddly and somewhat ironically was Polish – was told he would not be welcome. For most of the following year the sacked priest remained obstinately in place, supported by a large body of his parishioners. They hid the keys to the church, passing them round from house to house so that no one could be taken unawares and forced to yield them up.

At this point the archdiocese went to court to secure possession of the building. The scenes that followed would seem farcical if they had not left such deep scars in the community. The vicar-general, Miguel Cavalcanti, trooped up the hill with his bailiff and his injunction, only to find his way barred by a huge crowd holding a vigil in front of the church. He claims the Archbishop then telephoned Rome and 'spoke to a Cardinal . . . and was told by him to use military force'. The Archbishop and his vicar-general planned a surprise attack. 'We returned to see the judge and he suggested that we should take armed help with us. So we went to the police and spoke to the commander in secret. We spoke to the police, we spoke to the judge, we spoke to our lawyer, and we got ourselves organized. On the agreed day the police went to the area, surrounded the church with a full battalion, and half an hour later we arrived with a legal official . . . We went up to the church door and from there onwards it was pretty straightforward. They started to try to gather their supporters at short notice but there wasn't enough time. Our strength had been the secrecy of it all. When everything was in place we broke down the church door, went in, prayed, handed over to the new vicar, and then left. This time they lost.'

The legacy of the battle of Morro da Conceiçao is the saddest Sunday scene I saw anywhere: a church in open schism. The church the people of the parish built is securely in the hands of the archdiocese, and when I visited it it was packed with pilgrims to the shrine of Our Lady of the Immaculate Conception. Those still loyal to Father Reginaldo meet for a 'celebration' just across the road in the courtyard of Helena's school. Father Reginaldo is now married, and has been banned from celebrating Mass. Some odd twitch of the thread of faith makes him obey the proscription, and he has trained Helena to act on his behalf. This curious act of obedience means that she – devoted to the Faith and the community as she is – must perform a defiant act of rebellion every Sunday. Robed in white and flanked by two other women celebrants, she says Mass under his instruction.

The sound of the Mass in the real parish church across the road all but drowns out the small service in the schoolyard, and a van mounted with loudspeakers circles the square broadcasting pious slogans. The heroism that built the parish church and the courage that fought to defend it have been reduced to a medieval burlesque, as Morro da Conceiçao's rival preachers compete for the attention of the faithful in a noisy religious bazaar.

The great debate about Liberation Theology is now over. But it was not settled by the Recife police or Cardinal Ratzinger's modern inquisition. It was settled by what happened thousands of miles away from Morro da Conceiçao in Berlin on 11 November 1989. Once the Berlin Wall had collapsed and the failure of Communism became a fact of history, the danger that Liberation Theology would become a Trojan horse for infecting Catholicism with Marxism disappeared. 'When the Soviet Union and the Socialist countries were a reality,' argues Father Jon Sobrino, 'capitalism felt there was a real threat – there was a real power, missiles, weapons, tanks. But with that threat gone, what can we do with a couple of books to bring capitalism down?' Pope John Paul's analysis is the same, although the tone of his comments is, of course, different: 'Today, after the fall of Communism, Liberation Theology has collapsed as well. The bishops [of Latin America] have confirmed that these ideologies are neither a power nor a problem.'

There is a tragedy in this outcome for the people of Latin America. Liberation Theology, as Cardinal Arns realized, was a way for the people of the region to claim their own history. The Church was part of their European heritage, but with a new theology they demonstrated that they could reinvent that heritage in the context of their own distinctive historical experience. The fact that the collapse of their new theology was brought about by events in Germany must have stirred a weary feeling that they were still in thrall to Europe.

11

Certain Coincidences

After all the years of confrontation, the decades of trench warfare between two great ideologies, the moment the leader of the Communist world stood face to face with his Catholic counterpart should have been one of high drama. Instead, the meeting between Pope John Paul II and Mikhail Gorbachev in December 1989 seems to have been marked by platitudes of stunning banality. This is Gorbachev's account of their conversation: 'Underlining the honourable mission of His Holiness in the modern world, I noted certain coincidences both in his and my statements. "That means a simple thing – there should be coincidences in our basic thoughts." In response John Paul described our *perestroika* as the process that allowed us to look for common ways of arranging people's everyday life, probably better corresponding to the demands of different people, nations and human rights.'

Somewhere between the Pope's visit to Poland in 1979 and Gorbachev's visit to the Vatican ten years later, history had moved beyond their quarrel. The two men who sat opposite one another in the Vatican apartments that day had both been titanic figures of the twentieth century: between them they could lay claim to having managed perhaps the greatest revolution ever and added immeasurably to the sum of human happiness. Yet by the time they met they seemed already to be figures of the past. The Berlin Wall had fallen the previous month, and for both that marked the summit of their achievement and the beginning of a period in which they seemed to be out of step with the world around them.

Mikhail Gorbachev was to suffer a coup, humiliation at the hands of Boris Yeltsin in its immediate aftermath, then humiliation again at the hands of the voters when he tried to rebuild his career in a democratic Russia by standing for president. John Paul remained a force to be reckoned with much longer, partly because he could not be removed from office, and partly because the institution that owed him allegiance was infinitely more enduring than the Soviet Communist Party — next to Catholicism's two millennia, Communism's seven decades are a blink of the eye. But John Paul, like Gorbachev, has often given the impression of being unsure how to respond to the change that he himself has unleashed.

John Paul has had such a profound impact on the secular world that we judge him by secular standards. He has influenced so many people, expressed his views on so many different issues in public and private life, and exerted his authority so freely in so many areas that the judgements on his papacy vary widely. And the inconsistencies seem glaring, especially those between the champion of human rights and freedom in the Communist world and the authoritarian who crushed dissent within the Church, and those between the revolutionary in Eastern Europe and the reactionary in Latin America. But John Paul's standards are not those of the world: they are those of the Church. Judged by Catholic rather than secular criteria, his record appears more coherent.

The Gorbachev Foundation in Moscow has been collecting evidence of attacks on Catholic churches in Russia. One of the former president's aides explained that the Vatican is widely identified with the capitalist West, and John Paul is thought of as a 'Western' leader. The Russian Orthodox Church has become the focus for a new and exclusive Russian nationalism, and Russians seeking scapegoats during the painful transition to a market economy find a convenient villain in the Pope. Russia's Catholic minority is suffering as a result.

The belief that John Paul and Ronald Reagan formed a so-called 'Holy Alliance' to undermine the Soviet empire has been fostered by the evidence that has come to light of intelligence-sharing between the White House and the Vatican. When the conspiracy theorists of the KGB read the headlines generated by Carl Bernstein and Marco Politi's biography *His Holiness* they must have cheered. Here was the proof that the fall of Communism really had been a plot hatched by a sinister coalition of CIA Cold Warriors and zealous monsignors.

It is certainly true that first Zbigniew Brzeziński and then Richard

Allen, his successor as national security adviser when Ronald Reagan moved into the White House, ensured that John Paul II benefited from American intelligence-gathering. On one occasion in December 1980 Brzeziński telephoned John Paul directly – 'I suspect I must have been one of the very first people to just phone him; and it wasn't that easy to just get through' – to pass on evidence gathered from American satellites, 'incontrovertible information', he says, that the Soviets were preparing for an invasion. Brzeziński had no doubts about the Pope's capacity to process the information with the right political instincts: 'This Pope is not just a theologian,' he said. 'He is a first-class world political leader. I once joked and said to him, "When I talk to President Carter I sometimes think I am talking to a religious leader, and when I talk to you I have a feeling I'm talking to a number-one power statesman."'

Richard Allen says the new administration showed the Pope satellite photographs of Soviet missile emplacements just as if they were 'sharing intelligence with, say, Helmut Kohl or François Mitterrand'. He describes intelligence-sharing as 'a legitimate function between sovereign states – after all the Vatican is a sovereign state and can legitimately be treated that way'. He was trying to suggest that the relationship between the Vatican and Washington was part of the normal currency of diplomatic life, but I still found it odd for a superpower to pass the fruits of its espionage to the leader of the world's largest religion.

It is difficult to see how that kind of intelligence transaction could have had much of an impact on the way events in Poland unfolded. The Pope had no 'divisions' to mobilize if the Soviets decided to invade. The Church was a powerful force in Polish politics, but it was still first and foremost a religious institution. Yet the belief that the Americans and the Vatican had struck a secret pact persists, and the Pope's stand in Latin America is cited as further evidence. In the climate of crude black-and-white judgements fostered by the conflicts there, John Paul might appear to be fighting with the Americans and against much of his own Church in the region. But his record does not support the idea that he has been a lackey of American foreign policy. During the Gulf crisis of 1990 and 1991, the Pope remained resolutely opposed to the American-led Operation Desert Storm, which forced Saddam Hussein out of Kuwait: true to his non-violent convictions, he pushed publicly for a negotiated solution long after the rest of the world had accepted the inevitability of war. In January 1998 he visited Cuba, the last Communist outpost in the Western hemisphere, and the longest-standing pariah of American foreign politics. He declared the United States' economic embargo against the island 'deplorable'.

Throughout his twenty-year reign he has been almost as vocal in his condemnation of unrestricted free markets as he was in his attacks on Communism. His encyclicals on social and economic issues, such as *Centisimus Annus*, published to mark the centenary of Leo XIII's radical *Rerum Novarum*, and *Labor Exercens*, on the relationship between labour and capital, consistently stress the importance of bringing to bear moral restraints on the operation of unfettered capitalism. When Mikhail Gorbachev spoke of 'certain coincidences' between the two men's thinking, he was referring to the doubts they shared about the free-market ideology emerging in 1989 as the dominant orthodoxy across the world. Gorbachev told me that at their meeting in the Vatican they discussed 'the many problems and the injustice in the capitalist world, in particular concerning the developing world – the illness, poverty and sorrow there'. He rather cheekily claimed the former scourge of Communism as 'one of the brightest representatives of the left'.

The attempts to analyse John Paul's papacy as if he were any other world leader fail because he is working to a different agenda. When he first became Archbishop of Kraków he concentrated on the work of the Church and steered clear of political involvement. He did not become engaged with day-to-day politics until he concluded that it was necessary to clear that space the Church needed to operate freely. The same priorities dictated his actions as pope. His pilgrimages to Poland may have had a profound political effect, but that was secondary to his primary objective, which was to secure the rights of the Church.

The failure of the secular analysis of John Paul's actions explains why he has disappointed so many people; the way his triumph in Eastern Europe has been described only tells half of what he sees as the full story. On the first evening of his pivotal visit to Poland in 1979 he said this in his sermon in Warsaw's Victory Square: 'Christ cannot be excluded from man's history anywhere in the world, from any geographical latitude or longitude. Attempts to exclude Christ from man's history are directed against man.' The visit was a master-class in the meaning of human dignity, and that is how it has gone down in political history. But for John Paul, the religious dimension and the Christian message are at the heart of what it is to be human. His belief in the pre-eminence of religion explains the apparent contradiction between his condemnation of priests who were directly involved in politics in Latin America, and his pursuit of a political agenda of his own in Eastern Europe. For John Paul, the political game was a means to a religious end, and he believed that Latin-American priests like the Cardenal brothers were working towards an objective that was purely political.

John Paul turned the relationship between Catholicism and Communism neatly on its head, so that Catholicism appeared to the world as a force of revolution and Communism was revealed as a force of reaction. Then he apparently performed a further somersault when he adopted the intolerant and authoritarian habits of Catholicism's old rival in the way he ran the Church. That is the most troubling contradiction of his record in the 1980s, and it goes to the heart of the way he has run the Church in the 1990s. The key to understanding it lies in the true nature of the Polish Church, which became apparent only with the fall of Communism.

Many of those who rallied to the Church in Poland's Communist years did so because it was a force of opposition to the regime, not because they had faith. Just as the Church gave strength to political dissidents, so the dissident movement gave strength to the Church. And, perversely, the Communist authorities colluded in some areas with the Church's attempts to impose its moral agenda as a way of buying its compliance in others. Mieczysław Rakowski was the deputy prime minister in charge of the education ministry in 1983, and remembers trying to introduce a school textbook on sex education. He describes it as 'chaste in comparison to what is being written on the subject today', but the bishops did not like it, and the government was forced to pulp the entire print run. 'The Church liked to claim it was persecuted by atheists and Communists,' Rakowski says, 'but those same Communists watched very carefully that no "Western disease" crossed into Poland. There was no way even the mildest pornographic magazine could circulate while we were in power.'

Since 1989 Poles have been engaged in a reassessment of the nature of their Church, and it has put a severe strain on the relationship between a pope and a people that played such a critical role in the history of the late twentieth century. John Paul's 1991 visit to Poland, the first after the Communist cloud was lifted from the country, should have been a celebration. Instead, it is remembered for the Pope's anger at the way his compatriots had used – or, as he saw it, abused – their new-found liberty. He had fought for their freedom to believe, not their freedom to challenge the Catholic belief system. Like a disappointed father, he shook with rage as he lectured the crowds: 'We cannot talk here about the freedom of man. It is a freedom that subjugates. We cannot create a fiction of freedom that supposedly liberates man. It is a freedom that demoralizes. Understand that I cannot but care and suffer about all this, and so should you.'

The growing gap between the Polish Church and Polish society was crystallized in the Dec affair of 1997. Professor Wacław Dec was a respected and popular gynaecologist in Łodz, south-west of Warsaw. He was an ardent Catholic, had made sacrifices for his faith under Communism, and had a record of 'pro-life' commitment in his practice: he always encouraged those patients with unwanted pregnancies to opt for adoption rather than abortion. But when the Catholic politicians who dominated Poland's first post-Communist government proposed a tightening of the abortion laws, he spoke publicly about what he saw as the likely consequences: illegal abortions in unsafe conditions and abortion 'tourism' to Russia, Germany and the Czech Republic.

In May 1997 Professor Dec was killed in a road accident, and since he was a figure of some consequence one of the bigger churches in Lodz was earmarked for his funeral. It was only when the arrangements were published in the papers that an awkward silence told his children that something was wrong: their father had been declared a 'professed sinner', and was to be denied a Church burial. The Professor's daughter describes how she tried to persuade the local archbishop to relent: 'I approached Archbishop Ziółko, knelt down before him and kissed his ring, pleading for a moment's talk. I said we simply wanted to bury our father, that we didn't want to turn the occasion into any declaration of beliefs; that our father loved human life in all its forms, that he only represented women's rights, arguing that our society needed to be prepared for the anti-abortion legislation. The Archbishop interrupted me abruptly and said, "You obviously didn't know your own father." He got into his car, slammed the door and drove off.'

The Professor's funeral was eventually performed by the Army chaplain at the Military Medical Academy where he had worked for many years. It produced something quite unprecedented in Poland: huge crowds came out to protest *against* the Church. The hierarchy quickly recognized that the episode had been badly handled, and I found almost no one in the Polish Church willing to defend what had been done. But it does reveal the natural reflexes of the institution in which John Paul developed his understanding of Catholicism's relationship with society. The Church was an effective force of opposition precisely because it was such a well-developed alternative society, with its own values and institutional system of discipline. Its leaders saw no reason to change that simply because Communism had been vanquished. The abortion debate has raged more or less continuously in Poland since 1989, and was intense at the time of John Paul's visit there in 1991. The Pope plunged in with both feet: 'The principle of absolutely refusing to admit the dimension of the holy into social or governmental life means introducing atheism into society and government,' he said.

The Pope's background may help explain his readiness to use discipline, but that is not the same thing as excusing it, and it remains difficult to square some of the things the Archbishop of Kraków said during the Second Vatican Council with some of the things John Paul II has done in the 1980s and 1990s. He was one of the champions of the Declaration of Religious Liberty, and during the debate on the Church in the Modern World he criticized the draft under discussion in these terms: 'It is not the Church's place to teach unbelievers . . . Let us avoid any spirit of monopolizing and moralizing. One of the major faults of this *schema* is that the Church appears authoritarian in it.'

Rebels like Hans Küng and Leonardo Boff threaten John Paul's view of the Church because they bring the standards of the secular world to bear on the way it is run. Hans Küng's judgement on the contradictions of John Paul's papacy is ruthless, and makes no allowance for the Catholic approach, which attempts to reconcile them. He calls them a 'contradiction between foreign policy and domestic policy'.

'You have a pope who is affirming all the time that he is for human rights,' he told me, 'but that, of course, is valid for the world, not for the Church.' The tenth anniversary of the withdrawal of his licence to teach came two months after the fall of the Berlin Wall. He wrote then:

Comparison with the East German regime before 9 November is now inescapable. On the outside, demonstrations of power, above all during papal visits; on the inside fear, compulsion, abuse of power, hypocrisy, denunciation, silence imposed by penance, humiliations, and lack of ecumenical hospitality. The Vatican shows itself to be Europe's last absolutist state.

Küng claims that since his own confrontation with Rome the crackdown on dissenting theologians has grown more and more intense, and his picture of the way the Vatican works today is sinister: 'The Congregation for the Doctrine of the Faith collects denunciations every day from all over the world. And if someone does not obey, he will be deposed. They will say, "We don't burn people at the stake any more." They don't burn people physically, but they burn them psychologically instead.'

Cardinal Poupard, the suave Parisian who took over Cardinal König's portfolio at the Secretariat for Non-believers, quotes with evident admiration John Paul's judgement on Gorbachev in the mid 1980s: 'Le problème pour Gorbachev, c'est changer le système sans changer de système' – which, roughly and inelegantly translated, means, 'Gorbachev's problem is to change the way the system works without changing the system itself.' That neatly encapsulates the challenge John Paul himself has faced in the 1990s as he sought to master the next phase of the Council's revolution.

12

A Notification

Dawn comes to Cochin with tropical speed, but the sluggish scene on the waters of the harbour slows it to timelessness. A huge and crudely hewn boat passes, carrying a new roof of woven coconut leaves to the bank opposite. One man punts ferociously at the front, his companion steers languidly from the back, and together they manoeuvre their craft, its load barely clear of the water, to catch the breeze in a tattered sail as they slip-slop their way across.

A canoe with four men comes to check the night's catch. Two beat their paddles on the hull as they move gently up the line of the nets, and their companions use the rhythm to ease the task of hauling them in. Clumps of green swirl across the slow-moving brown water, atolls and reefs of grasses and branches eddying in the currents. And, in the distance, stuccoed fronts, eaten by age and humidity amid the palms, evoke the seaports of southern Portugal and stir thoughts of colonial adventure.

Christianity came here when the memory of the historical Christ was still alive in the minds of men. St Thomas the Apostle is said to have stepped ashore in Kerala in southern India in AD 52. Five years earlier, a Roman merchant named Hippalus had discovered the monsoon winds, which shortened the journey across the Arabian Sea to a matter of weeks instead of months. According to legend, St Thomas landed at the ancient harbour of Musiris, where he founded a Christian community – the first of seven – before working his way north and east across the sub-continent to his martyrdom at Mylapore near Madras.

The point at which the apostolic feet first touched the soil of East Asia is marked by a monument of stunning vulgarity, a truly grotesque example of Western cultural imperialism. You bump your way for miles along narrow, broken roads, past pools and palm trees, and through villages where the people smile at you in friendly perplexity when you ask the way. Just as you are about to give up hope you reach a lagoon that opens on to the Arabian Sea, and on your right as you drive along the water's edge are two enormous fixed cantilevered fishing nets. Kublai Khan's traders brought the design to the region: each net is some fifteen feet square, and it takes a team of four to operate the system of counterweights when they are lowered into the water at high tide. There is an unspoken reproach to modern efficiency in their cumbersome beauty and the unhurried drill of the men who work them.

Ahead, complete with colonnaded arms reaching down to the water, stands an enormous blue and white replica of St Peter's in Rome. This magnificent piece of devotional kitsch announces itself as the 'Mar Thoma Pontifical Shrine – Cradle of Christianity in India'. There is a series of buildings next to the church in an even more startling colour scheme of red and white checked brick, one of which houses an elderly brother with a scruffy beard and a brown habit. An appropriate donation will secure his prayers for your good intentions, a quick lecture on St Thomas's journeys, and a visit to the mini-basilica.

The star attraction is concealed behind a pair of curving green glass doors under the dome. 'On the auspicious occasion of the 19th century celebrations of the Great Entrance of St Thomas to India,' as the official leaflet puts it, 'the Holy See thought to offer a befitting gift to St Thomas Christians in Kerala.' In 1953 Cardinal Eugene Tissèrant (who, a decade later, celebrated the Mass that opened the Second Vatican Council) came to Kerala bearing the Right Arm of the Apostle. A twist of a silver capstan and the glass doors slide back to reveal some eight inches of bone: the arm that touched the wounds of the Son of God.

Now Thomas, one of the Twelve, called the Twin, was not with them when Jesus came. So the other disciples told him: 'We have seen the Lord.' But he said to them, 'Unless I see in his hands the print of the nails, and place my finger in the mark of the nails, and place my hand in his side, I will not believe.' Now eight days later, his disciples were again in the house, and Thomas was with them. The doors were shut, but Jesus came and stood among them, and he said, 'Peace be with you.' Then he said to Thomas, 'Put your finger here, and see my hand; and put out your hand, and place it in my side; do not be faithless, but believing.' And Thomas answered him, 'My Lord and my God.'

Doubting Thomas was the most modern-minded of the apostles. But the doubts I found on the continent where he preached the gospel were of a distinctive kind. In Europe we doubt the existence of God, but Christianity remains the dominant religion for those who believe. In Asia the presence of a spiritual dimension in day-to-day life is widely accepted; the doubts are about which religion holds the truth.

The second evangelization of the region came with the arrival of the Portuguese in the fifteenth and early sixteenth centuries. In mainland India, the Catholic population is now spread right across the country, but in Sri Lanka the way in which pockets of Catholics are dispersed still reflects the pattern of colonial conquest: most are concentrated along the coast, where the Portuguese established their forts.

The Sri Lankan Church is small and fractured; it is just over a million strong and a third of its members are in Jaffna, cut off from the Church in the south of the island by the civil war. But it has some of the strength of a Church that has survived persecution. When the Dutch expelled the Portuguese and became the island's new colonial masters in the eighteenth century, Catholicism was suppressed. It survived underground, in part due to the heroic efforts of one Father Joseph Vaz. A Goan, Father Vaz slipped into the country in 1687 disguised as a beggar, and until his death twenty-four years later kept the Church alive by administering the sacraments in secret. He was an Oratorian, and by one of those curious twists of the thread that draw the Catholic story together, his picture has pride of place in Newman's chapel at the Birmingham Oratory.

No one would claim Sri Lanka as one of the great centres of world Catholicism, but in 1997 it earned itself a niche in Church history: the island produced the first victim of the ancient penalty of excom-munication since Vatican II. Though in his seventies when we met, Father Tissa Balasuriya gave me the overwhelming impression of a small boy intent on mischief. He was decked out in the trappings of an Asian prophet: a flowing white robe with hair of a colour and sweep to match. But the engaging falsetto giggle, and the way his eyes lit up whenever he produced a particularly outrageous idea suggested an adolescent taste for anarchic fun. *Mary and Human Liberation*, the book that got him into trouble, seems to me, first and foremost, a tremendous tease.

He knew he was choosing a dangerous target. The name of his

own order, the Oblates of Mary Immaculate, is a reminder of the special devotion the Catholic Church accords to the Virgin Mary as the Mother of God. The teachings that have grown up around her are thoroughly confusing to outsiders, and the way she keeps appearing in places like Lourdes and Fatima confirms the scepticism of those who believe that the Church feeds on superstition. Within the Church, Marian doctrine has often been a litmus test for dividing conservatives and progressives. During the Second Vatican Council one of the most arcane but fiercest debates turned on the question of whether she stands above the Church or should be regarded as one of its members. Cardinal König's eloquence managed to secure only a slim majority for the liberal position. And John Paul II's passionate and traditional devotion to Mary is well known.

Mary and Human Liberation takes the conventional idea of the Virgin and turns it inside out. Instead of a humble, other-worldly figure, eternal mother and virgin, Father Balasuriya offers us a feminist icon and political activist, a woman who played a full part in her Son's revolution against the establishment of the time and the ruling colonial power. He has arrived at this picture with the same kind of reversal of traditional theological methods that the Liberation Theologians used in Latin America. The old version, he explained to me, was based on a 'descending Mariology'. 'First we define Mary as Immaculate, Virgin, the Mother of God, and then we draw certain conclusions. The other is based on an ascending Mariology, where you see how she lived, how her life is shown in the scriptures.'

The problem is that there is not very much to go on, as Father Balasuriya freely admits. He makes much of the social radicalism of the Magnificat, the prayer with which Mary praises God in St Luke's gospel.

> He has shown strength with his arm,
> He has scattered the proud-hearted,
> He has cast the mighty from their thrones,
> And lifted up the lowly,
> He has filled the hungry with good things,
> And sent the rich away empty.

But even that was probably invented by St Luke, drawing on Old Testament sources, and most of the picture Father Balasuriya draws of Mary's life is pure conjecture: 'Not much of it is written,' he says, 'so we have to use our imagination.' He has made up his own Mary to suit his political message.

He has some fun while he does it. He questions the famous apparitions of the Virgin on the grounds that Our Lady of Fatima and of Lourdes failed to show a sufficiently well-developed social conscience.

For instance, at Lourdes, Mary appears to Bernadette and speaks of herself as the Immaculate Conception; but she does not say anything about the conditions of the working class of the day . . . Much less did Mary, appearing at Lourdes, even hint at the enormous harm being done in Africa by French military and economic expansion in the colonial empire. It would be interesting to know whether Mary ever appeared to British Christians to challenge them concerning the British presence in Ireland or India.

The way a rather cheeky book was transformed into an international *cause célèbre* seems to have taken everyone, including the main protagonists in the drama, by surprise, and the passions generated by the Balasuriya affair have uncovered some of the most sensitive pressure points in the Church today. The Sri Lankan bishops were stirred into action by plans to turn *Mary and Human Liberation* into a video. The book attracted little attention when it was first published in 1990, but the attempt to popularize it two years later alerted the Church. According to Bishop Malcolm Ranjith, whom Father Balasuriya regards as his principal persecutor in the local hierarchy, they were duty-bound to consider the contents of 'a film for common use among the faithful at the grass roots'.

Bishop Malcolm is an intelligent and articulate man, widely tipped for a cardinal's hat. But he believes the sensitivities of those less well-educated than himself should be respected. 'Very often,' he told me, 'those who protest are not necessarily the priests, bishops or theologians, but the common people.' The faithful, he argues, experience 'a sense of loss in their life' when traditional Catholic teaching is 'shattered or cast into serious doubt', because 'basic concepts of theology have become the foundations for their faith and their life'.

I find that kind of intellectual paternalism profoundly offensive. It patronizes ordinary members of the Church, relegates them to the role of children in their faith and implies they occupy a lower rank in the hierarchy of souls. It is the kind of logic totalitarian societies use to justify censorship and it represents a rejection of everything we have learned about the way knowledge can bring power to ordinary people. But if you spend some time in the fishing community where Father Balasuriya grew up, it makes perfect sense.

Negombo is around an hour's drive from the Sri Lankan capital, Colombo, and you know you are approaching Catholic country when the shrines start springing up along the roadside. The area is known as 'Little Rome', and the spirit that inspired the monument to St Thomas in Kerala has been at work here too. The main church is a vast pink neo-classical confection, tricked out with freshly painted white statues and flourishes like a wedding cake. It dwarfs the modest shops and shacks gathered around its feet, its ceilings are so high that crows fly across the frescoes, and giant saints line the nave and side-aisles. What can these people make of the eight-foot Joan of Arc towering above them as they pray? And why is St Augustine of Hippo, Africa's most famous theologian, as white and blond as a Swede?

This is Mary's church – *Ecclesia Beatae Virgini Dedicata*, as its west front declares in uncompromising Latin. Women in mantillas mumble the rosary before Mass, and signs of Marian devotion are everywhere. Beyond the harbour, along the coast where the fishing families live, Mary is an even more powerful presence. One of her churches is built on a point, which the boats pass every dawn on their way to the fishing grounds. There is a statue of the Virgin high in the walls of the tower facing the water, and each morning the fishermen lower the sails of their junks for a moment to pray to her for a good catch before they make for the open sea. Mary is woven into the culture here in a way John Paul would recognize from the peasant communities in the Tatra mountains around Kraków. The church boasts another statue of the Virgin, which is thought to bring good fortune, and once a year it is carried at the head of a procession into the village. It is a tiny thing, and can be easily accommodated in a home; it is moved with song and ritual from house to house, and left for a week or so at each so that its blessings will be widely dispersed. This is the old faith of the dark, numinous St Mary's Church in Kraków. Its roots long pre-date the Second Vatican Council, and it is easy to see why the bishops were reluctant to risk disturbing them.

Father Dalston Forbes, a theologian and, like Father Balasuriya, a member of the Oblates of Mary Immaculate, points out that most of the new theological work in Sri Lanka since the Council has been written in English, and so is even more inaccessible to people like the Catholics of Negombo: 'The upper élite know what's happening,' he said, 'but ordinary Catholics are not used to feminist theology, Liberation Theology and modern exegesis. So it comes as a shock to them.' The prospect of *Mary and Human Liberation* being widely distributed as a video raised the spectre of a head-on collision between pre- and post-Conciliar Catholicism.

In December 1992 an 'Ad Hoc Theological Commission' of four, Father Forbes among them, was set up to study Tissa Balasuriya's book, and the following month its author was summoned to appear before them. Everyone has their own story about why things then went so horribly wrong: Father Balasuriya says he wasn't given a chance to explain himself properly; Bishop Malcolm blames him for blabbing to the press; and Father Forbes says he was bewildered by the way the hierarchy took matters into their own hands without giving their own commission time to consider the book further.

The turbulent priest was told not to translate his work into Sinhalese, and in the summer of 1994, some four years after *Mary and Human Liberation* first came out, the Bishops Conference of Sri Lanka issued a statement through the *Catholic Messenger* in which they 'admonished the faithful to refrain from reading this book, as it could be detrimental to their faith'.

The affair might still have sunk without much trace, as a curiosity in a far-flung province of the Church, had not Rome weighed in with its full authority. The month after the statement from the Sri Lankan bishops had been released, Cardinal Ratzinger's Sacred Congregation for the Doctrine of the Faith announced that it was taking the matter out of the hands of the local Church. Even some of Father Balasuriya's staunchest allies concede that his book contains theological errors that go beyond a clever joke about Mariology. In the course of reflecting on the Virgin's freedom from stain of sin, *Mary and Human Liberation* calls into question the doctrine of Original Sin itself. His conclusions about sin – like his conclusions about Mary – are based on his observation of the world around him rather than the Church's traditional teaching. One of my BBC colleagues was injured during my visit to Sri Lanka, and Father Balasuriya and I spent an evening together in hospital while she underwent a minor operation. While we were there a baby was brought out of the operating theatre after being born by Caesarean section. 'Now how,' demanded Father Balasuriya, 'could anyone take that baby in the hand and say, "This is a child of Satan"? . . . I have no difficulty in believing that a child or a baby has an inclination towards being selfish, or that we are born into a world of sin, but I do not accept that a baby is born alienated from God.'

The Sacred Congregation for the Doctrine of the Faith argued that the way Father Balasuriya understands Original Sin negates the idea of redemption and therefore puts a question mark over Christ's redemptive mission on earth. Some of the finest minds in the Vatican were set to work on this obscure theologian's modest volume, and what they came up with provides an intriguing insight into the way those minds work. 'Some Observations on the book *Mary and Human Liberation*' is a meticulously footnoted and precisely argued dissection of the original text, carefully sectioned and sub-sectioned under such headings as 'Methodological Deficiencies' and 'Hermeneutic Principles Proposed by Fr Balasuriya'. It is quite clear that what really got under the Vatican's skin was the hint of insurrection. The note that accompanied the 'Observations' when they were sent to Father Balasuriya stated that he was required to 'withdraw the opinions that are erroneous and contrary to the faith'. Authority was the issue here, just as it had been in Latin America. Cardinal Ratzinger told me quite frankly that it was the revolutionary cast of the book that made it open to condemnation: 'He [Father Balasuriya] said that the whole edifice of dogmas was a means for the hierarchy to exercise power; in particular, the fear of sin, generated by the concept of Original Sin, served the hierarchy to keep the people down and preserve their power over them . . . His programme was to bring this edifice down and develop an ideology of liberation in its place, which differed slightly from the one in Latin America, but still had a lot in common with it.'

The heretic was sent a Profession of Faith to sign. Its thirty-five clauses leave absolutely no room for deviation from the strictest interpretation of orthodox Church teaching.

32. I also firmly accept and hold each and everything that is proposed by that same Church definitely with regard to doctrine concerning faith and morals.

In particular:

33.   I acknowledge that Christ, in calling only men as His Apostles, did not proceed from sociological or cultural motives peculiar to His time but rather He acted in a completely free and sovereign manner.

34.   Therefore, I firmly accept and hold that the Church has no authority whatsoever to confer priestly ordination on women.

35.   What is more, I adhere with religious submission of will and intellect to the teachings which either the Roman pontiff or the College of Bishops enunciate when they exercise the authentic Magisterium even if they proclaim those teachings in an act that is not definitive.

Father Balasuriya was being asked to sign away his freedom of thought. Just as those who wrote the prayer-books of my childhood believed that every moment of life was a fitting subject for prayer, the Sacred Congregation for the Doctrine of the Faith operates as if no corner of the mind is outside its jurisdiction. Even some of the inquisitors blanched at the document from Rome. Father Forbes called it a 'pot-pourri, a hotch-potch . . . a series of cuttings from different Councils, different articles of faith, from Vatican One and Vatican Two and from some of the documents of the Roman Curia'. Tissa Balasuriya refused to sign, and Father Forbes believes he was right. In so doing, as well as challenging Rome's authority, Father Balasuriya had touched on an even more sensitive nerve in the modern Church: the debate over the nature of Truth.

In January 1995, in the midst of Father Balasuriya's row with Rome, Pope John Paul II visited Sri Lanka. It was the final stop on a gruelling 20,000-mile tour through Asia and the Pacific. In the Philippines he had been buoyed up by a congregation of four million people at a Mass in Manila, but by the time he reached Sri Lanka he was exhausted and, to make matters worse, the air-conditioning in his popemobile went wrong. It blew out hot air on the twenty-mile journey from the airport to the capital. The high point of the visit had been intended to be the beatification of Father Vaz, the Oratorian from Goa who had kept the Faith alive during the Dutch persecution. Instead it is remembered because the local Buddhist leadership boycotted a meeting with John Paul. In *Crossing the Threshold of Hope*, his best-selling book published the previous year, the Pope described Buddhism as 'in large measure an atheistic system', and distinguished between the Catholic and Buddhist ideas of salvation. The Buddhist ideal of nirvana is, John Paul writes, 'almost exclusively negative', and 'a state of perfect indifference to the world'. In Buddhism, according to the Pope, 'We do not free ourselves from evil through the good that comes from God; we liberate ourselves only through detachment from the world, which is bad.'

Buddhist leaders in Sri Lanka found the remarks offensive. The aggressive enthusiasm of some Christian missionaries during the colonial period had left an unfortunate legacy of bad blood between Buddhists and Christians. The British had abolished Buddhism's special status as the state religion, and after independence Buddhist monks led a nationalist challenge to the country's Christian leadership. The Pope's book stirred ancient memories and Buddhist monks demonstrated on the streets of Colombo, demanding a papal retraction.

John Paul did his best to repair the damage at his arrival ceremony. He expressed his 'highest regard for the followers of Buddhism'. 'I ardently hope,' he said, 'that my visit will strengthen the goodwill between us.' The one thing John Paul would not do was apologize – for the simple reason that he did not believe he had said anything wrong. The circumstances of his visit and the realities of the time and the place might demand a conciliatory approach, but nothing could change the facts: Buddhism does not reflect the Truth as John Paul understands it. His ideological policeman, Cardinal Ratzinger, expressed the conventional Catholic view even more bluntly: he was quoted in the French weekly *L'Express* as describing Buddhism as 'spiritual auto-eroticism'.

John Paul believes that Truth is absolute. It is the theme of his most famous and uncompromising encyclical *Veritatis Splendor*, the Splendour of the Truth. Tissa Balasuriya believes that truth has no capital letter, and is relative, not absolute. One chapter of *Mary and Human Liberation* is dedicated to 'Presuppositions in Theology'. It argues that all theological ideas – including those of Jesus – must be understood in the context of the people, time and place that produced them: 'Even a founder's teachings are conditioned by the culture of that time.' As for the body of Truth built up over the centuries by the Church's theologians with the guidance of the Holy Spirit, 'The later evolutions are influenced by the course of history and the particular evolution of a religious community.'

This is relativism of the most outrageous kind, and the Sacred Congregation for the Doctrine of the Faith quite rightly concluded that they had the evidence they needed for a conviction. The problem was that Father Balasuriya's views were and are widely shared by other Asian theologians. Father Aloysius Peres, a Jesuit, has a reputation that attracts students from all over Asia to his centre just outside Colombo. He has dedicated himself to developing a theology rooted in the context of his time and place. The Sri Lanka of the late twentieth century is seventy per cent Buddhist, and Buddhism, he believes, has been the principal civilizing influence on the island for centuries. Father Peres has immersed himself in the study of the belief system so peremptorily dismissed by Cardinal Ratzinger and Pope John Paul II, and believes that his mission is blessed by the Second Vatican Council. It was, he told me, 'the first Council which gave us a positive appreciation of other religions. It gave us a mandate that was long overdue.'

Father Peres sees the Balasuriya affair as 'a typical incident that shows the conflict that Vatican II has created'. He regards that as a mark of 'the success of the Council'. It was not, he says, a reforming Council but a 'renewal Council'. 'Now, renewal is a very chaotic thing. Reform is programmed – from top to bottom, from centre to periphery. Renewal is something that is caught at the periphery and moves into the centre – and it shakes the centre.'

In May 1996 Tissa Balasuriya was given a deadline by which he must sign the profession of faith or risk excommunication. He refused to do so, but was granted a stay of execution while an increasingly ill-tempered correspondence bounced backwards and forwards between Rome and Sri Lanka. On 7 December 1996 he was summoned to appear before the papal nuncio in Colombo and read a Notification of Excommunication. He was warned that it would be published and take effect unless he signed the profession of faith forthwith. The Notification is datelined 'Rome, from the offices of the Congregation for the Doctrine of the Faith, 2 January 1997, memorial of Saint Basil the Great and Saint Gregory of Nazianzen, Bishops and Doctors of the Church'.

. . . In publishing this Notification, the Congregation is obliged to declare that Father Balasuriya has deviated from the integrity of the truth of the

Catholic faith and, therefore, cannot be considered a Catholic theologian; moreover, he has incurred excommunication 'latae sententiae'.

The Sovereign Pontiff John Paul II, at the Audience granted to the undersigned Cardinal Prefect [Joseph Ratzinger], approved this Notification . . . and ordered it to be published.

In strictly legal terms, it simply meant that Tissa Balasuriya could not give or receive the sacraments, or exercise jurisdiction in the Church. Yet although it stopped him acting as a priest it did not stop him being one. Father Balasuriya remained a member of the Oblates of Mary Immaculate, and continued to live in the congregation's house in Sri Lanka.

But there was real pain in the way he spoke about what had happened to him – the pain of someone who feels rejected by their family. Tissa Balasuriya has served the church for most of his adult life; he joined the Oblates in 1945, studied in Rome and was ordained there in 1952. His parents, who had initially opposed his ordination, came to Rome for the ceremony and together they were granted an audience with Pius XII the following day. Most of Balasuriya's inheritance from his father went towards the Centre for Society and Religion, created in the early 1970s to advance his work with the poor. His excommunication, he told me, was 'painful in the sense that the Mother Church, to whom I have given my life, should treat me like this'.

The official Church line is that he inflicted the wound upon himself. Marcus Fernando, Archbishop of Colombo, told me that it came down to the requirement to accept the rules of Church membership: 'You have either to believe totally or you are not in that denomination. You cannot have half of it, or three-quarters of it. It has to be a hundred per cent or you are not what you profess to be.'

I suggested to Father Balasuriya that if you belong to a club it is not unreasonable that its other members should expect you to obey the rules. 'This is not,' he reminded me sternly, 'just a club. The Church is a necessary community and I have a right to belong to it – a birthright. Nobody can send me out of the Church.' However questionable his theology may be on some points, it is difficult to disagree with his view of the Church. Vatican II defined it not as an institution but as 'the People of God'.

Father Aloysius Peres likes to tell a story from Sri Lankan literature to illuminate his analysis of the Balasuriya affair. 'It is about an elephant and a chameleon – a tiny little animal. The elephant threw his weight around too much in the forest and didn't allow the other animals to behave as they wanted. And the chameleon said, "I'll take him on." He entered the elephant's trunk and started scratching and gnawing at the elephant's brain, and the poor elephant fell ill. It was a revelation: a little animal can put a big elephant in difficulty.'

Excommunication did not silence Tissa Balasuriya, and for Asia's theologians, his treatment by the Church became a test case.

13

Don't Judge the Sounds

Providence chose to bring together Father Dominic and the BBC in an unconventional manner. He woke me from my Sunday-morning stupor by saying, 'Crap!' very distinctly and with firm emphasis from the pulpit of the Church of St Thomas More in Chelsea. The parish has a claim to be one of the richest and grandest in the world, but no one turned a hair: they had grown accustomed to the ways of the visiting priest from Delhi. But I was just a visitor and was intrigued.

Six months later we were sitting in a boat together on the Ganges watching the sun rise over the holy city of Varanasi. Father Dominic had become our guide on our journey through his native India. I asked him how many times Hindus can be reincarnated before the life-cycle is over, and he shouted the question over to the boatman who was piloting our camera crew through the bits of bamboo biers, charred wood from funeral pyres and floating oil lamps that littered the surface of the river. 'Eighty-four thousand,' came the answer across the water.

What takes place on the ghats – the giant steps that lead down to the holy river – is especially bemusing to anyone familiar with the rites of the Roman Church. We are accustomed to think of religious ritual as something ordered and structured, an event that progresses from a clearly defined beginning to a definite end. The scenes acted out by the Ganges are recognizable as religious ritual, but they seem improvised and idiosyncratic, and they begin and end without warning or apparent reason. Everyone piles down the steps, singing his or her own hymn, and splashes into the water for a purifying dunking without any thought of form or ceremony. Prayer and daily chores are cheerfully combined: a group of women were doing their laundry in the river, and one had stuck cow dung all over the riverbank walls to dry so that she could sell it as cooking fuel.

The informality of the scene is a reflection of the belief system that inspired it. 'You can be an atheist, a monotheist or a polytheist and still remain a Hindu,' Father Dominic told me as we bobbed past a gaggle of priests sitting under umbrellas. There are 330 million Hindu gods and demons, and a religion with so many deities, so self-evidently based in myth, has none of the Catholic hang-ups about sharing its claim to the truth, or distinguishing between historical truth and symbol.

That might explain the tolerance of those on the ghats that morning. We had come to film a Catholic priest, Father Francis Barbossa, who had developed a representation of Christ's passion in traditional Indian dance. It was a beautiful, expressive performance, and attracted a crowd. They applauded appreciatively, and none seemed put out by the Christian theme. Imagine the effect of saying Mass in Mecca, or getting out a prayer mat in St Peter's Square.

It is that very tolerance which, somewhat perversely, worries Cardinal Ratzinger, who believes that the religions of the East present some of the most serious challenges the Church will face in the next millennium. He is already brandishing a new piece of jargon in anticipation of the battle: the problem with Hinduism, says the Cardinal, is its 'inclusivism'. Each new religious force that appears in India, he argues, 'is integrated into the comprehensive and diverse edifice of religious traditions and somehow deprived of its strength'. Many Hindus, he says, 'have a certain affection for Jesus, whom they view as a sublime, pure figure' – a cause for rejoicing in Rome, one might have thought. Not so. They revere him, the Cardinal went on, as 'a figure that is part of the whole religious edifice of India, and they grant him equal status with many others', and that leads to 'this real danger of inclusivism, which fails to reveal the individual and new character of Christianity'.

Hindus do not proselytize – you are either born Hindu or you are not – but Hinduism has the capacity to swallow other religions whole, rather than consuming them bit by bit by picking off individual members. Cardinal Ratzinger fears that the One Holy, Catholic and Apostolic Church will be absorbed and tamed in the rich mix of India's beliefs. Only in Asia, and especially in India, does Catholicism meet religions as ancient and well-developed as itself but entirely outside its traditional frame of reference. 'India is unique,' says Alan de Lastic, the Archbishop of Delhi. 'There is no other nation in the world which has within its confines all the great religions.' Islam and Judaism are Christianity's close cousins, and Islam is a long-standing competitor in the battle for souls. But Hinduism, Buddhism, Sikhism and Jainism come from another family altogether. Hinduism, especially, is ancient, robust and vast. Its roots stretch back at least a thousand years before the birth of Christ, and it is practised by 80 per cent of Indians. In crude figures, that is some 670 million people, or two-thirds of the membership of the Catholic Church worldwide.

The banks of the Ganges are as awe-inspiring as St Peter's Square. Stand there for a moment and you immediately understand the inadequacy of the old Catholic doctrine *'nulla salus extra Ecclesia'*, there is no salvation outside the Church. In Varanasi the impressions tumble over you so fast they are impossible to process – the cavernous shops selling everything from silk to cigarettes, the snaking lines of little boys carrying garish lamps on their heads, the magnificently painted elephant blocking the traffic in a narrow street, the wedding parties, performing monkeys and brass bands, and the way that the gas lights in the old town down towards the river flicker over the faces. The sheer mass of humanity is overwhelming. There is too much of God's creation here to be left out of the plan of salvation.

And yet that is what Asian Catholics were once required to believe. I spoke to one elderly bishop who recalled having it drummed into him by his theology teacher at the Gregorian University in Rome: 'I would have been about twenty-one at the time and this professor went on and on, banging the desk and trying to impress us, "Salvation is only possible within the visible Catholic Church." I still remember that somewhere inside myself I couldn't agree. I was thinking that in my own country only a tiny handful will be saved . . . then thinking of the whole of Asia, where Christians are less than one per cent. Surely God's plan of salvation could not be so bad?' He was forced to suppress his doubts: in those pre-Conciliar days the style of teaching did not encourage debate.

At Vatican II the Church's attitude to other religions underwent a radical reassessment, and the Asian bishops played an important part in it. Angelo Fernandes, the retired Archbishop of Delhi, remembers going to Rome for the Council as a second-class citizen. While the European bishops had national colleges around the Vatican and arrived with an impressive support staff of theologians, the Indian team 'had no college of our own, no typewriters, no experts. All that we did had to come out of our heads and our own experience.' But they were given the chance to make use of that experience.

When the draft of one of the key Council documents *Gaudium et Spes*, the Church in the World, was attacked for being too conservative in its approach and too Western in its orientation, the Archbishop was one of seven Asians 'roped in to try to apply some sort of remedial treatment'. He remembers the benevolent but patronizing attitude of some of the Western bishops. 'One of them asked, "What can we do for these people far away there in the East?" I put my hand up and said, "Excuse me, all of you, I come from there, and if this Council is to be a universal one you have to take cognizance of our existence."'

The Asian bishops were rewarded with a profound change in the Church's attitude to other religions. Paragraph 16 of *Lumen Gentium*, the Pastoral Constitution of the Church, contained the seeds of a revolution: 'Those who have not yet received the Gospel,' it begins, 'are related in various ways to the People of God.' The paragraph then lists the different groups of mankind who can be saved.

Nor is God distant from those who in shadows and images seek the unknown God, for it is He who gives to all men life and breath and all things, and as Saviour wills that all men be saved. Those also can attain to salvation who through no fault of their own do not know the Gospel of Christ or his Church, yet sincerely seek God, and moved by Grace, strive by their deeds to do His will as it is known to them by the dictates of their conscience. Nor does Divine Providence deny the help necessary for salvation to those who, without blame on their part, have not yet arrived at an explicit knowledge of God, yet with His Grace strive to lead a better life. Whatever good or truth is found amongst them is looked upon by the Church as a preparation for the Gospel.

For the generation of priests ordained after the Council, like Father Dominic, it was an inspiration. The Council message, he said, was that 'there are seeds of truth and rays of hope in other religions too'. If social injustice provided the context in which the Latin-American Church responded to Vatican II, the experience of being a minority faith defined the response of the Church in Asia. Like the Latin-American Church, the Indian Church held its own conference to interpret the teachings of the Council: a year after the Latin-American bishops met at Medellín, their Indian counterparts gathered for the Church in India Seminar at Bangalore. It began a process of the 'Indianization' of the Church, vividly symbolized at the 'Indian Rite Mass', which was celebrated in the course of the seminar. Today, the use of Indian language and ritual in the celebration of the Mass is commonplace – but in 1969 the scene, as described in Benny Aguiar's essay on the Indian Church in *Modern Catholicism*, was dramatically new: 'A hundred priests walked barefoot to the altar, the chief celebrant vested in a saffron shawl wrapped around his shoulders. Nuns and lay people squatted on the floor. As the priests came in, they made an *anjali hasta* [a profound bow with hands joined] to the crucifix. Instead of kissing the altar, they touched it with their fingers, which they then brought to their foreheads. Then followed the lighting of the seven wicks of a tall, slender brass lamp, which signified Christ, the Light of the World. At the Offertory there was the *aarti*, the waving around of a *thali* or brass platter filled with fruits, a broken coconut, some joss-sticks and the bread and wine. At the Elevation, the celebrants prostrated themselves full length on the floor in a gesture called the *panchanga pranama* . . .'

The Bangalore seminar passed a resolution encouraging the development of Catholic ashrams. The ashram is a distinctively Indian phenomenon: a place of contemplation and spiritual searching, centred around a 'guru', and open to all who seek the truth through meditation. Catholic ashrams soon sprang up all over India, and they have become the vanguard of the Indian Church's encounter with other religions.

The ashram at which I met Sister Lioba, of the Institute of the Blessed Virgin Mary, is in Varanasi. Everything about the way it is organized is designed to ensure that it does not present an aggressive challenge to Hinduism in this holiest of Hindu cities. Hundreds of people come to hear the guru, Father Amildev, preach in the ashram's makeshift meeting-hall. It is a heroic performance simply in terms of physical endurance. His fortnightly prayer meetings last from ten in the morning until four in the afternoon, and he is on his feet throughout with only a short break for lunch. Occasionally, a certain weariness of imagination shows through: when we visited the ashram he asked for prayers for us – which was kind – but strung out the theme to a slightly desperate stage when he blessed each of us individually and our camera. Almost all of those who come are Hindus, and traditional Catholic symbols have been redesigned to make them feel at home. The circular chapel looks more like a temple than a church. Instead of a holy water stoop inside the door, there is a pool just outside where people dip their hands as in the Hindu rite of purification. Before Mass there was a *parikrama*, the procession with which Hindus express their respect for the divine presence, and each member of the congregation received a *tika* – the coloured marking with which Hindus adorn their foreheads.

Most of the pilgrims are also very poor. None is given direct material help as a matter of principle – indeed, they are asked to contribute to a collection on behalf of the ashram just before the lunch-break. But they are offered the hope that Christianity will make a difference to their material condition. There was a large box under Father Amildev's podium where they could place their petitions, and they bring bottles so that they can take home holy water he has blessed. Sister Lioba said that some of them 'take it internally', and during the prayer session those who had been cured of sore throats and other ailments were encouraged to declare themselves.

Because they are excluded by the caste system, those who come to Matridham ashram are natural targets for conversion. But Sister Lioba and Father Amildev recoiled at the suggestion that they are looking for converts. They do sometimes baptize new members of the Church, but they insisted it is rare, and seemed almost embarrassed by the idea. Their determined humility about the power of their faith is in part a recognition of the realities of life as a minority religion. They once converted a high-caste Hindu woman, who joined the community at the ashram. Her brother was ashamed by this act of apostasy and tried to kidnap her, and his threats to her life became so serious that she had to be taken into protective custody by the police. The natural tolerance at the heart of Hinduism has not prevented the development of a fanatical and sometimes violent tendency within it, and the group who run the Matridham ashram are conscious that their state is a stronghold of the fundamentalist Hindu party, the BJP.

Between 1994 and 1998 some forty attacks on Catholic priests and nuns were recorded, many in the neighbouring states of Bihar and

Madhya Pradesh where the Church runs similar centres for those excluded from the caste system. One priest was tortured with cigarette ends and beheaded. Two others and a seminarian were hacked to death after having their ears and noses cut off with axes. And, in an attack that caused particular concern because it was carried out with the apparent complicity of the local police, a Father Christudas was stripped naked and paraded through the streets of a rural town by students at his own school.

But the way in which Father Amildev and Sister Lioba approach conversion is not only from prudent caution: in India the Council's endorsement of respect for other religions has worked its way through to an entirely new approach to evangelization. Once, the Church held that it was right to compel people to accept the Faith; in the days when it taught that non-Catholics could not be saved that was perfectly logical. Today, Indian Catholics seek to do no more than offer the Christian message in the hope that those outside it will respond. 'Our duty,' says Archbishop de Lastic, 'is to preach and proclaim Christ.' But he stressed that conversion must be a 'free personal act', something that is 'left to each individual person by a gift of God'.

The change had led to curious ironies in the position of many Indian priests. Father Dominic is a member of the Societas Verbi Divini, the Society of the Divine Word, a missionary order founded by a German priest in Holland in 1875. The SVD has been working in Asia for more than a hundred years, and has trained thousands of young men for the priesthood. Most of its members are now Asians working in their own countries, not Europeans proselytizing abroad. Father Dominic and the other priests of his generation would almost certainly not be what they are had it not been for the missionaries. But they see their mission in terms that would have been incomprehensible to the congregation's founders. 'What we have to do is help people discover their own faith and to live their faith . . .' he told me. 'If people can be led to discover their own values in their own religion and live as better human beings, that's a great achievement for a missionary.'

The new openness to other faiths has led to a burst of creative energy among India's theologians. Just as Latin America's theology entered a period of exhaustion and uncertainty after the collapse of Communism and the conflict with Rome, Asia's thinkers picked up the torch of innovation. And the keen eyes of Cardinal Ratzinger swivelled from West to East. 'Asian theology is still a very young theology and is in a stage of experimenting, which I find appropriate and interesting,' he said. But he added an important qualification: 'I think it is also appropriate that it is guided in that process by the older Churches and theologies.' Cardinal Ratzinger may sound benign when he talks of 'guiding' Asia's theologians, but his track record suggests that he will use all the power at his disposal to impose Rome's will on them if he feels it necessary.

When I visited the staff at the Viyadoti College in Delhi I discovered that they saw this as a real threat. The college's governing body had just been told to expect an Apostolic Visitation, an official commission that would study the way they are teaching theology. The college is run by the Jesuits; there are now some three and a half thousand Jesuit priests in India, which makes it the largest province of the Society of Jesus anywhere outside the United States. They are in the forefront of the new ideas in India just as they were in the development and implementation of Liberation Theology in Latin America. The teaching at Viyadoti – the name means Wisdom and Light – is certainly radical: Mother Teresa was criticized for dealing with the symptoms of poverty instead of attacking its causes.

Viyadoti's theological star is Father Samuel Ryan, one of the grand old men of Asian theology. He is careful in his choice of words, but he comes close to arguing two positions that would bring him into direct confrontation with the Vatican: that there is not much to choose between Catholicism and any other religion, and that the way Rome exercises its power is not just a hangover from European colonialism but a legacy of the Roman Empire. 'All religions,' he told me, 'are God's gift to his people . . . They're all imperfect in themselves.' When I asked him directly whether he would put all religions on an equal footing he equivocated: ' "Equal" often has a mathematical conno-tation. They're not on an equal footing, they are different . . . The differences are as important as what is in common, they make for the wealth and richness, both of God's approach to us and of the human experience. Therefore I hesitate to use the words "equal" or "equal footing", just as we do not speak of the rose and the lotus being on an equal footing.'

As to the Church's claim to have a unique understanding of the

Truth: 'For me, as a Catholic, the revelation in Jesus Christ is unique and Christ himself is unique, but this experience of uniqueness enables me to listen sympathetically to and to understand in some measure the sense of uniqueness and the language of uniqueness that I perceive in other religions.'

I asked Father Ryan about the forthcoming official inspection of the college and the evident anxiety he and other Asian theologians felt about the attentions of Rome. He said: 'An enthusiastic evangelization of the whole world was planned and attempted in the colonial era, but the contradiction between preaching the gospel of freedom in a situation of colonial conquest and exploitation was not attended to. Now that colonialism, at least of the political type, is on the decline . . . the gospel is presented as an invitation, as a grace and a privilege and not at gunpoint. If the old mentality persists, hiddenly, subconsciously, you can feel anxious.'

'You think there's still a bit of the colonial beast at work in the Vatican, do you?'

'This is a possibility. It is the duty of those concerned to examine themselves . . .' Father Ryan replied.

The college rector, Father George Mia, gave us a flavour of the way in which the new generation of Indian priests is being taught by inviting us to attend one of his lectures. His purpose was to reinterpret the New Testament in the light of the idea that elements of God's Truth are found in other religions. He chose the Gospel of St John for his text. Some of it was intriguing. Father Mia argued that the constant references to things that happen 'so that the scriptures may be fulfilled' was a clue to the fact that Christ's life fulfilled scriptural messages in non-Biblical religions. To illustrate the point he quoted a verse from Hindu scripture which has a very Christian echo: 'From untruth lead me to truth, from darkness lead me to light, from death lead me to immortality.' Some of it seemed like sophistry. Father Mia told his students that when Christ said, 'No one comes to the Father except through me,' He was really saying that only by following His example as a loving son can humanity experience God as a father. It is a nice idea, but surely Christ was saying that He is the true way to salvation. It is difficult to fault the logic of all those missionaries who used that text as their justification for exporting the Christian faith all over the world.

Talking to Father Mia I began to feel that I was being led gently but firmly beyond the boundaries of the Church. 'God,' he believes, 'is a mystery so great that it cannot be exhausted by any one religion,' so it is not just acceptable but necessary to look for truths in other religions. No one person, he argues, can fully experience God, not even Jesus, because he is limited by his humanity. I had always thought that Christ was both fully human and fully divine – indeed, I cannot see that the Christian faith means very much at all if that is not true.

The sense of being cut adrift from my intellectual moorings became positively vertiginous at the Samiksha ashram in Kerala. It is set in lush gardens on the banks of a wide, slow, muddy river all set about with palm trees. The guru was bearded, saffron-robed and barefoot. He leads meditation in a small round building above the riverbank. His followers in the search for truth sit with their legs tucked neatly under eight-inch high stools rather like kneelers. They are instructed to 'think you are a tree', and 'sense your rootedness in the earth'. 'Don't judge the sounds, just listen,' the guru tells them as the noise of the forest, undisturbed by any twentieth-century dissonance, seeps through the open doors. 'Reach for the divine in the centre of your being.'

The guru is also known as Father Sebastian, a member of the Society of Jesus who has studied in Germany where he heard both Hans Küng and Cardinal Ratzinger lecture. He is a devoted subscriber to the *Tablet*, the influential London-based Catholic journal, which makes its way from Hammersmith to the backwaters of Kerala each week. Father Sebastian has the precision of thought of the well-trained Jesuit mind, and he helped to crystallize my unease about the ideas that he and the new theologians of the Viyadoti College are developing. He distinguishes between spirituality and religiosity, and he describes spirituality as 'the experience of being gripped by the divine spirit, and at that level one does not ask what religion one belongs to'. The belief that spirituality can be directed through an institutional religion lies at the heart of Roman Catholicism. The idea of a truly Catholic Church, which embraces believers from Delhi to Dorset, becomes meaningless without some kind of definition.

Father Sebastian was an enthusiastic champion of Tissa Balasuriya's campaign against his sentence of excommunication. He described excommunication as 'a cruel punishment for the Roman Church to use on someone in this century'. He had no doubt that it was intended as 'a signal of warning for the rest' of Asia's new theologians, and added, 'I hope Rome will take note of the protests coming not only from Asia, but from all over the world.'

Almost every one of the Asian theologians and priests I spoke to voiced their support for Father Balasuriya, although even the most radical in their thinking accepted that he had moved outside the boundaries of Catholic teaching. His case became the focus for a debate that went well beyond the arena of Asian theology: it came to be seen as a test of the Church's human-rights record. There were protests from Latin America, the United States and Europe about the way the Church had dealt with him. The *Tablet* weighed in with thunderous leader columns:

There is a widespread opinion in the Church that the treatment of Fr Tissa Balasuriya, whatever judgement may be made upon his writings, and even if he himself has also been obdurate, is indefensible. Must we wait 200 years before Rome gets round to an apology?

That was written in October 1997. In January 1998 a discreet announcement stated that Rome had found it possible to accept Father Balasuriya back into the Church. A small ceremony in Colombo marked the lifting of his excommunication. There was no apology, but there seems little doubt that the constant pressure had made itself felt in Rome. I asked Cardinal Ratzinger whether he accepted that the affair had been badly handled. 'Our political experience is limited,' he said, 'and one will have to find ways and means of how to do this in a more transparent way and explain it better to people if, God forbid, such a thing should happen again.' That is about as close to an admission of poor judgement as the Sacred Congregation for the Doctrine of the Faith is ever likely to get.

Father Aloysius Peres said that while the Sacred Congregation may have intended the Balasuriya affair to be a warning to Asia's theologians, it has turned out to be a warning to the Vatican about the independent spirit of the Asian Church. It has also been a reminder of the way open societies have rewritten the rules by which the Church conducts its business. Father Balasuriya himself believes that 'With the fax and the e-mail and the broadcasting stations of the world I do not think dictatorship is possible any longer.'

The way the new openness to other religions has influenced Asia's Catholics touches on essentials of the Faith, and the debate over Asian theology could have a profound impact on the direction of the Church in the third millennium. But, as it prepares to join battle, the Vatican has once again been forced to confront the difficulty of imposing its discipline in the modern world. The strength of opposition to its actions from within its own ranks is especially worrying. A generation after the Council, pluralism is becoming part of the Catholic mindset.

14

The Very Sick

Finding a Milingo Mass in the prosperous countryside of northern Italy is like tracking down an illegal rave in the Home Counties. There is no official publicity, but somehow or other word of the location gets around among the aficionados. All we had by way of an address was the name of an industrial estate, and we got lost several times among the vineyards, cornfields and rich little towns around Bergamo before we reached it. There were no signs at the entrance to the estate, but the queues of cars and buses showed the way. The accents came from all over Italy – even from Naples and Calabria hundreds of miles away – and there were Austrian, French and Swiss voices, too.

The building at the end of their pilgrimage looked no different from the warehouses around it, a solid, squat rectangle of concrete. But instead of housing light-engineering parts or paper packaging, it had been roughly arranged as a church – a red-painted concrete divide had been erected at one end to provide space for a sacristy, and stations of the cross had been hung on the walls. There was a hamburger stall at the main entrance, and the impression that this was a live music event rather than a religious ceremony was strengthened by the presence of burly bouncers controlling the crowd. We were given a strict lecture about what we could and could not film, and one told us: 'We'll take your tape away if you break the rules.'

Most disturbing of all were the sounds. Ave Marias and Salve Reginas were sung as the building filled up, but above them there rose the keening of those possessed by demons. They were described by the officials as 'the very sick', and they were gathered in a group just to the right of the altar. Before Milingo's arrival, most of them were simply whimpering in anticipation of the struggle to come, but every so often one would erupt into an ecstasy. I saw a woman close to the front of the crowd being restrained by six bouncers lest she do violence to herself or those around her. She screamed with a ghastly, wrenching scream that seemed drawn from the depths of her being.

The Milingo story is one of the oddest in the modern Church, and just as Father Balasuriya's difficulties illuminate the conflict between the Vatican and the Church in Asia, so the strange case of the former Archbishop of Lusaka reflects the tensions within the post-Conciliar Church in Africa. It was not until 1942, when Emmanuel Milingo was twelve years old, that the White Fathers – a missionary order – opened a school close to his village of Mukwa in eastern Zambia, and he began his education. Until then he had spent his time herding his father's cattle, but the White Fathers who taught him quickly realized his talent. A generous Italian doctor sponsored his passage through seminary, and after ordination he rose quickly in a Zambian Church desperately short of local priests. He studied in Rome and Dublin, and first established a national reputation as a broadcaster during his time as the Zambian Church's secretary for communications. He became its leader at the remarkably young age of thirty-nine when he was consecrated Archbishop of Lusaka in 1969. Pope Paul VI, on the first ever visit by a pope to Africa, presided at the ceremony.

Four years later Emmanuel Milingo 'discovered the gift of healing'. He describes how a woman came to him with what sounded like the symptoms of psychiatric illness. She said she sometimes went for months consuming nothing but water and soft drinks, and 'She feared for her child because she did not think him a human being. She constantly heard voices speaking to her.'

Milingo says he tried praying with her, hearing her confession and celebrating Mass for her, all to no avail. 'Suddenly an idea glowed in my mind: "Look three times intently into her eyes and ask her to look three times intently into yours. Tell her to close her eyes a third time and order her to sleep. Then speak to her soul after signing her with the Sign of the Cross."' Milingo's career as a faith-healer had begun. It unleashed a firestorm in the Zambian Church. He attracted huge crowds with his faith-healing services – and was accused of being a witch-doctor.

The initial complaints to Rome came from other members of the Zambian episcopate, and Milingo's supporters in Zambia believe they were inspired by envy because of the popular enthusiasm he generated. According to Henry Msoni, a prominent member of the laity in Lusaka, 'even the head of state was frightened of him because of his healing sessions', and leaders of other Christian denominations began to resent that he was drawing their members away. Msoni says that some in the Catholic hierarchy suspected that Milingo was on the point of 'breaking away from Rome and forming his own Church'.

In February 1974, a year after he began his faith-healing, Archbishop Milingo received a letter from Rome. The Congregation for the Evangelization of Peoples – formerly the 'Propaganda Fidei', the curial department responsible for missionary churches – asked him to stop his healing sessions, which were by then causing a serious division in the Zambian Church. Milingo says he tried, but found popular demand impossible to resist: 'The people followed me wherever I was, at the office, at my home, and during my confirmation tours.' In 1977 the Zambian Episcopal Conference agreed that healing sessions could be held once a month, but that concession was withdrawn within less than a year, and in February 1978 Archbishop Milingo performed his last mass healing at the cathedral in Lusaka. So many people turned up that it had to be held outside.

He remained Archbishop of Lusaka, but relations with his fellow bishops became steadily more strained. In 1981 ugly gossip surrounded a member of the order of nuns the Archbishop had founded, the Pious Union of the Daughters of the Redeemer. One of the sisters was thought to be pregnant, and rumour ran that Milingo was responsible. The unfortunate nun had to submit to three medical examinations before the matter was laid to rest. The affair was symptomatic of the overheated atmosphere in a Church now riven with dissent and ill-feeling, and a cardinal and a bishop from Kenya were sent to investigate Milingo's case.

In April 1982 the Archbishop was summoned to Rome. What followed seems truly medieval and makes the treatment of Leonardo Boff appear enlightened by comparison. When he first arrived, Milingo was kept almost as a prisoner in the Vatican. He was forbidden to communicate with anyone at home in Zambia, and told not to appear in public places in case he was recognized and questioned. He was given medical and psychiatric tests, and put through four rigorous examinations on doctrinal questions by the prefect of the Congregation for the Evangelization of Peoples. Much of the questioning focused on reports that he had been 'speaking in tongues' during a confirmation service. There were also accusations to answer about the misuse of archdiocesan funds. It was a frightening experience, he told me, especially for someone with his background: 'You come from the countryside, from a shielded area, and there you are up before these ecclesiastical dignitaries . . . It was terrifying.'

For eighteen months Milingo remained in a state of limbo in the Vatican. He was still technically Archbishop of Lusaka, a post he steadfastly refused to resign. Eventually he was granted a private audience with Pope John Paul, and he agreed to resign in return for being allowed to continue with his faith-healing. He says the Pope promised him, 'We shall safeguard your healing apostolate.'

Since then Milingo has lived in a kind of internal exile, rather like that once endured by Soviet dissidents who were too popular to be silenced altogether. He was appointed Special Delegate to the Pontifical Commission for Migration and Tourism. It would be nice to think that the Vatican official who dreamed that up had a sense of humour, but I rather fear that was not the case. The job, which Milingo freely admits is not very taxing, came with a modest but well-placed apartment just outside St Peter's Square.

His forays across Italy for healing sessions like the one I witnessed in Bergamo are regarded with extreme suspicion by most of the country's hierarchy, but he remains fully in communion with the Catholic Church, and is no less a bishop than any other. The curious mixture of harshness and tolerance with which he had been treated stands in contrast with the rigidity of the Vatican's initial approach to the Balasuriya affair and reflects Rome's indulgently paternalistic attitude to the African Church at large.

Father Bob Lavertu is a Canadian priest of the White Fathers order that educated Emmanuel Milingo. His parish of Serenje is 150 kilometres long and 130 kilometres wide – roughly the size of Belgium. Until 1954 there was no Catholic presence there at all; he describes it as the 'forgotten child' – a huge tract of land between Zambia's Northern Province, where the first Catholic missionaries came in the 1890s, and the region around Lusaka. Even today there are large areas of the parish in which the people see their priest no more than two or three times a year.

When he first came to Zambia in the early 1960s, Father Lavertu officiated at the funeral of one of the last links with the original missionary Church in Africa, a man who had been freed from an Arab slave caravan. The White Fathers would approach the caravans when they stopped to camp for the night, and if they found a sick man or woman among those destined to be sold into slavery they would bargain for their freedom. The first two missions in the region were founded with redeemed slaves. 'The days of Livingstone,' says Father Lavertu, 'are not so very far remote.' The great Scottish explorer and missionary who discovered Victoria Falls died in this part of Africa in 1873. When the Second Vatican Council was called, the African Church was still in its infancy.

Africa's representation at the Council was tiny: only 311 of the two and a half thousand Council Fathers were from the continent, and only sixty were Africans, the rest being missionaries or expatriates in what was still essentially a colonial Church. But as the bishops were deliberating their revolution in Rome, the spirit of political independence was sweeping the colonial powers out of Africa. The winds of change blew through the African Church too. Just as Vatican II liberated the creative powers of the Asian Church with its openness to other religions, so it released new energies in the African Church by its recognition of the value of non-European cultures.

The image of a universal Church, which so struck those who witnessed the Council's opening ceremony, was reflected in the documents that emerged three years later. Cardinal König regards it as one of the Council's greatest achievements that it was 'the first Council to recognize that we are not a Roman Church . . . that we have to accept the culture of India, the culture of Africa and so on'. The Church evolved a new mechanism to realize its aspiration to universality, and fixed on an inelegant piece of jargon to describe it: inculturation. Its most obvious manifestation is the mix of drums and African dancing and singing that have now become such a familiar part of the African Mass. Because the African Mass arrived at the same time as guitars and the vernacular appeared in European churches, we tend to associate it with the 'trendy tendency' in the Church. But when I attended an exuberantly choreographed service in Lusaka, I was struck by how old-fashioned it was. It was a magnificent spectacle, designed to reflect God's majesty in just the way the old Tridentine Mass was. The fact that the music was Zambian instead of Mozart did not make it any less formalized. It was a performance to be watched, and did not require the constant participation of the congregation, so that 'space for prayer', which priests of the pre-Conciliar generation remember with such affection, was preserved.

And it was certainly not democratic in spirit. The Dutch missionary at the Regiment Parish Church gave me a set of notes to explain the service. 'According to Zambian tradition,' it begins, 'people highly respect their chiefs and chieftainesses. They do this by dancing for them, thanking them through gifts and praising them.' The priest is accorded the respect due to a chief, and at the offertory 'bundles of assorted things, like beans, vegetables, tomatoes and groundnuts' are brought to him at the altar. Because the Mass I attended was a special occasion, a live goat was included in the gifts: it was carried up to the altar with its hoofs lashed round a pole, then taken out into the yard to be slaughtered later.

Medardo Mazombwe, the current Archbishop of Lusaka, says that inculturation is a kind of religious declaration of independence: 'When we celebrate the Eucharist, when we worship Christ, let us do so as Africans, as Zambians.' But that means something much deeper than drums in church on Sunday morning. Like Pope John Paul II, with his strong sense of the destiny of individual nations, Archbishop Mazombwe believes that 'culture is the totality of expression of a particular people', and argues that inculturation only becomes real if 'Christ and the African cultures accept each other and give each other the best of what they have'. The fertile but dangerous territory into which that process can lead the Church was hinted at by Paul VI when he ordained Milingo and eleven other bishops on his visit to Africa in 1969. 'There is in all traditions in Africa,' he said, in his sermon during the service, 'a sense of the spiritual realities. This sense must not be understood merely as what scholars of the history of religion at the end of the last century used to call animism. It is something deeper, vaster and more universal. It is the realization that all created realities, and in particular visible nature itself, are united with the world of invisible and spiritual realities.'

Like the culture that formed Karol Wojtyła in Poland, the culture that nurtured Emmanuel Milingo in the heart of Africa accepts a close relationship between the living and the dead. Cardinal Arinze, a

Nigerian who has risen higher in the Curia than almost any other African and is often tipped to be the first black pope, says the traditional religions of Africa make Africans natural converts. 'In the traditional religions,' he explained to me, 'there is a belief in God, in spirits good and bad, and in our ancestors, our mothers and fathers who have died and reached the "happy spirit land" as they would put it in those religions.' Traditional African religion, he says, 'has many elements that are good, that are true, that are noble', which Christianity can 'adopt unchanged, or adapt, retouch, polish or correct'. But Cardinal Arinze also warns that it has 'elements that have to be rejected'. Henry Msoni, who after years of service has acquired the status of a grand old man of the Zambian Church, is remarkably frank about the uncertain no man's land between Catholicism and the spirit world of Africa. 'We Christian Africans,' he says, 'are living a double life. We try to follow Christian values when we are at the church but immediately we leave the church we want to follow our own traditional and cultural values.' He gives this example to illustrate what he means: 'I go to church and I'll be praying the rosary very honestly, repenting to my God and thanking him for the good that he does for me. But immediately I leave the church I go to a friend and I say, "Hey, boy, can you accompany me to such and such a witch-doctor? Because my son is very sick and I want to find out who bewitched him."'

Archbishop Mazombwe says it is at the 'critical moments' in people's lives, the 'moments of suffering and deep feeling', that many African Catholics forget their faith and return to traditional African religion. It means that for a parish priest like Father Bob Lavertu the task of distinguishing between the good and the bad in African culture is a daily reality. And the kind of problems it involves are anything but abstract. When a married person dies, for example, tradition dictates that their partner should be 'cleansed' before they can resume their place in society. One way of cleansing is for a relative of the dead partner to sleep with the surviving widow or widower. As Father Lavertu delicately puts it, 'In the case of a person who is Catholic, and goes by Christian values, this creates a very painful conflict.' And the dark side of the belief in the spirit world so admired by Pope Paul and Cardinal Arinze is the widespread belief in witchcraft. For Father Lavertu that is a social as much as a religious problem. In remote areas like Serenje witchcraft is a criminal racket. 'The worst thing about witchcraft,' he says, 'is the suspicion that surrounds everything that is sickness or death.' He says that whenever a child dies, be it from malaria or one of the many other threats to young life in the deep countryside, 'someone in the family will suspect that the boy or his parents have been bewitched, and they go to a witch-finder'.

The witch-finders have 'clerks', assistants who fill them in on the small tragedies and personal rivalries of rural village life, and give them the inside knowledge they need to select a victim to blame for the death. They can turn a profit twice over: by charging for the ritual needed to identify the witch, and then charging again to cleanse the witch they have identified. 'They make a fortune,' according to Father Lavertu. And if they are not paid, they frequently resort to violence.

Father Lavertu spends much of his time meticulously documenting instances of 'witch-finding' and passing them on to the police. Witch-craft is illegal in Zambia, but his local force has only one vehicle to cover an area of 20,000 square kilometres, and that is often broken down. A delay of nine months before an investigation gets under way is not unusual.

The White Fathers also try to fight witchcraft through education. They have engaged the services of a former witch-finder's clerk, George, and in the garden of the mission he holds seminars in witch-finders' techniques. The tricks used to prey on people's credulity are really very simple: a coffee bean up the nose to produce a whistling sound that is supposed to be the voice of a spirit, or a little chemical mix to cause a cone of nuts to burst into flames.

I wish I had had George with me at Archbishop Milingo's Mass in northern Italy. His professional opinion might have been instructive. The Archbishop processed up the centre of his warehouse cathedral accompanied by a choir of nuns from his Pious Union of the Daughters of the Redeemer. Their voices were quite mesmerizing in their beauty, and as the procession approached the altar the wailing of those possessed by demons became more intense. The Archbishop explained to me later that the devils are affronted by sanctity, and therefore protest more violently as the Mass gets under way.

As religious pageantry in the medieval tradition, it was highly effective. The ugly shrieks of the demons served to underline the beauty of the singing, and the possessed twitched only yards from the rhythmic order of the nuns' choir. The presence of evil brought God's goodness into sharp focus, and the light stood revealed more clearly by the contrast with the dark.

A Milingo Mass is both compelling and revolting. There was a sad story behind many of the faces in the congregation, and they came in search of miracles. I met a Hindu couple, Indian immigrants, who had brought their little boy: he had been brain-damaged at birth. They knew little about Catholicism and cared less, but they had been drawn by the desperate hope of a cure. Other parents with children too sick to make the journey brought photographs for the Archbishop to bless. Amid so much genuine human sorrow the antics of those possessed by demons were an affront. They seemed to compete with one another in the extremity of their ecstasies, vomiting, cursing and writhing on the ground. There were two Masses, and most of the possessed stayed through both. I spotted one of the most energetic and witch-like of the women recovering from her exertions with a cigarette during the lunch-time break.

Milingo himself behaves with a bewildering mixture of orthodoxy and flamboyance. One moment he was giving a sermon on the importance of regular Sunday Mass attendance, the next he was laying on hands and driving out demons. Whatever qualms some of his fellow bishops may have about his activities, the enthusiasm of his supporters is undeniable. I found myself most shocked by the way they chanted his name, not God's, at the end of Mass.

Sister Leonia knows the deadly power of faith in witchcraft in Milingo's native Zambia all too well. Her efforts to stop the spread of Aids in the slums around Lusaka are hampered by the widespread belief that its victims have been bewitched. They really are 'the very sick', but she says, 'They don't realize what's going on. So many times, when they come to the hospice, the family says, "Sister, he or she has been witched" – they are really sure about it. So I say, "There is no medicine for witchcraft – what do you expect me to do?"'

Most of those who come to her for treatment have usually been to the witch-doctor first; ritual cuts in the arm as a means of cleansing the evil spirits is a frequent prescription, so the patients often appear with serious infections. The belief in witchcraft also undermines the Zambian government's education efforts. Sister Leonia says the Aids education programme has now reached almost everyone in the country, and you cannot move far in Lusaka without encountering one of the roadside billboards that warn of the risk of infection. But people who believe that they are more likely to be afflicted by evil spirits than a physical disease take little notice of health warnings.

When I raised the awkward subject of condoms with senior members of the Zambian Church I could not avoid the impression that they were guilty of perpetuating superstitions of their own. The case for promoting the use of condoms in the face of the Aids pandemic is so self-evidently reasonable that they have been forced into unreason in their attempts to justify the Church's teaching. The Archbishop of Lusaka is an intelligent man, and there is no reason to doubt his sincerity when he says he cares for his flock. Yet this was his considered view on condoms: 'I was reading some material from some doctor, who was involved in fabricating condoms, and he says whereas condoms can hinder a sperm from going through, they cannot effectively hinder an Aids virus. He was saying that an Aids virus is fifty times smaller than the mesh of a condom, and therefore its success is not assured.'

Father Steven Mwewa is Zambia's leading theologian. Here is his view on the value of condoms in the fight against Aids: 'Condoms are not watertight. We are told . . . the transportation here has an impact on those things; the climate in which they are made is not the same as the climate here.'

And from Henry Msoni: 'Now, some of us had an interest in trying to see what this condom is, and you find that it is being sold on the street in the sun. Now if a condom is sold in the sun what chances are there that it will protect the individual who uses it? It will break out of friction.'

The African Church is a loyal Church. The only Catholic in Zambia I found willing to question Rome's teaching on condoms was a European: Sister Leonia. It chills me to think that I belong to a Church that regards her as a heretic but Emmanuel Milingo as a bishop.

15

Invincible Ignorance

In the parish church at Kafue I watched Archbishop Mazombwe of Lusaka confirm 150 children and teenagers. The girls were dressed like child brides, white from head to toe, with hats and stockings under the punishing sun, and the boys wore neatly pressed white trousers and shirts. Their procession snaked its way like a gleaming ribbon beneath the trees of the parish compound, and the Archbishop brought up the rear in full Roman fig. It is a testament to his physical fitness that he survived the three-hour service. It is a big church, and several hundred people were crammed inside. There was no air-conditioning, and before long the heat became intolerable. So many had come to see the ceremony that benches had to be set up on the grass by the narrow windows, and dozens more watched from outside. The outside back wall of the church was being used as a classroom for a catechism lesson, and half a dozen teenage boys were listening to the gospel stories with rapt attention.

In the 1980s the Church in Africa was growing at a rate of some two million annually, and the Archbishop estimates that today thirty thousand people are received into the Zambian Church every year. 'In terms of baptisms,' he told me, 'the rate of growth is so fast we can hardly cope with it.' In areas like Serenje there are still places where the name of Christ is scarcely known, and a rich harvest of conversions awaits the missionaries. In terms of crude numbers, Africa is the Church's future.

When Archbishop Milingo speaks of his treatment at the hands of the Curia, his words carry a powerful echo of Africa's struggle to free itself from colonial domination. It was, he told me, 'humiliating'. He was made to relearn basic theology and required to take a course in

American immigration law to prepare him for his job on the Pontifical Commission for Migration and Tourism. Even among his critics in Lusaka, Archbishop Milingo is remembered as a pioneer of inculturation, and he has certainly fulfilled the spirit of the Council in the way he has made his faith an African faith. 'When I am in church I am not a servant of anybody,' he says, 'not anyone except for God. And since my religion has become my life I don't owe it to the white man – I don't owe it to anybody at all. The origin, yes, but the living as I live it, no. I cannot live it unless I, as an African, see that my identity is not lost.'

The huge crowds the Archbishop draws to his healing sessions stand in sharp contrast to the empty rows of pews in so many Italian churches on Sundays. For the Curia in Rome it is an uncomfortable reminder of the way the Church is changing. Even Milingo's altogether more conventional successor, Medardo Mazombwe, believes that the time is fast approaching when the African Church will become the leader instead of the follower of the European Church. He says the Church in Europe is 'ageing . . . It gives the impression of a Church going into slumber, while here on the other side of the world the Church is in its youth and somehow vibrant with life.'

Archbishop Mazombwe puts a benign historical gloss on the process of change. He points out that in the fourth century North Africa was a Christian place, with more than three hundred dioceses. 'It was Christianized and as time went on it was deChristianized. So we have to start the process of reChristianizing. The same is true in the West today: we can say that a number of Western countries have become deChristianized.' A history of two thousand years allows the Church the luxury of taking the long view of its current problems, but it is difficult to accept that the transformation it has undergone since the 1960s is simply, as the Archbishop puts it, 'like high tide and low tide'.

The Church has been shaken by an earthquake since the Second Vatican Council, and although the tectonic plates are still grinding noisily away it is beginning to be possible to discern what the landscape may look like when they settle. What were regarded only four decades ago as far-flung provinces have become the true centres of Catholicism, in numbers, ideas and vigour. And because the Church is an institution, the change can lead only to an argument about the distribution of power.

The troubled history of relations between Rome and Latin America has provided a warning of the shape the battle to come may take. When Cardinal Arns went to Rome in 1978, determined to elect a pope from outside Western Europe, he was flexing his Church's institutional muscles. In the 1980s when John Paul II and Cardinal Ratzinger cracked down on the Church in Latin America they were reasserting the centralizing authority of the Vatican. Their victory came at considerable cost. Some of the innovative thinkers in the Latin-American Church – like Leonardo Boff – have been driven out. The giants of the generation of bishops who flourished in the aftermath of Medellín are fast disappearing, and the Helder Câmaras are being replaced by the José Cardosos. At the grass-roots, priests like Father Tony Terry are disenchanted, and the enthusiasm that drove the parishioners of Morro da Conceiçao in Recife to build their own parish church is a thing of the past. An exhausted Latin-American Church has become vulnerable to raiding parties from born-again Protestant churches: in the first two years of the 1990s 710 new churches were opened in Rio de Janeiro, the vast majority of them Pentecostal. Only one new Catholic Church was consecrated during the same period.

In Latin America the theologians led the revolution and the bishops followed. The process is likely to be repeated in Asia. It is inevitable that the priests being trained in the new theology at places like the Viyadoti College will lead their Church before very long. Indeed, in the way they stress the 'Catholic' rather than the 'Roman' face of the Church, the leaders of the Asian Church are already beginning to show signs of the independent spirit that animated Cardinal Arns and his colleagues. 'The word Roman,' Archbishop Marcus Fernando of Colombo told me, 'is used because the Pope happens to be in Rome. For me the Catholic religion is not Roman, it is Catholic, meaning universal, meant for the whole world.' His fellow archbishop in Delhi, Alan de Lastic, speaks of the Church in terms of a kind of worldwide federation: 'In Delhi it's the Catholic Church localized in time and space, but in communion with all the other Churches and certainly in some way directed and helped by the Holy Father.' He describes the Pope as the 'principal source' of what he calls, in an intriguing phrase, 'the divisible unity' of the modern Church.

Bishop Malcolm Ranjith, despite the reputation for orthodoxy he established as the scourge of Father Tissa Balasuriya, looks ahead to a time when Asia's thinking is even more independent. He says, 'Very often those who do theology in Asia have studied at European universities . . . in a system based on Greek and Roman instruction.' He argues that until that inheritance is jettisoned 'Our theology is going to be looking at Asia with dark glasses which we picked up somewhere else.'

But the most striking illustration I found of the centrifugal forces at work in the Church was the worldwide web of rebels. Hans Küng in Europe, Leonardo Boff in Latin America and Tissa Balasuriya in Asia all talk to each other and support each other's causes. They believe they are all engaged in essentially the same struggle: a battle to build a new kind of Church. Leonardo Boff describes Balasuriya as a 'dear friend' and believes Asia's theologians have picked up the Latin-American idea of Liberation Theology and given it a new meaning: 'It is infusing Christianity with a non-Cartesian logic, a culture that is not Western,' he says, 'so that Christianity can have a . . . face of the orient. The Vatican is petrified by this concept.'

The new spirit of independence among the non-European Churches is a mark of the success of the Second Vatican Council. But it is also a challenge to the institutional structures of a Church built so rigidly around the centralizing authority of Rome. And as those structures creak under the pull from the periphery, they are also being corroded from within by secularism and the habit of disobedience.

If the vigour of the new Churches is a mark of the Council's success, the crisis in Catholicism's traditional heartland can be traced back to the great failure of the Church in the 1960s, the birth-control encyclical *Humanae Vitae*. In the Western Church – European and American – Catholicism is still about sex. The American Jesuit writer Thomas Reese has this anecdote about preparing an article about the Church in the next millennium: 'I had been using a computer program to search through 300 newspapers and magazines on the Internet, using keywords like "Catholic", "Vatican", "pope", "bishop", and "priest". After searching awhile the program asked if I would like to add the word "sex" because this word came up so often in news stories about Catholics.' In Europe and America, sex is driving a wedge between the Church's leaders and the led, and the gap between Church teaching and the realities of Catholic life is growing wider all the time.

On the issue of contraception, even those close to the Pope seem to have accepted defeat. Cardinal Lopez Trujillo, president of the Pontifical Council on the Family, talks round the subject with great volubility, rather than addressing it directly. I asked him whether he felt much pressure from parish priests or lay people for a change in the Church's teaching and was rewarded with a cascade of words about 'serious love' and the dangers of a 'contraceptive mentality', but even he seemed squeamish about saying, 'Don't do it.'

In February 1997 Cardinal Trujillo's council issued guidance for confessors: 'Some Aspects of the Morality of Conjugal Love'. It tells priests that 'In general, it is not necessary for the confessor to investigate concerning sins committed in invincible ignorance of their evil or due to an inculpable error of judgement. It is preferable to let penitents remain in good faith in cases of error due to subjectively invincible ignorance, even in matters of conjugal chastity.' In other words, don't ask too many questions in the confessional. It takes a very special kind of curial mind to come up with the idea that when the vast majority of Catholics disagree with Church teaching they are 'in invincible ignorance of their evil'.

The quarters of the Pontifical Council on the Family in the Curia's San Callisto buildings are a mix of grandeur and asceticism. I interviewed Cardinal Trujillo in a reception room filled with dauntingly ornate and outsized gold furniture with scarlet upholstery. His staff's offices are arranged on either side of a long, white-floored corridor. At one end is a wooden carving of the Holy Family presented to the council by John Paul II himself. Jesus sits between his parents holding a sceptre symbolizing the Church; Mary and Joseph are both very erect, their backs so stiffly straight it is almost as if they are at attention. All three figures have the kind of clear, level gaze that denotes a strong sense of purpose. It is an inspiring image of an idealized vision of family life, and one that had meaning in the world of romantic Catholic aspiration of Karol Wojtyła's Kraków. It is a long way from the experience of most Catholics growing up in the high-pressure societies of late-twentieth-century capitalism. The council's offices are cool and well ordered; family life is warm – sometimes heated – and often chaotic.

The number of Catholics who fail to live up to the Church's ideals about sex, marriage and family life is growing all the time. Increasingly they cease to see themselves as a failure, and conclude instead that the Church and its teachings are irrelevant to their lives.

It is probably true that the tug on the conscience that makes Catholics regard the collapse of a marriage as a moral failure and not just a human tragedy is still there. But the statistics in the Western Church demonstrate that it does not stop them getting divorced: in the United States, almost half of Catholic marriages end in divorce. As changing social attitudes sweep them further and further from their Church's teaching, the practice of denying communion to those who remarry seems cruel. There are three ways in which a divorced person who remarries may enjoy the right to receive the Eucharist. The first is to secure an annulment, an official Church ruling that the marriage they have left was never really a marriage at all. Annulments now have a well-established reputation as a cynical fraud. In the first nineteen centuries of the Church's life fewer than a hundred annulment cases were considered anywhere in the world. In 1968, 450 annulments were granted, most of them to the rich and well connected. In 1994 the figure was 72,744, nearly 55,000 alone in the United States.

The second road back to the Eucharist is to return to the original spouse. The third is to live as 'brother and sister' in the new relationship. The rules are plainly unworkable in most modern societies, and many priests quietly ignore them. But that simply adds another area to the list of those where Catholic practice and Church teaching are at odds.

Homosexuality is gradually joining that list too. Vatican II said absolutely nothing on the subject, and it is one of the many ironies of the aftermath of *Humanae Vitae* that it began a general debate about sexual ethics, and opened the way for the issue of homosexuality to be raised for the first time. In 1973, the United States Bishops Conference recognized that sexual orientation is not a matter of choice. But the Church's official teaching remains that it condemns homosexual acts, even if it no longer condemns homosexuals. As Cardinal Hume puts it, 'The Church has always maintained a very strong principle that sexual activity is confined to people who are married . . . The Church would always distinguish between homosexual orientation – which is neither here nor there – and homosexual activity. It cannot come to accept homosexual sexual activity.' It is a nice distinction, but it can inflict real pain on active homosexuals who wish to play a full part in the life of the Church. A report commissioned by the Catholic

Theological Society of America in 1977 concluded that 'A homosexual engaging in homosexual acts in good conscience has the same rights of conscience and the same rights to the sacraments as a married couple practising birth control in good conscience.' Since most heterosexual Catholics have concluded that the Church is being silly about contraception, more and more Catholics of both orientations are concluding that it is being equally silly about homosexuality.

The corrosion of the Church's institutional authority because of the failure of its teachings on sex is speeded up with every newspaper story about a paedophile priest or a bishop with a baby. Tissa Balasuriya believes that the Holy Spirit now operates through 'the mass media, the Internet, and the e-mail', which he believes helped him escape excommunication. If he is right, the Holy Spirit seems to have decided on the wholesale exposure of prelates who are at best failing to live up to their vows and at worst exploiting and abusing those who trust them.

The old Catholic instinct whenever scandal threatened was to reach for a cover-up. Open societies in Europe and America have made that an increasingly ineffective response, and the Church is now more and more willing to apologize and accept responsibility for the sins of its clergy. But hair-raising stories are still emerging. 'Elisabeth' had two children by the same priest. In the conduct of her affair with a cleric, she abided by the Church's teaching on contraception. The first child was put up for adoption, but she decided to keep the second. The priest lover remained a 'family friend', and Elisabeth did not explain to her daughter that he was her father. She has now joined a support group for women who have been left wounded after love affairs with priests, and of the many traumas with which she is struggling to come to terms, this is the most distressing: her daughter was working as an au pair in Paris, and the man she knew as a Father but not as her father came to visit her. He took her on what was ostensibly a day trip to see a shrine outside the city. 'The trip got longer and longer, and she had no idea where she was going.' By the time they reached their shrine it was dark, and her companion said it was impossible to drive back: 'He took her for a meal in the town and put his arm round her and behaved as if he was her boyfriend. Bought her jewellery and then they went into a hotel. And she was absolutely horrified when she found that he was sharing the room with her. I could not ask her the final question,' Elisabeth stammered. 'I just said, "What did happen?" And she just said, "He made love to me in a way that no man who wasn't married to me should have done."'

According to Richard Sipe, who published a study of sex and the priesthood in 1990, only about half the celibate priesthood is practising celibacy at any one time. In South Africa he found that 43 per cent of priests were involved with a woman, and 38 per cent had terminated a relationship within the previous two years. A study of fifty gay priests in the United States in 1980 revealed that only 4 per cent of them were sexually abstinent, and the rest averaged more than two hundred sexual partners each. Horror stories like Elisabeth's may be rare, but the pattern of departure from the celibate ideal is not.

All the women I met who had been sexually approached by priests expressed horror at the betrayal of trust. The failure of so many priests to remain chaste lies at the heart of the crisis of authority in the Western Church, because celibacy is so intimately bound up with the Catholic understanding of a priest as someone above human weakness and desire. Celibacy has been described as a 'cultic symbol of "the man set apart" for the service of the divine', and the celibate priesthood is emblematic of the pre-Conciliar elements that endure in the Church. It is both a medieval institution and a specifically 'Roman' Catholic one. There were married priests in the early Church, and celibacy was not finally confirmed as a formal requirement of the priesthood until the Second Lateran Council in 1139. And there are, of course, other Churches, notably the Catholic Churches of the East and the Orthodox Churches, with married clergy.

In England, the Archbishop of Westminster, Cardinal Hume, had to negotiate his way through Vatican sensitivities about celibacy when he was managing the fall-out of the Anglican Church's decision to ordain women: some of the fugitive vicars seeking refuge in the Roman Church were married men. The Cardinal draws a careful distinction between the ordination of women, which is regarded by Rome as a matter beyond debate, and the issue of celibacy, which is simply a discipline the Church has decided to impose on its clergy. Of the latter he says, 'There's no reason why that should not change, because it's Church law and not divine law.' He recognizes that 'We lose some very good men because of the issue of celibacy,' and the crisis in the numbers entering the priesthood is often cited as the most compelling argument for relaxing the discipline. It is sometimes said that half the world's Catholics are unable to receive the Eucharist on Sundays for the lack of a priest. But the Vatican remains resistant to change.

Cardinal Ratzinger concedes that celibacy is 'not a dogmatic tradition and therefore not entirely unchangeable', but the difference of emphasis between his position and that of Cardinal Hume illustrates how much room for political manoeuvre there is even between two men who agree completely on an apparently narrow point of Church teaching.

The prefect of the Sacred Congregation for the Doctrine of the Faith says celibacy is 'so deeply rooted in the understanding of priesthood that Church authority will hardly dare to touch it'. He calls history to the aid of his argument. 'Recent studies,' he claims, show that celibacy 'dates back almost to apostolic times, at least the second or third century,' but it is his idea of what priesthood means that lies at the heart of his objection to tampering with the celibate rule. Priesthood, he told me, is the 'dedication . . . of oneself in an act of fundamental renunciation, by recognizing God as one's own country, as the country of one's own life'.

The Second Vatican Council was inspired by the belief that the Church should engage with the world, but Cardinal Ratzinger's idea of 'renunciation' suggests a suspicion of all things worldly. In the act of sex man's place in the world is powerfully expressed. The ideal of celibacy is rooted in medieval superstition that the world is fundamentally evil – though no respectable theologian, and certainly not Cardinal Ratzinger, would admit to that.

At the heart of all the debates on the floor of St Peter's there were two distinct views of the Church. The old guard, the pessimists attacked by Pope John XXIII in his opening address, saw the Church as standing outside history, and believed that its duty was to preserve the unchanging Truth bequeathed to it by Christ; bishops who, as Cardinal König put it, 'were very afraid to change anything because they felt the Church has eternal ideas, the message of Christ, and we can't touch it'. The progressive majority accepted the principle that there were certain basic truths that could never be changed – 'the sacred deposit of the faith' – but also believed that there were many elements in Church teaching and practice which could and should be adapted to meet the demands of time and place. At the end of the Council the balance seemed to have swung decisively in favour of the progressives but, in fact, the tension between these two visions has never gone away. And as the millennium approaches, the fault-lines are becoming a more and more serious threat to the unity of the Church. They are both vertical and horizontal. The energetic and expanding new Churches of the developing world are children of the progressive model, and they have flourished precisely because they have rooted themselves in their own cultures, societies and political realities. The lay people of Europe and North America are equally the inheritors of the Council's ideas, but only by accepting that Church teaching can and should be reassessed in the light of changing history can they remain Catholics while integrating themselves more deeply into modern society.

In Rome, though, John Paul II has been building a team of pessimists: the key positions in his Curia are held by men who believe in the old pre-Conciliar model of a Church that stands in opposition to the world. There is a double irony in that. No modern pope has had as profound a political impact as John Paul, and his campaign in Poland seemed to be a fulfilment of the Council's promise to engage with the world. Equally John Paul's own brand of Catholicism is deeply rooted in a specific conjunction of historical circumstances – only the experience of living as a Catholic in Poland under Nazism and Communism could have produced a pontificate like his. Yet everything about the way he rules suggests he fears the corruption of the Church by its contact with the world, and the undermining of its universal message by relativism.

The champions of both sides in this intellectual joust are highly articulate and effective advocates. Leonardo Boff says the Church's doctrine should not be 'like a cadaver, a mummy of the past', but 'like a living organism in touch with different cultures which opens itself up to new feelings'. And he puts the case for daring to engage with change with evangelical fervour: 'We should have faith in the intrinsic power of Christianity. It doesn't need too many defences; we don't need to tell a light to shine, a light shines for itself. So we have to believe in the force of its truth, and not in the security we want to keep, which stops the shining light from radiating outwards.' He paints the two models of the Church on offer for the next millennium in starkly contrasting colours. He describes John Paul's Church as an 'Imperial Church' with a mission to 'conquer cultures and people and convert them to Christianity'. And he gives a provocative twist to the frenetic pilgrimages of a pope who has used modern transport and communications to spread the Catholic message more widely than any pope before him: 'I think the most important symbol [of the imperial Church] is the Pope, who travels throughout the world with a Cross preaching conversion to Christianity – this type of Church is not growing, it is shrinking, and it inspires fewer people because it is imperial and conquering.'

Against that he sets the model of the Church as a 'mass movement for Jesus in the various cultures of the world'. It is, he says, 'a model of a Church built around a network of communities . . . a Roman Church, a Latin-American Church, an African Church, an Asian church . . . all of these sister Churches united'. He describes this as a 'Christianity which places at its centre not sacred power but life itself, in all its forms'. In institutional terms that would mean the Roman Catholic Church disappearing altogether.

The way the pessimists express their views lacks that seductive grand sweep. Joseph Ratzinger's criticisms of Vatican II are inevitably tempered by his having been, as a young theologian, one of those who drove its reforms: he was *peritus* to Cardinal Frings, one of the leading Trans-Alpini, and wrote some of his then boss's most radical speeches. But today Ratzinger's approach to his job as the guardian of the Church's orthodoxy is guided by his conviction that the spirit of the Council has been betrayed.

There were, he explained to me, from the very beginning two different 'receptions' of the Council. On the one hand there were those – and he includes himself among them – who understood the Council as a 'reform effort, which meant continuity of the faith in the Church, faith developing but remaining true to itself'. On the other hand there were those who adopted the 'revolutionary interpretation' of the Council, which the Cardinal believes has close links with 'what we saw in politics in 1968', a reference to that year's student riots in Europe and America.

Joseph Ratzinger was a theology professor at Tübingen – Hans Kung's university today – during the student unrest of 1968, and the experience scarred him deeply. Just as the Year of Revolutions in

1848 turned Pius IX from a champion of liberalism into its scourge so 1968 transformed Joseph Ratzinger. Thirty years later he was still scandalized by the memory of a flyer put out by students that described the New Testament as 'a document of inhumanity, a large-scale deception of the masses'. He once said of the period: 'In these years I learned when a discussion had to stop because it was changing into a lie, and when resistance was necessary in order to preserve freedom.'

Cardinal Ratzinger believes that at the Council 'the idea was born that the Church could do with itself whatever it wanted. The concept of Church voluntarism was invented, meaning that the will of the Church is self-determining.' And as if to bring the history of the past three decades neatly full circle, he illustrates his point by returning to that first debate of the Council's first session – on the liturgy. In shocked tones that echo the pronouncements of his predecessors in the days when the Sacred Congregation for the Doctrine of the Faith was the Holy Office of the Inquisition, he denounces what he calls 'abuses of the liturgy, in which the priest or group of worshippers determine the proceedings for themselves and thus turn the liturgy from a matter of the universal community of the Church into a private congregation of a priest or group'.

Cardinal Schotte is Cardinal Ratzinger's conservative soul-mate and personal friend – his apartment is a five-minute walk from the Palace of the Holy Office across St Peter's Square. And he, too, returns to the debate over the liturgy as an illustration of where the Church has gone wrong. He began by telling me that 'It's still too soon to make an assessment on what liturgical reform has meant for the Catholic Church,' which is a fairly astonishing remark even for a leader of a Church that famously thinks in the long-term. The liturgical reforms of Vatican II are now so well established that no one under forty will really remember what Mass was like before they were introduced.

Cardinal Schotte's concerns about the liturgy echo those of Cardinal Ratzinger: 'We are not,' he says, 'any assembly that comes together and does its own thing.' He complained that he had been to Masses where the congregation 'enjoyed it, but when they left there was a kind of emptiness. They could do the same in a football stadium, for a rock concert or for some political manifestation.'

For both men the improvisation and local colour of the modern lit-

urgy touch on the question of Church authority: if you allow the people
to decide their own liturgy, Cardinal Ratzinger told me, 'It becomes
obvious that you cannot leave the Pope to decide things on his own –
that everyone has an equal right to free will.' There were surprisingly
few moments during my work on this project when a cardinal slipped
into unconscious self-parody, but that was one of them.

Even Cardinal Ratzinger's enemies concede that he has a remarkably
clear mind, and he left me in no doubt about how he sees Vatican II's
legacy: 'The two interpretations, the reformist and the revolutionary,
are still at variance and constitute the real conflict of the post-Conciliar
era.'

The argument has been fought with the bitterness of a family quarrel.
Many of those involved have known each other well all their lives.
Hans Küng and Joseph Ratzinger, for example, were young Turks
together as theological advisers during the Council. And the Vatican
runs a real risk by the way it has sought to drive the dissenters outside
the mainstream of the Church: it may lose with them the creativity
and energy released by Vatican II.

The Council offered the Church an institutional mechanism for
resolving the tensions within it, what is known as 'collegiality'. It was
Vatican II's answer to the Papal Infallibility declared by Vatican I in
1870, and it sought to restore the balance of power between the Pope
and his bishops, and between Rome and the Church in the wider
world.

Collegiality acknowledges that the Pope is one of many bishops,
just as St Peter was one of twelve apostles. It acknowledges the primacy
of the Bishop of Rome, but gives the bishops of the world the say in
the central government of the Church that they were denied before
the Council was held. It fell a long way short of turning the Church
into a democracy, but it did mark a step away from the 'monarchical'
system of government that the Vatican had held on to long after almost
every state in the world had abandoned it. The means by which the
aspiration to collegiality could be reflected in the government of the
Church was widely discussed during the Council. There was even a
proposal for a semi-parliamentary system, a synod of bishops at least
some of whom would be permanently based in Rome. It was to act
as a 'supreme, executive, decision-making council' of the Church,
and was to have power over all the Congregations of the Curia, just

as a government in parliament has power over all the departments of its civil service.

That idea came from one of the Eastern patriarchs; even in those revolutionary times it went well beyond the bounds of what the Roman Church could consider. But in the final session of the Council Paul VI announced the establishment of a synod of bishops, and its stated aims have a democratic flavour:

(1) To encourage close and valued assistance between the sovereign pontiff and the bishops of the entire world.
(2) To ensure that direct and real information is provided on questions and situations touching upon the internal action of the Church and its necessary activity in the world of today.
(3) To facilitate agreement on essential points of doctrine and on methods of procedure in the life of the Church.

But the way this would-be parliament of bishops was set up was fatally flawed by the ambivalence that ran through so much of Paul's pontificate. The synod was there only to advise, not to decide. It would be called at papal whim, 'when for the general good of the Church this will seem opportune for us'. And when he announced it Paul stressed that 'We always need a Curia for carrying out our apostolic responsibilities.'

Humanae Vitae, three years later, dealt the idea of collegiality a devastating blow. The issue on which almost every bishop in the world had strong views was decided without any episcopal consultation whatsoever.

John Paul II has silenced the stirring of Church democracy represented by collegiality. It is a development much mourned by the surviving giants of the Council. Cardinal König is publicly loyal to the man whose candidacy he sponsored in October 1978, but if pressed privately he will admit to grave concerns about the direction the Church has taken under this pontificate. And he is quite open about his conviction that the ideal of collegiality has been betrayed. König accuses the Curia of abrogating the power that rightly belongs to the bishops. 'I understand that the Pope needs a big office for the universal Church,' he says, 'but everyone in the Vatican behaves as if he's the Holy Father. They're taking over the job of collegiality – and they can't replace the bishops of the world.'

Cardinal Schotte, who as prefect of the Congregation for Bishops has the job of making the synodical system work, staunchly defends John Paul as 'the most collegiate pope you can imagine'. Collegiality is not, he insists, a 'question of power or power sharing', it is an expression of the bishops' inheritance from the twelve apostles. He told me it was wrong to look for 'models from secular society. A synod is not a parliament. A synod is not the grand council or the senate of wise men.' Instead it has become a system for rubber-stamping papal decisions.

There have been two memorable instances of the brutal use of Roman power to suppress dissent among the bishops. In 1980, John Paul called a synod on the family. Several senior bishops and cardinals saw this first synod of the then new papacy as an opportunity to reopen the debate about birth control, which had been impossible during Paul's glum final years. Archbishop Hurley was one of them and still smarts at his memory of the way discussion of the issue was forbidden by curial decree. 'It wasn't on the agenda,' he said, with grim finality.

Some bishops did speak their minds, and Cardinal Hume gave a famously elliptical speech that simultaneously reaffirmed his support for *Humanae Vitae* and begged for sensitivity to the views from the grass-roots. But it was to no avail. The synod had been called for the purpose of endorsing the Pope's own conservative views, and that is what it did.

It was the same story ten years later when a group of bishops wanted to raise the issue of celibacy at the synod on the priesthood. It must surely be the most widely debated aspect of the priesthood in the modern Church at large, but at the synod it was simply not discussed. Cardinal Schotte justified this on the grounds that the issue had been settled in 1971 at Paul's synod on the priesthood. I protested that two decades had elapsed between the synods. The Cardinal's response was revealing: 'It was twenty years earlier, but the arguments were still the same.' In John Paul's Vatican the passing of the decades counts for nothing.

The stubborn resistance even to the limited devolution of power involved in collegiality takes the Church leadership another step away from its members. Father Andrew Greeley, the Chicago-based statistician, conducted an opinion poll among Catholics in nine countries. It was a massive undertaking and the results were startling: a solid majority for a democratic overhaul of the Church. As Catholics look forward to a new papacy, they seem to want 'a much more democratic pope. A pope who would permit us to elect our own bishops . . . much more power and authority decentralized to the bishops . . . women priests and married priests . . . a pope who is surrounded by lay advisers' – in short, the kind of sweeping liberal agenda that is the stuff of curial nightmares.

16

A Sign of Contradiction

I live within sight of a fine twelfth-century Anglican village church, and the sound of its bells on Sunday mornings provokes a mixture of emotions. The first among them is resentment. We English Catholics are only half joking when we say we want our churches back. It is galling to belong to the Church that nurtured Michelangelo and be required to worship in a prefabricated box knocked up in the 1950s. The beauty of the pre-Reformation churches, which were built when England was still Catholic, only makes the affront worse. The second is a strong desire to walk across the lawn and up the lane to attend the service. Being a member of a minority is exhausting. I still miss the sense of belonging to the mainstream that marked my Sunday mornings in the United States. The third, I am ashamed to confess, is a certain smugness. English Catholics have done their best to avoid triumphalism as they watch the travails of the Church of England, but even Cardinal Hume is human. It is not something to be proud of, but a quiet tribal cheer goes up each time there is another high-profile conversion to Rome.

We may like the idea of a more democratic Church in the abstract, but the Anglican experience serves as a warning of what it could mean in reality. The Church of England has an elected synod, which includes lay people as well as clergy and bishops, and it decides how the Church is governed. I used to cover the bi-annual synod meetings during the brief period in the early 1980s when I developed an opportunistic specialism in religious journalism. They were conducted with a great sense of fun and a certain Trollopian drama, but there was none of the high seriousness of purpose of an event like the Second Vatican Council.

Democracy has given Anglicans almost everything on the liberal wish-list – including women priests – and the Anglican Church is an open society. By and large its disputes are conducted in a civilized and courteous manner, and almost every area of Christian teaching, up to and including the existence of God, is considered a legitimate subject for debate. Some clergy and even bishops hold views that make Tissa Balasuriya look like a crusty old reactionary, but there is no prefect of a Sacred Congregation summoning them to Lambeth Palace to account for themselves. And yet the pews keep emptying.

As president of the Council for Promoting Christian Unity, Cardinal Edward Cassidy is the Vatican official with primary responsibility for relations with the Anglican Church, and he says the issue of authority remains the main source of division between the two communions. 'You have to find an authority which is accepted within the Church. Where is the authority in the Anglican community? Is it in the Archbishop of Canterbury? Is it in Lambeth? Is it in the meeting of the primates?'

Modern Catholics may hold views that put them at odds with the Church hierarchy, but they retain a deep affection for some of the basic principles upon which the Church is founded: respect for authority, belief in an absolute truth and a conviction of the universality of the Christian message. Like Henry Msoni's African Christian who leaves Mass and then visits the witch-doctor, many of us lead a double life; we are Protestant in the particular and Catholic in general, liberal in the choices we make in our daily lives but traditional in our abstract ideas.

There is no will for a revolution in the Church. No one wants to use the fault-lines I have identified to break it apart. Even the rebels with the most radical vision of its future accord a special respect to the Pope. Hans Küng has made a direct assault on John Paul – whom he described, in a comparison that must have been especially painful, as an East European despot – but his real quarrel is with the idea of Infallibility, not the office of the papacy. And both Leonardo Boff and Tissa Balasuriya have been careful to make the Vatican and not the Pope the focus for their criticism. Father Balasuriya continued to insist that John Paul cannot have known what was being done in his name, despite all the evidence to the contrary. And the determination with which rebels like them have fought to avoid exclusion is in its way a testament to the affection the Church can inspire. Despite all the tensions I encountered in my journeys around the Catholic world, I found the sense of what is precious in the Church still strong.

There was a time when divisions of the kind that exist today would have led to schism: at the Protestant Reformation, a great chunk of Christian humanity floated off like a vast iceberg, leaving the Arctic cap. But schism has become the last resort of the right. The only serious split in the Church this century came when the French Archbishop Marcel Lefebvre refused to accept the legitimacy of the Second Vatican Council, and founded a traditionalist church based around his seminary at Econe in Switzerland – or as he would have put it, re-established the true Church, which had been destroyed by the Council. There is a flourishing Lefebvrist sect in America but the split was certainly not a second Reformation. There is something inherently silly about rebelling in the name of authority and tradition.

The threat to the Church's unity does not lie in the clean break of a schism. It lies in a more chaotic disintegration brought about by the twin forces of a new spirit of independence at what was once regarded as the Church's periphery, and a crumbling of faith in its traditional heartland. The shattering of a vast pane of glass is a more apposite metaphor than the shearing away of an iceberg. On the surface the Church seems calm as it approaches the end of its second millennium. The high-profile disputes I have described are a distant echo to the vast majority of ordinary Catholics – most Asian Catholics have probably never heard of Tissa Balasuriya, and Leonardo Boff's name is not much mentioned in English parish churches.

The non-Catholic world sees only an ageing pope who has long since lost his novelty value. John Paul continues to display an astonishing vigour in defiance of those determined to kill him off, and his longevity as a source of news stories is remarkable. Whether he is admitting the Church's failure during the Holocaust or lecturing the leaders of Nigeria about human rights, he still manages to find his way into the newspapers. But it tends to be on the inside pages. Even his 1998 visit to Cuba seemed more a matter of tidying up the unfinished business of history than preparing for a new era. The allegations that President Clinton had behaved indecently with a White House intern in the Oval Office surfaced in the middle of the trip, and the American television networks chartered private planes to fly their anchormen off the island and back to Washington. It told a sad truth about the place to which this sometime superstar of the Cold War had sunk in the news rankings.

But the surface calm of the Church is a false calm – like the calm before the Council. The danger posed by the coincidence of so many different sources of tension only becomes apparent when you stand back and look at the whole. It means that the next pope will face a pressing challenge. After two decades in office, John Paul has appointed more than 80 per cent of the cardinals eligible to vote, and according to the conventional wisdom that means the new pope will be a man in his image. But that is to ignore the Holy Spirit, and His recent track-record. An ecumenical council from a pope expected to be no more than a caretaker, a devastatingly reactionary encyclical from his most modern-minded successor, a pontificate that lasted for a month and the first non-Italian pope for 450 years – the Church has thrown up so many surprises during the last four decades that we have come almost to expect the unexpected.

Recalling the two conclaves he attended in 1978, Cardinal Hume says, 'You are looking for one thing alone: the man that you think would be the best successor to St Peter.' That objective, he said, took precedence over 'all political considerations and national consider-ations'. But John Paul II's papacy has demonstrated emphatically that a pope's national and political background can define his papacy. St Peter's arrival in Rome marked the beginning of that intimate relationship, so cherished by Hilaire Belloc, between the Church, the Roman Empire and Western civilization. For the past two thousand years all the successors to St Peter have worked within the terms dictated by that relationship.

The next pope will have to work within a new set of rules, because the Church has at last become something much greater than a Western Church. A pope from outside Europe would be a fulfilment of the promise of true universality so many felt on the opening day of the Second Vatican Council, and could have an electrifying effect. It would obviously underline the 'Catholic' element in Roman Catholicism, but it could also strengthen the unifying force implied in the idea of a 'Roman' Church. At present Rome is often seen to be imposing its discipline; that carries echoes of the imperial associations of its past, and encourages rebellion. With a non-European at its heart Rome might appear as a symbol of a new relationship in which the centre is the servant of the wider Church, not its master.

Politically the arrival of a non-European in the Vatican could have the effect of bringing the concerns of the developing world – such as poverty and Aids – to the top of the international agenda, in just the way John Paul focused the world's attention on Eastern Europe in the early 1980s. And it might even re-energize the Church in Europe, by giving tired European Catholics a sense of excitement about the richness and diversity of their Church, which I have been able to witness during my journeys to research this book.

Wherever the new pope comes from, he will need a well-developed capacity to admit error. Despite his fierce traditionalism in many areas, John Paul has shown a willingness to apologize for the Church's past wrongs – and that has paid dividends, notably in his relationship with Judaism. But if the next pope is to make the kind of institutional reforms necessary to reunite the Church leadership with its members, he will need to admit that Roman Catholicism has been wrong in its teaching as well as its actions. That will mean freeing himself from the creeping Infallibility that Hans Kung detected in Paul's decision to reassert the ban on artificial contraception.

A change in the ruling on contraception would bring millions of Catholics back into full communion with the Church, and destroy at a stroke the principal source of the gap between teaching and practice that has had such a corrosive impact on the Church's place in the daily lives of modern Catholics. It would also restore the Church's authority in the arena of sexual ethics and personal morality – something for which the need and the demand become ever more urgent as the bewildering choices offered to us by modern science multiply.

Equally the abolition of the celibate discipline for the priesthood would bring thousands of men into the Church's service, and dramatically reduce the scale of the sexual deviancy and abuse, which do so much damage to the Church's reputation. Both changes could be managed without undue fuss, since neither teaching is claimed as part of that central 'deposit of faith', which cannot be touched.

The issue of women priests is more difficult. Rosemary Goldie was among the first women admitted as observers to the Second Vatican Council. She recalls that during the debate over female 'auditors', as they were known, one bishop argued that they were unnecessary: 'You say there are no women here, but look around you in St Peter's. There are all these statues of women saints and, of course, the Virgin

Mary, who is with us all the time.' Still closely involved with the Vatican, she finds the misogyny that once ran deep there is diminishing, even though some older priests and bishops continue to find it difficult to deal with women. But a change in the Church's attitude to women does not mean a change in its teaching on the priesthood.

The male priesthood is regarded as a matter of truth, not simply of discipline. Cardinal Ratzinger explains it by distinguishing between the 'functional' and the 'sacramental' conceptions of the priesthood. If priesthood 'were a purely functional task', he says, 'then there is indeed no reason why women should not perform this service, as they are endowed with at least the same religious and intellectual gifts as men'. But the 'sacramental' conception is based on the conviction that Christ 'created the original form of priesthood by calling the Twelve', and since He did not choose to include women among them this established 'a sacramental form which we cannot manipulate'. That is an extremely difficult position to retreat from, and even more liberal leaders recognize that. When I asked Cardinal Hume if he could ever imagine women priests in the Roman Catholic Church he took a deep breath, gave an uncharacteristically uncertain look at his advisers sitting behind me, and said, 'No.'

But institutional reform does not hold the only key to the Church's future. The real revolution of Vatican II was to transform the Roman Catholic Church from an institution into an Ideal. In a Church that has no real temporal power, institutional discipline is difficult to maintain – Cardinal Ratzinger has been forced to recognize that by the spectacle of his favourite heretics becoming best-selling authors and international celebrities. As the Declaration on Religious Liberty acknowledged, only through truth freely received can the Church maintain the allegiance of its members.

The new pope will find the Church under severe strain as an institution, but it has also become a formidable engine of ideas. For an organization that is often regarded as a byword for reaction and spends so much of its energy trying to suppress dissent, it has shown remarkable intellectual fertility. That offers both a risk and an opportunity. In Asia intellectual innovation has cast doubt on the Church's claim to possess a unique Truth. But the power of ideas also gave John Paul his greatest triumph: the defeat of Communism.

The Church flourishes in adversity. The experience of persecuted papists in England, Latin-American martyrs and Polish anti-Communist dissidents suggests that its message is clearest when it is defined in opposition to an evident evil, so that its essential goodness is brought into relief. As John Paul sat with Mikhail Gorbachev in the Vatican in 1989 he was contemplating something outside the experience of any pope in the long history of the Church: a future without an obvious ideological enemy. With the defeat of Communism, there were no dragons left to slay.

Cardinal Poupard, appointed to succeed Cardinal König at the Secretariat for Non-believers, expresses the frustration of a crusading Church that no longer understands the enemy it must vanquish: 'In the name of the Holy See, I can hold conversations with atheists, anti-theists who fight against the Church,' he said. 'Non-belief, disbelief, agnosticism are much worse. What do you want me to debate with someone who merely drawls, "Ehh?" in a vacant way. This is what I call the "ehhhh?" generation.'

It was said with a contempt that only a true Parisian can muster. Cardinal Poupard draws the front-line between the Church and the modern world with elegant strokes: 'The anthropologists say that man is *Homo sapiens* – i.e. the man who thinks . . . we could also say *Homo economicus* – i.e. the economic man. I would say *Homo cocacolanus* – i.e. the man who drinks Coca-Cola. But I also say that man is always *Homo religiosus* – i.e. religious man.'

Coca-Cola, like McDonald's, is used everywhere as a code-word for the phenomenon known as globalization. It is not so much an ideology as an absence of ideology, but it is the nearest the Church has to the ideological adversary it needs to define its relevance to the world of the coming millennium. Father Michael Campbell-Johnson, an English Jesuit working in El Salvador, attacked globalization with evangelical fervour at one of the annual lectures sponsored by the *Tablet*:

In the guise of a solution, since the collapse of Communism a new spectre is haunting not just Europe, but the entire world: the spectre of unrestricted economic growth, accompanied by the neo-liberal mechanisms needed to generate it; globalization, privatization, deregulation . . . The results are predictable: the dehumanizing of people, or workers, of the marginalized . . . the submission of morality to the dictates of the market; the promotion of individualism, consumerism . . .

There is a hint there of the true challenge facing the Church of the future. Although the process known as globalization has complex political and social consequences, it is a relatively straightforward economic idea: it simply means the elimination of obstacles to the free movement of goods, money, people and information across the world. Some of those obstacles, such as tariffs and immigration controls, can be removed by political will, others, such as transport logistics and the practical problems of financial transactions, are being steadily diminished by technology.

Unlike Communism, the force that Father Campbell-Johnson believes it is trying to replace, globalization is a means to an end rather than an end in itself. Its prophets do not proselytize on its behalf: they believe it is a road to economic efficiency and profit, and persuade others of its virtues only as a means of opening the way towards those objectives. It cares not a jot whether a consumer, a worker or a manufacturer is a Catholic, a Hindu or nothing at all, and in and of itself it is – again in contrast to Communism – morally neutral. But in two critical respects it is Catholicism's enemy. The driving force behind the process of globalization is choice: a manufacturer's right to choose to seek supplies where the best deal is to be had and to place factories where the labour is cheapest, and a consumer's right to buy what pleases him or her. These judgements are based on purely material and economic criteria, and have no moral dimension. That is a direct challenge to the Catholic conviction that every decision carries with it moral baggage. A Church that is founded on the belief that every human action must be judged against universal principles of good and evil is facing a world in which the critical choices are those a teenager makes between different brands of trainers.

And the consequence of global economic structures is to rank human beings by their economic value. Judged on an economic scale, an American is worth infinitely more as a consumer than one of Sister Leonia's dying Aids patients. Equally a multinational would place less value on them both as labour than a fit young Chinese willing to work long hours for low wages in one of the sweat-shops of Guangzhou. For the Church the idea of judging the value of human life in those terms is an offence to human dignity. Father Campbell-Johnson's economics may be questionable, but they are rooted in the democracy of souls: to the Church, every human being has equal value as God's creation.

I feel ambivalent about Catholic attacks on the globalization process. Michael Campbell-Johnson's was revealingly frank: he argued for a 'levelling down' of world prosperity on the grounds that the whole world cannot share in the fruits of the current economic system. 'If a society based on abundance and consumerism cannot be universalized, it must be considered a false solution, an aberration that makes the overall situation progressively worse.' In support of his argument he was able to cite the texts of both John Paul II, who has written endlessly about the moral dimension of economic activity, and Father Ignacio Ellacuria, one of the six Jesuits shot dead in the massacre at the University of Central America in San Salvador.

Father Ellacuria wrote of a 'Civilization of Poverty'. Poverty, he said, 'makes room for the spirit, which now will not be choked by the concupiscent desire to have all kinds of superfluities, when most of humanity lacks what is necessary. Thus the gospel spirit will be lived out more easily, according to which it is not necessary to have much in order to be much; on the contrary there is a limit at which having is opposed to being.'

The glorification of poverty is an old Catholic reflex − and a thoroughly pernicious one. Of course poverty can ennoble if it is freely chosen. But, as the Jesuits of Latin America know all too well, the vast majority of the world's poor do not choose their condition, which denies them the ability to make any choices at all − they are too busy surviving. Material well-being brings freedom, and global markets are bringing more wealth to more people. Somewhere behind the Catholic attacks on the modern market-place there lurks the ancient Catholic perception that souls are more biddable when they are enduring hardship, and that the promise of a better life in the next world is more appealing to those who are suffering in this one.

Father Campbell-Johnson's unfashionable insistence on the moral dimension of economics is characteristic of a Church that believes itself to be the possessor of Divine Truth. That certainty can do terrible damage to the Church and the world − as the fall-out from the encyclical *Humanae Vitae* demonstrates. But it gives the Church's judgements value as examples of courage and conviction even when they are wrong. In *Humanae Vitae* Paul VI anticipated the furore it would cause:

There is too much clamorous outcry against the voice of the Church, and this is intensified by modern means of communication. But it comes as no surprise to the Church that she, no less than her divine Founder, is destined to be a 'sign of contradiction'. She does not, because of this, evade the duty imposed on her of proclaiming humbly but firmly the entire moral law, both natural and evangelical.

Paul returns constantly in the encyclical to the question of what it is to be human. John Paul's writings are centred around that, too, as indeed are Catholic concerns about the direction of neo-liberal economics. The Catholic answer is that humanity only fulfils itself if it accepts its spiritual dimension.

Everywhere I went I found men and women trying to make that vision a reality. Only a Church that aspires to universality can make a real attempt to find a common humanity. It is a noble enterprise, and the effort to achieve it is worth making even if the institution is strained to breaking point by the need to contain so many different interpretations of its meaning. There were deep disagreements between some of the people I met but they were united by a shared sense of purpose. They were trying to fulfil the promise implied in the theatre of a papal audience in St Peter's Square – the promise that the Church cherishes every individual and his or her story. It is an extraordinary promise for an institution to make, and the Church often fails to keep it. But, as I end this journey, I find it is the one treasure in the Church's hands for which I feel unqualified admiration. That, more than anything else, makes membership of the world's biggest club worthwhile.

Many of Sister Leonia's Aids patients are received into the Church in the last days or even hours of their lives. To non-Catholics these frantic deathbed conversions may seem tasteless and opportunistic, particularly in a place where the Church's teaching on condoms is an obstacle to saving life. But they are motivated by the deep conviction that each human life has a place in the divine order. 'It is my dream that they can get out of this world to another world,' she says. 'I want them to believe they can live together with God.'

The Church I saw has been badly battered by the upheavals of the last three decades, and there may be worse to come. But it is fulfilling the dream of universality incarnated in that multicoloured waterfall which flowed over the steps of St Peter's in October 1962, and Pope

John XXIII's call to optimism at the opening of the Council remains apposite as the third millennium approaches:

Now that human society has reached a turning point, it is better to recognize the mysterious designs of Divine Providence which, passing through the different ages of man, and his works, generally against all expectation, achieve their purpose and guide events wisely for the good of the Church – even those events which seem to conflict with her purposes.

Select Bibliography

Much of the information for this book was drawn from interviews with those who witnessed the events it describes at first hand, but to put their stories in the context of wider developments in the Church I have relied on the work of authors who have given the subject much more scholarly attention than I could hope to. The amount of published material available on the modern Church is daunting; the books that follow are those I found especially helpful.

Balasuriya, Tissa, *Mary and Human Liberation*, Mowbray, London, 1997.

Bernstein, Carl, and Politi, Marco, *His Holiness*, Bantam, London, 1997.

Brockman, James, SJ, *The Word Remains, A Life of Oscar Romero*, Orbis Books, New York, 1982.

Davies, Norman, *Heart of Europe, A Short History of Poland*, Oxford University Press, Oxford, 1986.

Greeley, Andrew, *The Making of Popes*, Futura, London, 1979.

Hales, E. E. Y., *Pope John and his Revolution*, The Catholic Book Club, London, 1965.

Hastings, Adrian (ed.), *Modern Catholicism, Vatican II and After*, SPCK, London, 1991.

Hebblethwaite, Peter, *Paul VI, The First Modern Pope*, HarperCollins, London, 1993.

Kaiser, Robert, *Inside the Council*, Burns and Oates, London, 1963.

Kwitny, Jonathan, *Man of the Century, The Life and Times of Pope John Paul II*, Henry Holt, New York, 1997.

Lernoux, Penny, *People of God*, Viking, London and New York, 1989.

McClory, Robert, *Turning Point*, Crossroad, New York, 1995.

Milingo, Archbishop Emmanuel, *The World Between, Christian Healing and the Struggle for Spiritual Survival*, Orbis Books, New York, 1984.

Noel, Gerard, *The Anatomy of the Catholic Church*, Hodder & Stoughton, London, 1980.

Pirie, Valerie, *The Triple Crown, An Account of the Papal Conclaves from the Fifteenth Century to Modern Times*, Spring Books, London, 1965.

Ratzinger, Cardinal Joseph, *Salt of the Earth, The Church at the End of the Millennium*, Ignatius, San Francisco, 1996.

Reese, Thomas, SJ, *Inside the Vatican*, Harvard University Press, Cambridge, Massachusetts and London, 1996.

Rocha, Jan, *Brazil, A Guide to the People, Politics and Culture*, Latin American Bureau, London, 1997.

Rosenberg, Tina, *The Haunted Land*, Vintage, London, 1995.

Rynne, Xavier, *Letters from the Vatican Council*, Faber and Faber, London, Vols. I–IV, 1964–6.

Stanford, Peter, *Cardinal Hume and the Changing Face of English Catholicism*, Geoffrey Chapman, London, 1993.

Szulc, Tad, *Pope John Paul II, The Biography*, Scribner, New York, 1995.

Weigel, George, *The Final Revolution, The Resistance Church and the Collapse of Communism*, Oxford University Press, New York and Oxford, 1992.

Index

Index

Index

Index

Index